HUMAN RESOURCE MANAGEMENT IN THE HOTEL INDUSTRY

HUMAN RESOURCE MANAGEMENT IN THE HOTEL INDUSTRY

M. C. METTI

ANMOL PUBLICATIONS PVT. LTD.
NEW DELHI - 110 002 (INDIA)

ANMOL PUBLICATIONS PVT. LTD.

H.O.: 4374/4B, Ansari Road, Darya Ganj,
New Delhi-110 002 (India)
Ph.: 23278000, 23261597

B.O.: No. 1015, Ist Main Road, BSK IIIrd Stage
IIIrd Phase, IIIrd Block
Bangalore - 560 085 (India)
Visit us at: www.anmolpublications.com

Human Resource Management in the Hotel Industry

ISBN 978-81-261-3234-8

PRINTED IN INDIA

Printed at Mehra Offset Press, Delhi.

Contents

Contents

Preface

Global managers have now realised that HRM strategies vary significantly from country to country and that the strategies used to manage human resources in one country are sometimes ineffective or irrelevant in another country. With the growing significance of developing countries in the global world (as suppliers of cheap resources, buyers, competitors, capital users and home for the majority of MNCs' foreign direct investment), both academics and practitioners need to know how HRs are managed in developing countries. This will contribute both to better theory and practice development.

The rapid increase in the globalisation of business and the growing significance of emerging markets suggest that the success of managers in this new century will depend on the degree to which they develop an understanding regarding the dynamics of managing human resources (HRs) in different parts of the globe. We have plenty of information regarding the management of HRs in the developed countries. However, there is a lack of information regarding the dynamics of human resource management (HRM) in developing countries.

The challenges of management of HRs in developing countries are complex and demanding. Academics can play a significant role in this regard by providing relevant information to policy-makers and researchers. It is also important for business students—as future business leaders, to gain an understanding of the different issues relating to the management of HRs in developing countries.

Author

Chapter 1

Introduction

WORKFORCE PLANNING AND EMPLOYMENT

There are a number of dynamics that increasingly make workforce planning and employment critical components of the organization's strategic plan. The United States economy has transitioned from a manufacturing base to a service base and is in the process of transitioning to a knowledge base. As the economy moves along this continuum, the success of the organization is increasingly based on the quality of its human capital, which is defined as the total current and potential capabilities of the organization's workforce. As this transition occurs, organizational strategies increasingly must be developed to develop the organization's primary resource: people. The quality of its human capital will allow an organization to differentiate itself in the market place, much as innovative products and services now do. In fact, for many organizations, human capital will become their core competency—the unique capability that distinguishes them from their competitors. To create this competency, an organization must be able to attract the right kinds of people in the right place at the right time.

The nature of competition has changed and is global. Markets and environments are frequently dynamic and volatile, and organizations have been downsized and right-sized to improve cost efficiencies. Globalization requires the organization to understand multiple cultures and how to attract, retain, and motivate persons from those cultures. The dynamics of the environment often require flexibility and adaptation at the lower levels of the organization. All this affects the workforce planning and employment practices.

Technology has not only changed the way work is done, it has also changed the knowledge, skills, and abilities needed to do the work. Organizations must plan to either attract those with the right skills to the organization or to develop those skills internally. The latter requires hiring individuals who have the capacity to learn and to grow.

Workforce demographics in the United States are changing. The workforce is aging and contains an increasing percentage of both women and members of minority groups. In addition, workers often come to the organization with deficient skill sets. The organization must plan how to replace the impending retirement of the "Baby Boomers" while developing the skills of those that follow. The organization must be actively engaged in planning to determine how to react to the dynamics just discussed to develop an internal workforce that is capable of accomplishing the organization's strategic goals. That is the essence of workforce planning and employment.

CONCEPT AND PROCESS OF HUMAN RESOURCE PLANNING

Human resources alignment means integrating decisions about people with decisions about the results an organization is trying to obtain. By integrating human resources management (HRM) into the agency planning process, emphasizing human resources (HR) activities that support broad agency mission goals, and building a strong relationship between HR and management, agencies are able to ensure that the management of human resources contributes to mission accomplishment and that managers are held accountable for their HRM decisions. This is especially important in light of the Government Performance and Results Act's (GPRA) push to align all agency activities, including HRM, toward achieving defined agency strategic goals and measuring progress toward those goals.

In fiscal year 1999, the U.S. Office of Personnel Management (OPM) embarked on a special study to determine how much progress Federal agencies have made toward aligning HRM with agency strategic goals in support of HRM accountability and agency mission accomplishment. Our key findings and conclusions are summarized as follows.

Many more agencies than expected include HR representatives in the agency planning process and integrate human resources management goals, objectives, and strategies into agency strategic plans. However, most agencies are still struggling in this area. Therefore, agency executives and HR leaders need to work together to fully integrate HRM into the planning process so that it will become a fundamental, contributing factor to agency planning and success.

Although some agency HR offices have begun focusing on organizational activities that assist agency decision-making, most are still emphasizing internal HR office efficiency efforts. While internal issues are important to the success of any HR programme, HR offices also need to examine the "big picture" and find ways to impact the success of the agency as a whole.

Most agencies are in some way measuring the efficiency and/or effectiveness of the HR function. These measures, however, are generally output-oriented, focus on internal HR processes and activities, and are used to make improvements to HR-specific policies and procedures. As HR refocuses its activities to broader organizational issues, HRM measures also need to be expanded to gauge the impact HRM has on agency goals and mission. Then, the measurement data can be used to inform agency-level decisions.

The relationship between HR and management is becoming more collaborative. HR executives are beginning to earn a seat at the management table. HR offices are becoming more consultative and involved in day-to-day line management activities. Nevertheless, there is still a long way to go if HR is to become a strategic partner at all levels. To do so, HR needs to build its own internal competencies to deal with organizational issues, educate itself on agency and programme missions, and find ways to offer creative and innovative solutions to organizationwide issues.

Although many National Performance Review (now known as the National Partnership for Reinventing Government) initiatives, such as downsizing, reorganizing, streamlining, and delegating HR authorities, were meant to improve HR's ability to focus on organizational issues, they have not taken hold as quickly or thoroughly as hoped. Therefore, HR is still doing most of the process work, and its ability to focus on alignment has been limited. However, as HR's role in agency planning, activities, and decision-making advances – and it is advancing – so too will the alignment of human resources management with agency mission accomplishment.

Alignment

Strategic human resources management...strategic alignment...alignment with mission accomplishment. These are just a few of the terms being used to describe the new, evolving role of Federal human resources management (HRM). What do these terms really mean? If you were to ask agency personnelists, managers, or employees, you would probably get a wide range of answers. So, it's important to establish from the beginning what we are really talking about. Human resources management alignment means to integrate decisions about people with decisions about the results an organization is trying to obtain. Our research indicates that agencies that successfully align human resources management with agency mission accomplishment do so by integrating HRM into the agency planning process, emphasizing HR activities that support mission goals, and building strong HR/management relationships.

In addition to being a vital contributor to agency mission accomplishment, HRM alignment is the ultimate level of HRM accountability, as demonstrated in the Hierarchy of Accountability. While HRM accountability must begin with basic legal compliance, it ultimately encompasses all four levels of the pyramid, including demonstrating how HRM supports achievement of the agency strategic goals.

Why Align?

Why the sudden emphasis on aligning HRM activities with agency mission accomplishment? Basically, it comes down to demonstrating the value of human resources management to the agency. In the past, one of HR's primary roles has been to ensure compliance with laws, rules, and regulations. Although this is still, and will always be, a necessary function, many recent developments have led to a strong emphasis on results.

The National Performance Review (NPR) took on the task of reinventing government to make it work better, cost less, and get results. NPR mandated many initiatives that changed the focus of HR from just compliance toward results, including downsizing the HR function, delegating HR authorities to line managers, calling for HR to demonstrate its business value, and enhancing customer service. Through these initiatives, management of human resources would become more responsive to mission-related needs because it would take place at the line level, and the HR staff would be able to expend more of its energy on broader organizational issues.

The Government Performance and Results Act (GPRA) of 1993 has also played a large part in focusing agencies on results. The purpose of GPRA is to improve Federal programme effective- ness, accountability, service delivery, decision-making, and internal management, thereby improving confidence in the Federal Government. This is achieved by demonstrating organizational results through strategic planning and performance measures.

Although the primary focus of GPRA is on programmatic functions, agencies are also required to describe how administrative resources, such as HR, are being used to achieve strategic goals. Further, the General Accounting Office (GAO) and the Office of Management and Budget (OMB) have evaluated many of these efforts, and are calling for agencies to improve their discussions of HRM alignment in strategic and annual plans. Therefore, the human resources function is increasingly being aligned to the agency strategic plan, which requires HR to show how it is supporting mission accomplishment.

Alignment has already occurred in other key administrative functions. When Congress developed a statutory framework to introduce performance-based management into the Federal Government, it initiated financial, information technology, and procurement reforms through such mandates as the Chief Financial Officer Act and Information Technology Management Reform Act. Human resources management is the administrative missing link to this comprehensive package.

The private sector has recognized that it is not just financial and technological capital that provide companies with the competitive edge, but people, or human capital. Without attracting and retaining the right people, in the right jobs, with the right skills and training, an organization cannot succeed. Therefore, people have been recognized as companies' most important asset. As the Federal Government moves toward a performance-based management approach, we, too, need to realize the importance of our human resources. A huge percentage of agencies' budgets is spent on human resources — salaries, benefits, training, work life programmes, etc. Nowhere else do you make that substantial an investment and not measure the return.

Not only do human resources provide the competitive edge, but several recent studies have confirmed that the quality and innovation of HR practices impact business results. These studies were able to draw a correlation between increased quality of HR practices and increased business success. Among other benefits, HR alignment with mission accomplishment increases HR's ability to anticipate its customers' needs, increases the agency's ability to implement strategic business goals, and provides decision-makers with critical resource allocation information. Finally, HR alignment is a vital process to advance agency accountability. By defining, maintaining, and assessing HRM goals and measures, communicating them throughout the agency, and using the information to make management decisions, agencies are able to ensure that the management of human resources contributes to mission accomplishment and that managers are held accountable for their HRM decisions in support of mission accomplishment.

STRATEGIC PLANNING

AGENCYWIDE PLANNING

To some agencies, strategic planning is a way of life. To others, it's an exercise. To almost all, it's a requirement. As part of GPRA, agencies, unless specifically exempted, follow a continuous, three step strategic planning process:

Strategic planning allows agencies to map out where they are, where they want to go, and how they plan to get there. Some agencies adopted the idea of strategic planning even before GPRA was enacted, whereas others are just beginning to understand its potential benefits. The results of the fiscal year 1999 Merit System Principles Questionnaire (MSPQ), an OPM Governmentwide survey of supervisors and employees, show that agencies are beginning to embrace not only the concept, but also the practice, of strategic planning.

HRM Integration in Agency Strategic Plans

The management of agency human resources is an integral part of how an agency is going to achieve its mission goals. Without people, there is no one to do the work. Therefore, integrating HRM into the agency strategic plan is the first step in aligning it with the mission. Even though GAO and OMB are pushing for improvement of HRM alignment discussions in strategic and annual plans, GPRA's primary focus is still on agency programmes, rather than corporate functions. Therefore, we assumed at the beginning of this study that not many agency strategic plans would have addressed HRM's role in mission accomplishment. We were pleasantly surprised. Out of the 31 strategic plans reviewed, 87 per cent had addressed HRM in some way. Below is a breakdown of how integration between HRM and the agency plan is achieved, a count of how many strategic plans have integrated HRM in a particular way, and some examples of actual agency approaches.

Although some agencies are clearly ahead of the pack, integration of HRM in agency plans is still evolving. When looking at the actual placement of strategic plan HRM discussions, they are generally segregated from the programmatic goals, objectives, and strategies. Considering that an agency's mission cannot be achieved without its people, this is an important point. Could this be an indication that human resources management is not yet recognized as a critical contributor to agency mission accomplishment?

In any case, it is clear that though there are some exceptions, as evidenced by some of the examples above full HRM integration into agency strategic plans have not yet been realized. The human resources issues addressed in agency plans provide insight into what aspects of human resources management are most important to agency management. In reviewing the plans, or even just by looking at the examples above, it is clear that diversity, recruitment, retention, employee development, and workforce quality are the major areas of interest. Although these could be looked at as process or output programmes, when they are designed and implemented well, they lead to the ultimate result: the right people, with the right skills, in the right positions to carry out the agency mission.

Agency HRM Strategic Measures

Defining practical, meaningful measures that assess the effectiveness of agency human resources management and its support of mission accomplishment is a topic that agencies have been struggling with. It is easy to measure a process –

how long does it take to complete an action? It is easy to measure productivity – how many actions were completed in any given time frame? But how do you measure the outcome of human resources management? How does an agency know if it has the right people, with the right skills, in the right positions to carry out the agency mission? Have any agencies found a way to do this? To help answer these questions, we looked to see if agencies are including HRM measures in their strategic plans, and what types of measures they have identified.

Not surprisingly, 71 per cent of the plans did not identify any HRM measures. Moreover, the meaningfulness and practicality of the 29 per cent of agency identified measures could be stronger. About one-third of the 29 per cent contain measures that are not really measures. They are lists of activities or projects that, when completed, will help to reach the goal. In other words, they are strategies labeled as measures. The other two-thirds of that 29 per cent have fairly good measures that are tied to specific mission or support goals and provide seemingly relevant information. However, even these fairly good measures tend to focus on HR processes (outputs) rather than intended outcomes. For example, some agencies measure the average number of employee training hours to measure workforce skill levels, rather than what skills are actually gained through the training or what skills the workforce actually possesses.

HR Involvement in Agency Strategic Planning

Now that we have seen what types of goals, objectives, strategies, measures, and other forms of HRM integration are present in agency strategic plans, we should look briefly at how these were developed. The legitimacy and ultimate value of these pieces of the plan will depend substantially on where they came from. Historically, members of the HR community have remarked on the difficulty they have had "getting to the table" with top agency management. Rather than being involved in agency planning from the beginning, HR is commonly consulted after decisions have been made in order to help implement any major changes. Considering the invaluable perspective HR has on how decisions will impact agency resources, HR professionals have been frustrated that they are not involved sooner in the planning process.

Therefore, it was surprising when 79 per cent of the agencies we talked to indicated that they do play a role in the overall agency strategic planning process. The roles vary from a peripheral consultant who reviews and comments on preliminary products to an integrated team member who actively helps to identify not only HRM agency strategic goals and objectives, but programmatic goals as well. Two or three of the responding agencies fall in the former category, a handful in the latter, and the rest somewhere in between. Later, we will discuss how some HR officials are able to elevate themselves to agency strategic partner, while most are still struggling to achieve this.

Patent and Trademark Office (PTO): HR's Involvement in Strategic Planning

The PTO's planning process tracks closely. HR, as well as the other administrative functions, is integrally involved in and present during all aspects of planning – the top management discussions, business line planning, and overall ranking and budgetary discussions. The administrative functions serve several purposes: to inform managers what resources are available to them; to determine what resources managers will need; and to discuss the impact programme initiatives will have on the agency.

When it comes to defining actual HRM goals, strategies, and measures, the roles also vary. In general, agencywide HRM-related goals, strategies, and measures are identified by the agency leader or other senior managers with HR collaboration. They decide what is most important to the agency based on the challenges the agency will face in years to come. Some use a more elaborate collaboration approach that involves agency management, HR officials, and other stakeholders, as is demonstrated in the presented examples from the Department of Commerce's Patent and Trademark

Office (PTO) and the Department of Veterans Affairs (VA). Then there are the agencies that use the functional strategic planning approach where the HR office is tasked with coming up with the goals, strategies, and measures itself. In these cases, HR generally uses some type of feedback from customers to identify what is important to the agency and should be included in the plan.

Department of Veterans Affairs Collaborative Approach

The Department of Veterans Affairs (VA) Office of Human Resources Management was integrally involved in the Department's strategic planning process. Although the programme offices were the drivers for the strategic goals, the administrative functions were integrally involved in establishing how resources can be attained, retained, and utilized to support the programmes that deliver services to their customer, the veterans. The HR staff worked with programme planners and line managers in an iterative and interactive series of meetings that provided HR with information on the Department's current and future business and corresponding human resource needs. The HR staff was able to translate this information into specific objectives with supporting strategies and performance goals that were incorporated into the VA strategic plan.

To further refine its priorities, HR held a conference attended by approximately 300 people representing its key stakeholder groups departmentwide including: HR professionals, political appointees, headquarters executives, field line managers, staff offices, unions, and veterans. A "real time" strategic planning process that included facilitation, formal presentations, and inter-active discussions led to the identification and prioritization of four critical human resources "strategic opportunities" that must be dealt with if VA is to successfully accomplish its mission. Top management at the conference committed to supporting the pursuit of these strategic opportunities, and, subsequently, teams including field and headquarters, line and staff representatives were formed around these opportunities.

Agency Annual Performance Plans

In addition to reviewing strategic plans, we also reviewed 28 agency annual performance plans to see how HRM is addressed. As mentioned earlier, performance plans are the yearly operational plans defining what the agency will accomplish in that fiscal year that will contribute to the longer-term strategic goals, and how they will measure accomplishment of these performance goals. Seventy-five per cent of the reviewed plans contain both HRM performance goals and measures. This is not surprising because these operational plans tend to be more process and budgets focused than strategic plans and therefore contain more detail about the resources needed to accomplish the performance goals. Therefore, administrative functions, in general, are represented more fully than in the strategic plan.

The development of the performance plan is invariably more functional than overall strategic planning. At most agencies, each programme and administrative function is responsible for defining its own goals and measures which it then forwards to the planning office for coordination into the annual performance plan. As with the strategic plans, the HRM goals, strategies, and measures identified by HR offices tend to focus more on processes or activities than on overall outcomes. These process measures can be helpful, but because operational goals, strategies, and measures.

HUMAN RESOURCES MANAGEMENT STRATEGIC PLAN

The Health Care Financing Administration (HCFA) has developed a very noteworthy approach to aligning human resources management with mission accomplishment. HCFA's Human Resources Management Group (HRMG), Learning Resources Group (LRG), and Office of Equal Opportunity and Civil Rights (OEOCR) collaborated to develop a draft Human Resources Strategic Plan that goes beyond each of these individual organization's human resources responsibilities and instead addresses the entire sub-component's human resources management responsibilities. It assigns accountability for specific HRM goals to HRMG, LRG, OEOCR, senior leadership, line managers, employees, the union, and/or other non-HR stakeholders. The HRMG, LRG, and OEOCR worked very closely with the HCFA strategic planning and evaluation office to tie the plan to HCFA's strategic plan.

Specifically, the plan includes challenges that HCFA will face in the future, HRM goals that will support HCFA in meeting those challenges, potential performance indicators and strategies for each goal, the roles and responsibilities of HRMG, LRG, OEOCR, managers, employees, and other stakeholders, and finally how to implement and assess its results. help determine achievement of mission goals, they should focus more on whether or not the intended outcome of the activity was achieved.

HR Strategic Plans

Approximately half of the agencies we talked to have developed separate Human Resources strategic plans. These plans generally serve one of two purposes. Either they provide direction for those agencies that have not integrated HRM into the agency strategic plan, or they are used as implementation plans which support agencywide HRM goals, strategies, and measures.

These plans are particularly important to those agencies that do not integrate HRM into the agencywide plan because it helps them map out where they want the HR programme to go. They seem less important to many of the agencies that have thoroughly integrated HRM into the agency plan. For example, the Social Security Administration (SSA) has not developed a specific HR strategic plan because HR's goals and measures are part of the agencywide approach. Then, there are some agencies that integrate HR extensively into the agency plan, but still prefer to have a separate HR operational plan supporting the agencywide plan, as is often done by other corporate functions such as information technology and financial management.

Most of these plans focus on internal HR office programme activities, rather than on agencywide accountability for the effective use of human resources in accomplishing the mission. Therefore, ownership of the plan belongs to the HR office, not the agency. The Health Care Financing Administration (a sub-component of the Department of Health and Human Services) is an interesting exception to this, as seen in the inset. As with agency strategic plans, the measures identified in HR strategic plans are typically process- oriented and tend to address what steps have been taken to achieve a goal, rather than whether the intended outcome of the goal has been achieved. A little over half of the agencies use management input in developing these plans, generally in the form of previous customer satisfaction surveys.

Strategic planning allows agencies to put down on paper where they are, where they want to go, and how they plan to get there. But the best planning in the world does nothing for an agency if it does not act on those plans. Strategic implementation of human resources management means performing activities that support agency mission accomplishment and measuring how well those activities contribute to achieving agency strategic goals.

Strategic HRM Activities

When we talk about HRM activities, we tend to focus on what the HR office, itself, is doing even though we recognize that supervisors would bear the responsibility of HR decisions in an ideal world. After all, NPR advocated deregulation and delegation and the downsizing and out- sourcing of HR office activities so that human resources management could take place at the line level, making it more responsive to mission-related needs. Additionally, the HR staff would be able to devote more time to broader organizational issues, thereby improving its contribution to mission accomplishment.

Unfortunately, deregulation and delegation, as reported in OPM's 1997 special study, Deregulation and Delegation of Human Resources Management Authority in the Federal

Government, have not taken hold as quickly or thoroughly as was hoped. HR is still doing most of the HR- related work and is the nerve centre for HRM activities. That is why the focus of this section is on the HR office and what it does to support mission accomplishment. So what are HR's contributions toward mission accomplishment? Although most line managers we interviewed cannot describe precisely which HR activities support specific agency strategic goals, they recognize that they could not accomplish their mission without HR's help. Ironically, the areas most often mentioned by managers as HR's most valued contributions are also the areas they feel need the most improvement: recruitment and staffing, employee development, and employee relations. They would like to see HR become more involved and innovative in these areas, but they also admit that it would be extremely difficult for them to get their jobs done without the help HR already provides.

With this system, HR can immediately identify available deployment candidates for selection as soon as disasters are declared. Additionally, the system allows HR to better identify employee training and promotion needs, match employee expertise with specific disaster site victim needs, and create a selection routine that rotates available employees, thereby avoiding employee burnout. Clearly, staffing, development, and employee relations are important HR activities that make a difference to agency goal accomplishment. However, there are other areas in which HR offices contribute to and align with mission accomplishment, such as the few described below.

Agency Reorganizations: Because of all of the downsizing, streamlining, and budget cuts that have been occurring in recent years, many agencies and sub-components have had to redefine their missions and restructure the programme areas that support those missions. Human resources staffs play key roles in some of these redesign efforts. Managers at the Federal Emergency Management Agency and the Department of Labour's Occupational Safety and Health Administration were particularly complimentary of all of the work the HR staffs did to redeploy and retrain the workforce, provide guidance on organizational development issues, and redesign performance standards.

Workforce Planning: In this time of budget cuts, downsizing, and an aging Federal workforce, workforce planning becomes extremely important to increasing agencies' overall ability to achieve their missions. Although few agencies have strong workforce planning systems in place, some are beginning to take steps in this direction. The Department of the Army has an automated civilian forecasting system that uses 15-year workforce data trends to project future employment patterns, up to 7 years. This is part of a developing workforce planning initiative. SSA has developed a methodology to predict the number of actual

Tracking Strategic Progress

Engineers at NASA's Kennedy Space Centre have designed and implemented an excellent strategic management tool: the Goal Performance Evaluation System. This computer system implemented a major performance management change by linking individual employee performance goals all the way up through the Centre and Agency goals.

The system tracks the status of performance plans, and allows organizations to track results achieved against their mission. Managers can access the system to see what their units and individual employees are contributing toward the agency strategic goals. The system functions as a strategic management tool, an employee performance management system, and a Centre-wide communication tool. Kennedy and Johnson Space Centres have piloted the computer system with very positive results. retirements and is developing a workforce transition plan that will identify current and future required skill sets, determine how the workforce can obtain these skills, and set action plan milestones. Additionally, OPM is in the process of developing a workforce planning model that will assist agencies in this area.

Linking Performance Management to Mission Accomplishment: When managers and employees are interviewed, they almost always cite the performance management system as a way they are held accountable for meeting agency goals. So, does this mean performance management systems are aligned with agency strategic goals? In most agencies, the answer is "not yet" – at least not fully. Recently published research has identified over a dozen agencies and agency sub- components that have started to formulate systematic approaches to aligning performance management to strategic goals. Most are starting by linking top management performance plans and contracts to agency goals and rating and rewarding executives based on achievement of those goals.

Many of these agencies are planning to cascade the alignment down to the employee level. OPM's 1999 publication, A Handbook for Measuring Employee Performance: Aligning Employee Performance with Organizational Goals, is a very useful tool to help agencies link employee performance to the goals of the organization and measure employee accomplishments. A couple of agencies actually mandate the linkage of employee level plans to agency goals, while others are using team-based performance management approaches that include performance targets, informal team assessments, and awards that are linked to mission goals. The National Aeronautics and Space Administration (NASA), as shown in the inset, actually has an automated system that assists in the linkage. Nevertheless, as the General Accounting Office (GAO) concluded in its study, Performance Management: Aligning Employee Performance with Agency Goals at Six Results Act Pilots, aligning performance management systems with organizational missions and goals is still a "work in progress."

HR Self-Assessment: A handful of agency and sub-component HR offices are actually assessing how well their programmes align with agency mission accomplishment as part of recently established HR self-assessment programmes.

These assessment programmes focus on the compliance of HR activities with law as well as how effectively HR programmes are achieving their objectives in support of mission accomplishment. Because these assessment programmes are fairly new or are in the process of being revamped, it is too soon to tell the success they will have in measuring HR's impact on organizational mission accomplishment.

HRM Measurement

In the end, HR can only determine its value to the organization by measuring it. Earlier in this report, we saw that most agencies had at least defined HR output measures in agency strategic plans, annual performance plans, and/or HR strategic plans. This is an encouraging trend, but we need to look further at whether these measures are actually being tracked and used for decision- making. The best measures in the world are meaningless if not used. HRM measures in the strategic and annual performance plans are usually tracked by the HR office and forwarded to the planning office for distribution and sharing of the information.

A few agencies, such as NASA, SSA, and Education, report actually using the information for decision- making and tracking whether goals are being met. NASA even posts the information on its web page. However, we found that most agencies look at available data without really evaluating how the information can be used to enhance goal attainment. HR staffs find that measures from HR strategic plans tend to be more useful than those in the agency strategic or annual plans, at least at the functional level. As discussed earlier, HR strategic plan measures tend to focus on internal HR programmes, policies, and processes, and can therefore point to deficiencies in these areas.

HR officials can then use this information to make improvements to the problem areas. From an organizational perspective, however, the measures are generally not very helpful in determining achievement of HR goals because they are process rather than outcome oriented. Few agencies have implemented elaborate systems to track HRM goals and measures. Nonetheless, there are quite a few interesting approaches some agencies are using to measure their HRM performance.

Benchmarking is a systematic process of measuring an organization's products, services, and practices against those of a like organization that is a recognized leader in the studied area. Many Federal HR offices are using this practice to identify ways to improve service and align with business results. The most common benchmarking effort Federal HR offices have participated in is the National Academy of Public Administration-Hackett Group HR Benchmarking Study. There are at least 19 Government agencies involved in the benchmarking of 22 HR processes within four areas: administration, risk management, employee development, and decision support. The study also helps to gauge HR alignment through decision support categories such as resource planning, organizational planning, and strategic HR planning. Most participating agencies see the value in the information but have not devised strategies for how to use it.

The Balanced Scorecard in Action

The Veterans Benefits Administration's New York Regional Office implemented a balanced scorecard that uses outcome measures linked to organizational goals at the team, core group, and division-wide levels. The purpose is to determine how successful its operations are and where improvements are needed. This "balanced scorecard" measures five performance areas: customer satisfaction, speed, accuracy, cost-per- claim, and employee development. For each element in the balanced scorecard, teams are awarded points based on how well they are performing, and the scorecard is aligned with individual employee assessments and incentive pay.

Veterans' expectations are used to define customer performance targets, and employee measures are derived from climate surveys, team development data, and technical skills inventories. HR has played an important role in designing the balanced scorecard, including developing measures, peer assessments, and other tools, as well as helping managers understand the approach and how to manage under it.

The Balanced Scorecard is a framework many agencies are using to translate strategy into operational terms by measuring a full range of perspectives: financial, customer, internal, and learning and growth. Vice President Gore advocated the use of this type of balanced set of results to evaluate agency performance at the Global Forum on Reinventing Government, January 1999. The scorecard is generally used at the business unit level, as with the Veterans Benefits Administration. To date, most agencies are in the beginning stages of implementing balanced measurement approaches.

Activity Based Costing (ABC) is a method of cost management that determines the true cost, including overhead, for a service or product. Finding the true cost allows agencies to discover cost improvement opportunities, prepare and actualize strategic and operational plans, and improve strategic decision-making. This cost management methodology involves identifying activities, determining activity costs, determining cost drivers, collecting activity data, and calculating the service cost. ABC is being explored by a number of agencies. The Patent and Trademark Office is using ABC agencywide, and the General Services Administration is using it to determine HR costs, as described on the following page.

Measuring True Cost and How to Use It

Both the General Services Administration (GSA) and the Department of Commerce's Patent and Trademark Office (PTO) have successfully used Activity Based Costing (ABC) to determine the true cost of human resources management services. The General Services Administration began tracking HR costs due to customer complaints that services were too expensive. The problem was that no one, including HR, knew the actual cost of HR services. By using Activity Based Costing, GSA was able to compute the HR activity costs and make comparisons to other Government and private sector organizations using the Hackett Benchmarking Study data. HR demonstrated to managers that its costs were actually relatively low, and it had the data to prove it.

The Patent and Trademark Office (PTO) has engaged in agencywide Activity Based Costing. All senior managers were trained in the process, and each functional area, including HR, formed teams to identify activities, activity-based drivers, and primary products. PTO has used the information to close out fiscal year 1998 financial activities and to plan the fiscal year 2000 budget. ABC has helped determine the full cost of agency activities, the proper distribution of costs, and has even influenced service rates. An additional benefit to the system is that it has encouraged strategic thinking. Managers see how much a function, such as HR, costs and starts asking what value that function really adds to the programme. This challenges HR to show its value and return on investment.

The Malcolm Baldrige and the President's Quality Award Criteria are each based on a set of core values and concepts that integrate key business requirements into a results-oriented framework. Using the criteria as a framework for management practices and measurement can help agencies to improve performance, facilitate communication and best practice sharing, and serve as a tool for managing performance, planning, training, and assessment. HR measures are 15 per cent of the total Baldrige framework score. Several agencies, most notably the Department of Navy's Inspector General's Office, have successfully used the criteria to assess agency mission programmes.

STRATEGIC RELATIONSHIPS

The lynchpin that holds all of this planning and implementation together is the relationship between HR executives and staffs and agency management. In the past, there was often much contention between the two groups because of HR's role as "gatekeeper," enforcing the laws, rules, and regulations. Now, with the role of the human resources staff shifting toward achieving organizational results, HR and management need to work together to further HRM's ability to have an impact on agency decisions and achievement of goals. So, let's take a look at how well these relationships have been fostered thus far.

Corporate HR and Top Agency Management

The relationship between corporate HR and top agency management varies greatly by agency. A few agencies, like SSA, NASA, Air Force, and GSA, have been able to develop strong working relationships with management in which HR is a full member of the agency decision-making body. Most other agency HR executives have not been so fortunate. They are generally brought into the agency decision-making process during the implementation phase rather than being consulted in the beginning on how decisions may impact agency human resources or vice versa.

For some agencies, it has been a hard road "getting to the table." For others, it has been more of a natural transition. In exploring how to elevate HR's role to management partner, agencies where this has been achieved attribute their success to a combination of the following factors: Reporting relationships - In agencies where there is a direct reporting relationship between the head of HR and the head of the agency, HR generally has a more visible role in agency decision-making.

Management advocates - In agencies where there is a strong HR advocate in senior management, HR enjoys more involvement in the agency decision-making. Credibility - HR representatives who are formerly programme managers tend to earn more credibility from the other managers. This type of individual knows, first hand, what the programme concerns are and how HR decisions will impact the programme, and can speak the same programmatic language.

The Social Security Administration: How HR Stays at the Table SSA's HR Office has a good record of contributing substance, creativity, and innovative solutions to dealing with agency issues.

For example, when SSA heeded NPR's call to downsize administrative staffs, the HR office devoted substantial time and resourcefulness to redeploying these displaced employees to direct service jobs. For the headquarters employees who did not want to leave the area, HR helped to create a direct service office at headquarters and bring work there. Not only does this demonstrate HR's ingenuity in turbulent times, but it is a fitting example of how SSA values its employees. Traditionally been part of the culture. Therefore, it is natural for the HR leader to have a voice in agency decisions.

Value - In all cases, HR has to bring value to the discussion in order to be considered a member of the management team. If you have little or nothing to offer, you will not keep your seat at the table. Because HR executives have little control over agency reporting relationships, management advocacy, executive appointments, and agency culture, they need to focus their efforts on providing value to agency business discussions. But what kind of value can HR bring to the agency decision-making table? Other corporate functions have no problem demonstrating their value.

The Chief Financial Officer has the money. The Chief Information Officer has the technology. Without money and technology, an organization is severely hindered. But HR has the people, and without the people, the organization has no one to do the work. So why has HR not been able to capitalize on this strength? We were able to identify two reasons.

First, HR has not historically had the statistics or data that can excite management and show how HRM influences agency success. Second, HR has focused on internal operations rather than activities that impact the entire agency. These facts are recognized by the Strategic Human Resources Roundtable, an OPM-sponsored working group of Governmentwide HR Directors that meets periodically to discuss HR's role in GPRA. This group acknowledges that to address these shortcomings, HR needs to ask itself what are the HRM concerns that will gain management's attention, and does HR have the data that can help address those concerns? SSA has done this, as is demonstrated in the above inset.

The HR Office and Line Management

Now that we have explored the relationship between HR executives and top agency managers, we need to look at how the HR office interacts with its line managers and if there has been any movement toward a more cooperative, consultative relationship. HR's role is changing, but is HR changing with it? As discussed earlier, NPR advocated HR delegating, downsizing, and outsourcing so that it could start concentrating on broader organizational issues rather than transactional processes. As we have seen, this is beginning to occur at the corporate level, but what about the line level?

The problem is that delegation to managers has not taken hold very quickly, but HR offices have already been downsized. Therefore, HR is still expected to do the transactional work it did before, while also focusing on broader organizational issues, and doing all of this with an average of 20 per cent less staff. It is not hard to understand why agency HR offices are struggling to redefine their role to strategic partner. Just how far have they gotten?

HR as Consultant: Most agency managers we interviewed acknowledge that their HR office has become more consultative. Rather than telling a manager he/she can or cannot do something, HR professionals are more helpful in finding solutions to HR issues.

HR as Contributor to Mission Accomplishment: These same managers also recognize the importance of the HR office to mission accomplishment. There is so much that HR does for managers in terms of recruitment and staffing, employee development, and employee relations that managers would have difficulty doing it on their own. However, HR does have its limitations, particularly the size of the staff in relation to the amount of work it has to do, its knowledge of the mission, and skill gaps resulting from downsizing.

HR as Strategic Partner: Few, if any, agency managers feel that their HR office is a true strategic partner. Few HR offices are included in business planning from the beginning, generally being brought in to implement a decision that has already been made. For HR to become more involved in line-level decision-making, managers would like the office to: C have greater knowledge of the organizational mission, and C get more involved and innovative in broad, organizational HR issues that impact most on the organization, such as recruitment and workforce and succession planning.

HR has made some headway, as demonstrated in the following NASA example, but clearly has some distance to go in being involved in line management decision-making. Now let's look at the other side of the coin – how managers are involved in making decisions about HR programmes. Most line HR offices involve managers at least at an informal level, generally through satisfaction surveys or informal discussions. A few have HR/management councils that get together

NASA's Centres Working Together

NASA has 10 field centres, and each of these centres maintains a strong sense of its own identity and purpose and a strong enthusiasm for its mission. At the same time, each centre can identify the linkage to the agency mission. This sense of empowerment appears to help motivate the centre HR staffs to actively support that identity and purpose. Personnel officers generally participate in deliberations on centre affairs. HR staffs are proactive in their work by making site visits, attending line staff meetings, asking managers for input on HR issues, and briefing managers about changes in HR programmes. Managers are impressed with HR's availability, knowledge, and resourcefulness. This symbiosis is portrayed well in results from various employee surveys, data trends from the Central Personnel Data File, and third party evaluations of the HR programme. Periodically to discuss human resources issues. This is as close as agencies get to real integration of managers into the HR programme decision-making process. Generally, managers do not feel that they have a large impact on the direction of HR programmes and therefore feel little ownership for them.

Accountability

With the developing relationship between HR and management, both at the top and line levels, along with NPR and GPRA mandates, accountability should become a shared responsibility. Managers are making more and more HRM decisions while the HR staff is becoming more involved in broader organizational issues. This means that both the HR staff and managers are ultimately accountable for effective, legally compliant HRM.

Is this shared accountability occurring in Federal agencies? Approximately half of the responding agencies agree that HRM accountability is shared between the HR staff and managers. Managers are accountable for the business results achieved through good human resources management, the HR staff is accountable for HR compliance, and both are accountable for the overall effectiveness of the agency HRM programme. However, the other half still feels that the ultimate accountability falls on the HR staff. They are the ones responsible if actions are found non-compliant, and little attention is given to whether managers' HRM decisions are an effective use of resources. OPM's HRM Accountability System Development Guide goes into quite a bit of detail on shared accountability and can assist agencies in understanding the concept, determining who is accountable for what, and devising strategies for how to hold them accountable.

Strategic alignment of human resources management has come farther than we expected to find when we embarked on this study. There is definitely a trend toward integrating HR into the business planning process, measuring aspects of human resources management and its contribution to the organizational bottom line, and establishing a collaborative working environment between HR and management. Nevertheless, there are several indications that human resources management is not yet recognized as a critical contributor to agency mission accomplishment. HRM alignment is still evolving, and there are several steps agencies can take to help it along. Fully integrate human resources management into the business planning process.

Although many more agencies than expected include HR representatives in the agency planning process and integrate human resources goals, objectives, and strategies into agency strategic plans, most are still struggling in this area. Agency executives need to recognize the value that HR can impart to discussions about agency activities, priorities, and goals. In turn, HR leaders need to understand agency mission needs and be able to contribute substantive, creative solutions to meet these needs. Once these realizations occur, HR will no longer be segregated out as a support function but will become an integral, contributing factor to agency planning and success.

Agency Decision-Making

Because of NPR mandates to downsize, streamline, and improve customer service, HR's recent improvement efforts have focused on the efficiency and effectiveness of traditional HR programmes and processes. These are important endeavors. However, in response to GPRA's call to measure performance and demonstrate value, it is time to start concentrating efforts outside of the traditional realm of HR and on to broader organizational issues. When HR demonstrates that it can have an impact on agency direction, then it will gain credibility with agency executives and earn a seat at the table. To generate that type of impact, HR needs to develop strategies based on actual business needs, which will require involving management in the planning process. In addition, it must address Governmentwide concerns about the workforce capabilities of the future, such as workforce planning, succession planning, training needs assessments, skill gap analyses, etc.

Measure HRM Outcomes

HR's role is evolving. Therefore, HRM measures need to evolve as well. As HR becomes more involved in broader organizational activities, HRM measures should evaluate the impact these activities have on the organization as a whole. At this point, measures typically focus on outputs and processes and are generally internalized to the HR function or office. The data are used mostly to make improvements to HR-specific policies and procedures. While this kind of measurement is important, measures should also focus on organizational outcomes. Information from these measures should then be used to inform agencywide decisions and find solutions to agencywide concerns.

Advance the collaborative working environment between HR and management.

To facilitate all of the changes recommended above, HR has to have a strong, collaborative working relationship with top agency and line management. Since there is no tradition in most agencies of HR as strategic partner, much depends on personal relationships established by HR officials with top managers and key line managers. Meanwhile, HR and agency management need each other more than ever. Authorities are being delegated to line managers, HR staffs are being downsized, and top agency management is being asked to show how its resources are being used to support mission accomplishment. HR must be able to make the case that everyone in the agency, from the agency leader down to the HR function, must share accountability for ensuring that the use of human resources not only complies with Federal laws, rules, and regulations, but adds to the success of the agency.

This shared accountability is beginning to occur. HR management is beginning to earn a seat at the table. HR line offices are becoming more consultative and involved in day to day management activities. Nevertheless, there is still a long way to go in becoming strategic partners. First, HR needs to build its own internal competencies to deal with organizational issues, change, and strategizing. Further, it needs to educate itself on agency and programme missions in order to understand what is important to those organizations and be able to offer creative and innovative alternatives and solutions to organizationwide issues. Finally, it must continually assert the absolute criticality of effective HRM to organizational success.

This all looks so easy on paper. Do this, do that, and you will be aligned with the mission and able to demonstrate your contribution toward it. Obviously, it is not that easy. Private sector, public sector, and some Federal entities have been struggling with this issue even before GPRA was enacted – and that works to our advantage. There is a wealth of information out there that can help – hundreds of articles, books, and studies have been written, numerous tools have been created, and many organizations have already tested a number of approaches. We can learn from all of these successes and failures.

But the only way to begin is to begin. To help start you on this path, we have included a rather extensive, though certainly not all-inclusive. In support of its programme to foster development of agency accountability systems, OPM will also offer assistance to individual agencies in developing strategies for strategic alignment and has created a Governmentwide clearinghouse that will provide information on additional real life, successful approaches that agencies are employing (currently available on the OPM web page). It is in all of our interests to ensure that Government establishes and maintains a highly skilled workforce that can handle the demands of the 21st century. To achieve this goal, we must all work together.

For some reason, people tend to think that the Federal Government has fallen far behind the private sector, and even other public sector entities, when it comes to aligning human resources management with agency mission accomplishment. Although we did not talk directly with private or non-Federal public sector representatives, we conducted a fairly in-depth literature search that tells a somewhat different story.

Private Sector

There are many conflicting views on where the private sector is in regard to HRM alignment. For instance, the

Conference Board recently conducted a poll of 155 private sector HR executives, and 63 per cent responded that HR is "never, rarely, or only sometimes" a major player in the companies' strategic process. A Price water house-Coopers poll indicates that although 75 per cent of the responding 70 companies reported that HR's effectiveness is measured by its contribution to business results, only 27 per cent include HR from the beginning of the business planning cycle. Further, 43 per cent rated HR's planning and policy effectiveness as only average while a mere 6 per cent rated it as excellent.

Other private sector surveys and studies over the past few years, however, have found that HR has been integrated into the strategic planning process, HR executives and top company management are strategic planning partners, HR is recognized for the importance of its role in implementing organizational change, and HR is viewed as critical to the success of the business.

Clearly, there are many private sector organizations that exemplify "best-in-class" alignment strategies. They have implemented such alignment approaches as the Balanced Scorecard, Return on Investment, Activity Based Costing, Malcolm Baldrige Award-type criteria, and more. They recognize the importance of their employees to business results, and HR is considered a valued strategic partner. However, even with a number of "best practices" out there, the research agrees that HR alignment, even in the private sector, is still a work in progress.

Non-Federal Public Sector

According to recent research, the non-Federal public sector is in much the same boat as the Federal sector. As the Government Performance Project pointed out in its recent study, State governments run into many of the same HR problems as the Federal Government – rigid rules, lack of strategic management decisions, absence of statewide HR data, lack of workforce planning or the ability to plan for the future, etc. State governments have begun making HR reforms, such as reducing job classifications and streamlining hiring procedures. However, as with the Federal Government, States are focusing more on the efficiency and effectiveness of programmes than how they support the bottom line.

That is not to say that local, State, and even foreign governments have not been able to align themselves with mission accomplishment. A few cases can be most instructive for Federal agencies as they ponder this issue. The City of Hampton, Virginia HR staff has played a large role in increasing the performance of government services through improvements to work environment, organizational structure, work design, employee behaviours and organizational systems.

The state of Washington is developing and enhancing HR information systems in support of mission accomplishment, is using personnel data to identify improvement initiatives, and includes the Director of Personnel in the Governor's Cabinet. The Canadian Treasury Board and HR Council of the Federal Government of Canada are developing approaches to measuring HR efficiency, effectiveness, and mission contribution. There are many other examples of how the public sector is moving toward aligning HR with mission accomplishment. Nonetheless, the research indicates that the non-Federal public sector, too, is only in the beginning stages of this transformation.

Chapter 2

Methods and Techniques

WORKFORCE PLANNING

Workforce planning is the process of determining how to staff the organization with the right employees at the right time and in the right place. As discussed, workforce planning is increasingly indistinguishable from organizational strategic planning in those organizations where human capital is the critical factor in organizational success. For the purposes of discussion and explanation in this section, it is assumed that organization has completed its strategic-planning process and determined its strategic goals and objectives. The purpose of workforce planning then becomes to determine the characteristics needed in the organization's workforce to facilitate achievement of those objectives.

In this scenario, workforce planning is strategic planning at the HR level and involves similar processes, including a SWOT analysis, which occurs at the organizational level. In simplistic terms, the HR function, under the leadership of the SPHR, must determine the numbers and types of employees needed and evaluate the availability of both internal and external individuals having the correct characteristics. Based on these analyses, a determination can be made as to the proper HR programmatic activities required to achieve the correct workforce composition.

Workforce planning then involves three stages: forecasting workforce needs, determining internal and external supply of employees, and developing appropriate strategies to achieve forecasted needs in relationship to projected supply. These three processes are discussed in the following sections.

FORECASTING WORKFORCE NEEDS

The organization's strategic plan and allied business plan provide guidance as to the number and type of employees that the organization needs during the planning period. Expansion, retrenchment, new products or services, introduction of new technology, entrance of new competitors in the market, economic conditions, employee retirements, workforce turnover, and so forth must be considered when forecasting workforce needs. Forecasting is the process of using both historical data and predicted scenarios to determine workforce needs during a stated planning period. Following is a discussion of several forecasting methods that are often used.

Trend Analysis

Trend analysis involves studying historical organizational employment levels to predict future employment levels. For example: If, on average, employment levels in the organization have increase 5% per year, it might be logical to forecast a 5% increase for the next planning period. A more accurate forecast using this method might be to evaluate trends in separate departments or other organizational sub entities and then aggregate the increases (or, potentially, decreases) at the organizational level. Doing so provides more specificity as to not only the numbers of employees but also the types of employees needed.

Trend analysis assumes that history will repeat itself. In today's more volatile times that might not be the case. However, trend analysis provides some data on which a final forecast can be made.

Ratio Analysis

Ratio analysis is a forecasting technique that assumes a set relationship between one variable and another, and that the relationship allows for the prediction of workforce needs. Assuming no increases in productivity, an organization might be able to predict total workforce requirements based on predicted total sales or total productivity. For example: If, historically, it takes five employees for each 100,000 unit of product produced, a projected increase of 1,000,000 units per year will require an additional 50 employees.

Organizations often have standard staffing tables that can be used in ratio analysis. As an example, a restaurant chain would know how many servers, cooks, managers, and so forth are needed to staff a restaurant. Based on a projected expansion in terms of number of restaurants, increase in workforce needs can be forecast.

Turnover

Analysis of historical turnover—in reality a type of trend analysis—provides additional data for forecasts. Average turnover rates provide an indication of the number of new employees required just to maintain current employment levels. Obviously, turnover is affected by many environmental factors, most notably unemployment rates, so other variables must be considered when using these data for forecasting.

Nominal Group Technique

The nominal group technique is a group-forecasting and decision-making method that requires each member of the group to make an independent forecast prior to discussion of any forecasts. Members of the group meet and independently develop a forecast. Each member must present his or her forecast before any of the forecasts are discussed. After all presentations are made and clarifying questions addressed, the group works to come up with a final forecast.

Delphi Technique

The Delphi technique is another group forecasting method in which experts independently develop forecasts that are shared with each other, but in this approach the experts never actually meet. Each of the members refines his or her forecasts until a group consensus is reached.

The nominal group and Delphi techniques are used to avoid the phenomenon known as group think. Group think occurs when group members, in the interest of developing group cohesiveness, reach consensus without fully considering what might be divergent forecasts.

Managerial Judgment

Managers and executives are asked, based on their experience and knowledge, to develop forecasts. Forecasts, like budgets, can be a top-level overall estimate or a bottom-up aggregation of multiple departmental estimates. Top-level forecasts provide a gross indicator of needed employment levels, but do not indicate where those employees should be allocated in the organization. Bottom-up forecasts, provided by managers in the various departments, provide a better idea of allocation of the workforce and the types of employees that are needed. However, bottom-up forecasts tend to overestimate workforce needs as each manager tries to increase staff size.

Statistical Forecasts

Statistical analysis was discussed in the section on research. Various statistical procedures, including regression analyses, can be used to develop forecasts based on scenarios or theorized relationships between variables.

Computer Modeling

Many organizations use sophisticated forecasting software. This permits the organizations to evaluate workforce needs under various scenarios.

Multiple Methods

In the final analysis, no single forecasting method is likely to be accurate every time. Most organizations use multiple methods to develop different forecasts. Ultimately, it is likely to be a top-level manager, using intuition based on accumulated knowledge and years of experience, that makes the final determination of the most likely forecast.

Determining Internal and External Supply of Employees

Not only must the demand for employees be determined, but workforce planning must include an analysis of the potential supply. Forecasts must be made of the supply of candidates for jobs within the organization and the supply external to the organization in the relevant labour market. Methods of forecasting supply, internally and externally, are discussed in the following section.

Internal Supply

The internal supply of candidates can be determined using a number of methods, such as replacement charts, succession plans, human resource management information systems, and departmental estimates. A brief discussion of each of these methods follows.

Replacement Charts

Replacement charts are manual or automated records indicating which employees are currently ready for promotion to a specific position. If needs are forecasted for a particular job, replacement charts provide data with which to determine the supply of internal candidates to fill the openings.

Succession Planning

The concept of succession planning is similar to replacement charting except the time perspective is different. Succession planning is the process of identifying candidates for future openings. It is a longer-term plan for developing candidates to fill positions. Traditionally, succession planning has been reserved for only high-level positions. However, because of the increased importance of human capital in many organizations, succession plans are being developed for the orderly replacement of lower-level employees.

Human Resource Management Information Systems

Many human resource management information systems frequently contain data on qualifications or skills of current employees. After workforce demand is forecast, the database can be queried regarding the supply of potential internal candidates that possess the necessary qualifications or skills.

Departmental Estimates

Organizations are not static. Most organizations and their component departments experience constant flows of employees both in and out. Analysis of this movement provides valuable information to forecast internal supply. Table provides the formula used to forecast internal supply within a particular department in the organization and common sources of employee movement in and out.

Table: Estimated Internal Labour Supply for a Department

Current Staffing Level – Outflows + Inflows = Internal Supply

Inflows	*Outflows*
Transfers from other departments	Retirements
Hires from the external labour market	Resignations
Recalls from layoffs	Death
Returns from leaves of absence and sabbaticals	Promotions to other departments
	Transfers to other departments
	Terminations

External Supply

There is a huge amount of information available to assist in the forecasting external supplies of labour. State and local economic and workforce development agencies typically can provide data on the labour supply availability. The United States Department of Labour has data available for virtually any location and publishes annual forecasts of labour supply by occupation, and the Bureau of Labour Statistics provides a wide variety of labour force information that is available online. In addition, various professional organizations regularly analyze labour availability within their respective professions. The availability of external candidates is affected by:

- Economic conditions
- Unemployment rates
- College and high school graduation rates in the relevant labour market
- Net migration in or out of the area
- Relative skill levels of potential candidates in the labour market
- Competition for labour in the labour market
- Changes in the skill requirements of the organization's potential job openings

You should be familiar with the various methods of forecasting both demand for and supply of employees and candidates.

Determination of Strategies

The analysis of demand and supply for labour leads to develop appropriate strategies to achieve the planned level of employment. The result of the analysis can result in one of three conditions:

- Equality In which case the strategy becomes one of retaining current employees.
- Insufficient number of employees In which case the strategy becomes recruitment.
- Too many employees In which case the strategy becomes decruitment.

Retention of employees involves strategies designed to maintain or improve job satisfaction and organizational commitment. They are discussed throughout this entire book as they apply to a particular programme area. For example, retention strategies involve creating pay equity and providing desired benefits when compensation and benefits strategies are being developed. Both recruitment and decruitment (organizational exit) are discussed later.

It would be very similar if the analysis reveals that only one of the conditions from the preceding list exists. However, that is not often the case and the SPHR frequently finds that some departments are currently staffed appropriately for future needs during the planning period, whereas some departments have too many employees and others too few. Thus, strategies of recruitment, decruitment, and retention must be developed simultaneously and interdependently because the recruitment objectives of one department can often serve to fulfill the decruitment objectives of another.

It provides a basis for understanding two major programmatic activities that are discussed later: recruitment and selection. Assuming that an expansion of the workforce is required, strategy determination is affected by the forecasts of yield rates and the timeframes required for each step in the recruitment and selection process. Yield rates are a comparison of the number of applicants or potential applicants at one stage in the recruitment/selection process with the number of applicants that remain available at the next stage.

To determine programmatic activities and action plans, the SPHR must work backward from the total number and types of employees that will be needed, including dates on which they will be needed. Based on experience, moderated by any projected changes in timeframes or yield rates, the planning process must incorporate an evaluation of the scope and timing of activities to produce the desired results. In the case, the SPHR must lead the organization in a determination as to the timing of recruitment efforts and the number of actual contacts that must be made to produce the 10 new employees at the appropriate time.

WORKFORCE PLANNING AND EMPLOYMENT LAW

Since the early 1960s there has been great legislative activity in the area of employment law. Most of this legislation has been enacted to prevent employment discrimination. The SPHR should be familiar with these laws and guide the organization in not only compliance with the legal requirements of the law, but also in its intent. The following regulations, executive orders, laws, and precedent case law are discussed in this section:

1. Civil Rights Act of 1866
2. United States Constitution
3. Equal Pay Act (1963)
4. Civil Rights Act of 1964
5. Executive Orders 11246 (1965) and 1375 (1967) and 11478 (1969)
6. Age Discrimination in Employment Act (1967)
7. Consumer Credit Protection Act (1968)
8. Fair Credit Reporting Act (1970)
9. Rehabilitation Act (1973)
10. Vietnam Era Veterans' Readjustment Assistance Act (1974)
11. Privacy Act of 1974
12. Pregnancy Discrimination Act (1978)
13. Uniform Guidelines on Employee Selection Procedures (1978)
14. Immigration Reform and Control Act (1986)
15. Worker Adjustment and Retraining Notification Act (1988)
16. Employee Polygraph Protection Act (1988)
17. Americans with Disabilities Act (1990)
18. Civil Rights Act of 1991
19. Uniformed Services Employment and Reemployment Act (1994)
20. Congressional Accountability Act (1995)
21. Fair and Accurate Credit Transactions Act (2003)
22. Precedent Case Law
    - Griggs v. Duke Power (1971)
    - McDonnell-Douglas Corp v. Green (1973)

- Abermarle Paper Company v. Moody (1975)
- Washington v. Davis (1976)

Civil Rights Act of 1866

The Thirteenth Amendment to the United States Constitution was passed in 1865 at the end of the Civil War and abolished slavery. However, it did not guarantee equal rights for all groups and states began passing laws limiting the rights of newly emancipated slaves in a number of areas, including employment. In response, the Civil Rights Act of 1866 was passed.

It prohibits illegal discrimination based on race or ethnicity in the formation or enforcement of contracts. The act also allows for punitive and compensatory damages in cases of intentional racial discrimination. Its impact on preventing discrimination is limited to cases in which an actual employment contract exists and it doesn't cover other types of illegal discrimination based on sex, age, and so forth.

United States Constitution

The Fourteenth Amendment of the United States Constitution was passed in 1868 largely because the states were not complying with the provisions of the Civil Rights Act of 1866. It states, in part:

- No state shall make or enforce any law which shall abridge the privileges or immunities of citizens of the United States; not shall any State deprive any person of life, liberty, or property, without due process of law; nor deny to any person within its jurisdiction the equal protection of the law.

This seems to imply that all persons should be treated fairly and equally in matters of employment because the courts consider employment to be a property right. Had all employers and governments abided by this requirement and complied with the intent of the Civil Rights Act of 1866, the massive employment legislation of the twentieth century would not have been necessary.

Equal Pay Act (1963)

The Equal Pay Act of 1963, which is an amendment to the Fair Labour Standards Act, is covered comprehensively, "Compensation and Benefits." The act prohibits discrimination in the payment of compensation based on sex for jobs that are similar in terms of skill, effort, responsibility, and working conditions.

Civil Rights Act of 1964

The Civil Rights Act of 1964 is the most comprehensive and far reaching legislation dealing with employee relations. Title VII of the act prohibits discrimination in employment as follows:

1. It shall be an unlawful employment practice for an employer–
   - To fail or refuse to hire or to discharge any individual or otherwise discriminate against any individual with respect to his compensation, terms, conditions, or privileges of employment, because of such individual's race, colour, religion, sex, or national origin; or
   - To limit, segregate, or classify his employees or applicants for employment in any way which would deprive or tend to deprive any individual of employment opportunities or otherwise adversely affect his status as an employee, because of such individual's race, colour, religion, sex, or national origin.

The outcome of the act, along with its amendments, has been to create protected classes. Those are groups specifically identified in the law for special protection from illegal discrimination. They are as follows:

- Race (African-American, Native American, Hispanic-American, and Asian-American)
- Colour
- Religion

- Sex (women)
- National origin
- Employees over 40 (Age Discrimination in Employment Act)
- Disabled (Americans with Disabilities Act)

The act creates the Equal Employment Opportunity Commission (EEOC) in the Department of Labour to administer and enforce the act. The act prohibits retaliation against individuals exercising their rights under the act. This includes both voicing opposition to the organization's employment practices and filing complaints with the EEOC.

Employers covered by the act are:

- Those that have 15 or more employees for each working day in each of 20 or more weeks in the current or preceding calendar year.
- All private and public educational institutions.
- Federal, state, and local governments.
- Public and private employment agencies.
- Labour unions with 15 or more members.
- Joint labour/management committees for apprenticeships and training.

The act also imposed certain record-keeping and reporting requirements on employers. Covered employers must keep employment-related records that can be requested by either the Equal Employment Opportunity Commission or the Office of Contract Compliance Programmes. Those records include documents associated with recruitment and selection, promotions, discipline, compensation and benefits, training, and so forth.

In addition certain employers are required to submit an annual report to EEOC. The most common annual report is the EEO-1, which is required to be submitted by the following employers:

- Employers with 100 or more employees, except for state and local governments.

- Federal contractors with at least 50 employees and contracts of $50,000 or more.
- Financial institutions with at least 50 employees and that hold government funds or issue savings bonds.

The EEO-1 requires the workforce be reported by race and gender for nine categories of employees:

- Officials and managers
- Professionals
- Technicians
- Sales workers
- Office and clerical
- Craft workers (skilled)
- Operatives (semiskilled)
- Labourers (unskilled)
- Service workers

EEO-1 is required for private businesses. Other industries might also be required to report on a different form, but the reporting requirements vary. For example, EEO-4 is a similar form for state and local governments, but is only required biannually. Several exceptions in the law permit discrimination that would otherwise be prohibited. They are as follows:

- Business necessity: A practice that is job-related and necessary for the safe and efficient operation of the organization may be permitted even if it negatively affects certain employees covered under the act. For example, a Ph.D. in physics may be required for research physicist positions even though some groups might be less likely to possess that degree.
- Bona fide occupational qualification (BFOQ): Permits an organization to exclude persons from consideration on a basis that would otherwise be illegal. For example, a film company wanting to hire an actor to play the female lead role could exclude all males from consideration.

- Seniority systems: Systems giving preferential treatment based on seniority are generally legal.

Executive Orders 11246 (1965), 11375 (1967), and 11478 (1969)

Executive Order 11246, as amended by Executive Order 11375, requires federal contractors and subcontractors with contracts in excess of $10,000 in any 12-month period to comply with Title VII of the Civil Rights Act of 1964 and to take positive steps to eliminate employment barriers for women and minorities.

A 2002 amendment to the executive order permits contractors and subcontractors that are religious organizations to hire only individuals of a particular religion. This amendment is controversial and is subject to being overturned by congressional action.

A contractor with contracts of more than $50,000 and 50 or more employees must develop and implement a written affirmative action plan to increase the participation of protected classes in the workforce. Executive Order 11246 creates the Office of Federal Contract Compliance Programmes (OFCCP) within the Department of Labour to implement and monitor compliance under the orders. Noncompliance can result in cancellation of current contracts and ineligibility for future contracts with the federal government.

Executive Order 11478 prohibits discrimination in employment practices by the United States Postal Service and federal government agencies on the basis of race, colour, religion, sex, national origin, handicap, or age. The executive order also requires federal agencies to prepare and implement affirmative action plans for federal employees. States and local governments often have additional requirements for affirmative action activities with respect to governmental contracts issued at that level.

Age Discrimination in Employment Act of 1967

This act, commonly referred to as ADEA, prohibits employment discrimination against employees who are at least

40 years of age. It has been amended several times, including the Older Workers' Benefit Protection Act of 1990.

The act covers employers that have 20 or more employees in each working day for 20 or more weeks in the current or preceding year and is administered and enforced by the EEOC. The act prohibits discrimination against employees over 40 in hiring, promotion, compensation, retirement, layoff, discharge, and any other terms, conditions, or privileges of employment. Employers may not retaliate against employees for exercising their rights under the law. In general, an employer may not require a mandatory retirement age. However, certain groups of employees—airline pilots, for example—may be subject to mandatory retirement based on safety requirements. In addition, highly paid executives over the age of 65 may be subject to involuntary retirement if they were in the position at least two years before the retirement and are entitled to immediate retirement benefits of at least $44,000.

Exceptions to the act are as follows:

- Bona fide seniority systems, even though they might adversely affect workers over 40, are generally allowed. For example, an employee who is 35 years of age with 15 years of service might be entitled to certain employment rights and benefits over an employee who is 55 but has worked with the company for only 5 years.
- Certain benefits may be adjusted based on age on the principle of equal costs or equal benefits. For example, an employer may provide less life insurance coverage to an older employee as long as the cost of the insurance is equal to what is spent on employees less than 40 years of age.
- The employer may take appropriate disciplinary action against covered employees if it does so for good cause.
- The employer may discriminate against persons over 40 using the requirements of BFOQ. For example, an

advertising agency could discriminate against someone over 40 when hiring a model for children's clothing.

Consumer Credit Protection Act (1968)

This act provides protections for employees whose wages have been garnished.

Fair Credit Reporting Act (1970)

This act, often referred to as the FCRA, regulates the process of obtaining and using credit and other types of information on employees. Consumer reporting agencies (CRAs) are businesses or persons that are paid a fee to assemble, analyze, evaluate, or report information on individuals for third parties. These reports are referred to in the regulations as consumer reports. The most common use of CRAs is to obtain credit reports on current or prospective employees. However, other vendors who provide background checks or perform investigations for a fee are also covered by the act. The employer must certify to the CRA that it is in compliance with all applicable provisions of the FCRA.

An employer that wants to obtain a consumer report on a current employee or applicant must advise the person of its intent. In addition, the employer must obtain written consent from the employee or applicant to obtain the report. There are certain exemptions to the pre-investigation notice and consent that are covered later in the discussion regarding the Fair and Accurate Credit Transactions Act.

An employer making a decision based wholly or in part on the consumer report that negatively affects the employee or applicant (failure to hire, termination, disciplinary action and so forth) must provide that individual with a pre-adverse action disclosure. Included in the disclosure is a document, prescribed by the Federal Trade Commission (FTC), which provides employees with information on their rights and a copy of the report. In general, the employer must then provide a reasonable amount of time, usually five business days, to refute the findings. After the final decision is made and effected, the employer must give the employee or applicant another notice that includes

- The name, address, and telephone number of the CRA
- A statement indicating that the employer, not the CRA, made the decision regarding the adverse action and that the CRA would not be able to provide specific reasons why the action was taken
- Notice of the right of the individual's right to obtain a free copy of the report from the CRA within 60 days
- Notice of the right of the individual to contact the CRA to dispute the accuracy of the information and to provide more complete information

Rehabilitation Act of 1973

This act prohibits employment discrimination based on disability. Those covered by the act are as follows:

- Contractors or subcontractors that have federal contracts in excess of $2,500
- Depositories of federal funds
- Organizations receiving federal grants or aid assistance

Contractors that have contracts in excess of $10,000 must take affirmative action to hire the disabled, and contractors with contracts of more than $50,000 and at least 50 employees must also develop and implement affirmative action plans to hire qualified individuals with a disability. These plans may be integrated with affirmative action plans required under Executive Order 11246 and the Vietnam Era Veterans' Readjustment Assistance Act. The OFCCP monitors compliance with the law. Failure to comply can result in cancellation of current contracts and ineligibility for future federal contacts. As amended, the Rehabilitation Act definitions of handicap and requirements for accommodation are very similar to those of the Americans with Disabilities Act, which are discussed in greater depth later in this section.

Vietnam Era Veterans' Readjustment Assistance Act (1974)

This act prohibits discrimination against disabled veterans, veterans of the Vietnam era, veterans who served on active duty in during a war, campaign, expedition, or military operation and recently separated veterans. Recently separated veterans are those that have been released from active duty less than three years. The act applies to the federal government and employers having at least $50,000 worth of federal contracts and 50 or more employees. Contractors meeting this threshold are required to:

- Develop and implement a written affirmative action plan to employee covered veterans.
- List job opportunities with the local unemployment office. Exceptions are temporary positions lasting less than four days, jobs that are to be filled internally, and certain top-level positions.
- Prepare and submit an annual report (VETS-100) that reports hiring practices with respect to covered veterans.

The requirement for filing a VETS-100 report has been changed so that only employers with $100,000 or more in federal contracts are required to file the report. The act is administered by the OFCCP. Failure to comply with the provision of the act can lead to contract cancellation and disbarment from future federal contracts.

Privacy Act of 1974

This act applies only to federal government employees and prohibits the release of information contained in an employee's personnel file, with limited exceptions, without the employee's written release. Federal employees also have the right to review their personnel files.

In general, employees other than those of the federal government have no such rights. State and local laws may impose restrictions on the release of employee information, both for private and public sector employees. The Health

Insurance Portability and Accountability Act (HIPAA), protects disclosure of medical information.

Employers must be very careful in releasing employment-related information on employees. Release could subject the employer to tort action under common law for invasion of privacy, defamation of character, and so forth.

Pregnancy Discrimination Act (1978)

This act is an amendment to the Civil Rights Act of 1964 and prohibits discrimination in employment matters based on pregnancy, childbirth, or related medical conditions. An employer must treat pregnant women the same for all employment purposes, including fringe benefits, as other employees who are similar in their ability or inability to work. Employer policies must apply equally to pregnant employees as to other employees. For example, if the employer provides temporary disability insurance for its employees, pregnancy must be considered the same as any other temporary disability. Employers may not require a pregnant employee to leave work because of the pregnancy if she is able to perform the essential function of the job. However, the act does not require any special accommodations or benefits for pregnant employees that are not provided to other employees.

The Pregnancy Discrimination Act might present problems when the pregnant employee is employed in hazardous occupations or subject to exposure to chemicals that could impose health risks for the fetus. Although the employer might believe it wise to temporarily transfer the employee to another position, to do so involuntarily is a violation of the act. The Supreme Court has ruled that the health of the fetus is the responsibility of the employee.

Uniform Guidelines

The Uniform Guidelines on Employee Selection Procedures (UGESP) is considered to be the most comprehensive document regarding the legality of employee selection procedures. They are administrative regulations published in the Code of Federal Regulations. The document provides guidance as to how employers should manage their various employment systems (recruitment, testing, selection, promotion, discipline, and so forth) to comply with federal employment law prohibiting discrimination. Two approaches for proving that illegal discrimination has not occurred are addressed in the guidelines: no disparate impact and job relatedness/business necessity. These approaches are discussed next.

No Disparate Impact

The regulations provide guidance on the determination of adverse impact, also referred to as disparate impact. Adverse impact occurs when members of a protected class are negatively affected by employment decisions. As employees alleging illegal discrimination must prove first that they are a member of a protected class and then that they have been the victim of disparate treatment or adverse impact. Disparate treatment is a relatively simple concept; it means that members of a protected class are treated differently from others. For example, requiring a woman to take a strength test but not requiring the same of a man. The determination of adverse impact is a bit more complicated and there are many statistical methods of doing so.

However, UGESP provides a relatively simple way of determining whether adverse impact has occurred. The methodology is referred to as the 4/5ths rule and can be used for analysis both internally and externally. Internally it can be used to determine whether an employer procedure or policy is adversely impacting a protected class. It also can be used to analyze the organization's workforce in relation to the external workforce to determine whether underutilization exists. Both methods are described in the following sections.

Internal Analysis of Employment Practices

Under UGESP, adverse impact occurs when the selection rate for a protected class is lower than 80% of the selection rate of the group with the highest selection rate. Selection rate is a broad term and can be applied to a number of practices. For example:

- Selection for an interview
- Passing an interview
- Selection for a position
- Selection for promotion
- Selection for training
- Performance awards and bonuses

As an example, an organization just finished a large recruitment effort that resulted in the hiring of 200 employees. The data regarding the number of employees interviewed and the number hired are shown in Table. The organization wants to determine whether its hiring practices resulted in adverse impact.

Table: Internal Adverse Impact Analysis

Group	*# Interviewed*	*# Hired*	*Selection Rate*
Hispanic Males	30	20	60%
White Males	100	80	80%
African-American Females	100	65	65%
Asian-American Females	50	35	70%
Totals	**310**	**200**	

To determine whether the selection rates identified in the table resulted in adverse impact, the adverse impact threshold must be determined. This is determined by calculating 4/5ths (80%) of the highest selection rate. In this case, the highest selection rate is that of white males and is 80%. The adverse impact threshold is 4/5ths of 80% or 64% (.80 x .80). Any selection rate below 64% is an indication of adverse impact. In this case, Hispanic males have been adversely impacted. At this point the organization might elect to modify the practice, abandon the practice, or justify the practice using job relatedness and business necessity.

Application forms cannot ask about an individual's protected class status, but the employer might be required to prove that such employment practices as the application process, prescreening process, and inventory process do not create adverse impact. This is referred to as applicant flow data. There are two ways to collect this data. The first, and preferable, way is to request that the applicant complete a separate EEO information form. The form must be kept separate from the application. The second way is visual inspection. For example, a receptionist can record perceptions of race and gender when the individual reports for an interview.

Analysis of the Workforce

The organization might want to know whether the internal workforce mirrors the demographics of the external workforce. This analysis is required if the employer is required to prepare affirmative action plans and otherwise can be used to evaluate the organization's diversity efforts.

Table given below compares the composition of the organization's workforce, in percentages, with the composition of the relevant labour market. The organization wants to know whether its practices have resulted in adverse impact and underutilization of a protected class.

Table: External Adverse Impact Analysis

Group	*% of Internal Workforce*	*% of Labour Market*	*4/5ths of Labour Market*
African-Americans	15	20	16
Asian-Americans	10	8	6.4
Native Americans	4	4	3.2
Hispanic-Americans	21	25	20

In this example adverse impact and underutilization are shown for African-Americans because they compose 15% of the internal workforce, but the adverse impact threshold is 16%. Note that Hispanic-Americans compose 21% of the workforce when they compose 25% of the external labour market. However, 21% is above the adverse impact threshold of 20%.

Remember that it is the outcome of an employer's practices, not the intent, which determines whether adverse impact and potentially illegal discrimination has occurred. A seemingly neutral practice engaged in with good intent can be found to be illegal.

Job Relatedness

An employer might not be illegally discriminating against a protected class, even if its employment practices result in adverse action for a protected class. For the purposes of UGESP, practices are referred to as tests. Recruitment, interviews, job simulations, and actual tests are all referred to as tests. All tests must be job-related and they must be valid predictors of performance on the job.

Content validity is used to prove that the practice is job-related. Job-related means that the practice (test) actually contains elements of the knowledge, skills, and ability required in the job. Criterion validity is used to prove that the test or practice is a valid predictor of future performance. Concurrent validity and predictive validity are two methods of validating the capability of a test to predict future performance.

However, it is not enough to prove that the tests are job-related. The practices must also be reasonably related to the safe and efficient operation of the organization. This concept is known as business necessity. The organization must prove that it would incur significant expenses, or suffer some harm, if it did not use the particular practice. For example, an organization could argue that a mathematical aptitude test is highly correlated with performance on a particular job and that not using it would cause the organization to select employees who would fail on the job, thus resulting in increased cost associated with high turnover. The organization could also argue that high error rates caused by these employees result in expensive rework.

Immigration Reform and Control Act (1986)

This act, often referred to as IRCA, was passed for two purposes. The first is to prohibit employers from hiring persons who are not permitted to work in the United States. Passed largely to reduce illegal immigration, the act prohibits the hiring, recruiting, and referral of undocumented workers and unauthorized aliens for a fee. Compliance with the act requires that the employer

- Not knowingly hire unauthorized aliens
- Verify the employee's identity and work status
- Maintain records regarding the employee's identity

Employers must verify the identity of the employee and eligibility to work in the United States by completing and signing a Form I-9. The form must be completed within 72 hours of hiring and kept for a minimum of three years or one year after the employee leaves employment, whichever is greater.

The second purpose of the act is to prohibit discrimination in hiring and termination based on national origin or citizenship status. Employers may not discriminate in the hiring or termination of individuals based on

1. Nation status
2. Citizenship status
    - As a citizen
    - As an alien lawfully admitted for either temporary and permanent residence
    - As a refugee granted asylum

The employer may not retaliate against an employee for exercising any rights under the act. In addition, an employer may not refuse to honor documents that show immigration status nor may the employer require additional documentation beyond that required in the act. Finally, the act does not prohibit employers from giving preference in employment to a United States citizen over an alien if the two have equal qualifications.

With very limited exceptions—union hiring halls, for example—the act applies to all employers. However, the discrimination provisions of the act apply only to employers with four or more employees. The act originally was enforced by the United States Immigration and Naturalization Service (INS), but responsibility has now been transferred to the Department of Homeland Security.

Employers who fail to comply with the form I-9 requirements can be subject to fines ranging from $100 to $1,000 per violation. Each instance of not documenting an employee can be found to be a separate violation. Additional fines can be imposed for falsification of documents and knowingly accepting fraudulent documents. These fines can range up to $5,000 per incident for repeated incidents. Repeated hiring of unauthorized aliens can result in fines up to $10,000 for each alien hired. Finally, employers who consistently violate the act can be subject to criminal prosecution.

Worker Adjustment and Retraining Notification Act (1988)

This act, most frequently referred to as the WARN act, requires advance notification to employees in the event of mass layoffs and plant closings. The act applies to employers that employ 100 or employees (excluding part-time employees) or 100 or more employees that in the aggregate work 4,000 hours per week, excluding overtime. Subsidiaries and independent contractors may be considered in the calculation for coverage if they have common ownership.

The employer must provide 60 days advance notice to employees, their designated representative, the dislocated worker unit (unemployment office), and the chief elected official in the governmental unit to which the organization pays the highest taxes when any of the following events occurs at a single site of employment during any 30-day period:

2. The permanent or temporary shutdown of a plant that results in 50 or more employees, excluding part-time employees, losing their jobs

1. A mass layoff if
   - -50 or more employees, excluding part-time employees, are laid off and the layoffs constitute at least 33% of the workforce or
   - 500 or more employees, excluding part-time employees

There are exceptions to the notification requirements that might permit less than a 60-day advance notice in the cases of

2. Natural disasters
1. Business conditions that could not have been reasonably foreseen

However, if a reduced notice exception exists, the employer must give the notice as soon as it is practical to do so. The notice must include an explanation for the shortened notice.

Failure to provide notice can result in significant costs to the employer. Former employees or their designated representative (a union) may sue the employer for back wages, including health benefits, for each day of violation up to the full 60 days. For example, if the employer provided notice but closed the plant or executed the layoff 30 days after the notice, it could be liable for an additional 30 days of compensation. The actual amount that can be awarded is reduced by any compensation or severance payments made during the violation period. Employers may also be subject to fines for violation of the act. You should be familiar with the conditions under which WARN notification is required.

Employee Polygraph Protection Act (1988)

The act, often referred to as EPPA, restricts most private employers from conducting polygraph (lie detector) tests on prospective and current employees. It is enforced by the Wage and Hour Division of the Department of Labour. Pre-employment polygraph tests are not permitted, with the following exceptions:

- Local, state, or federal governments and certain federal contractors involved in law enforcement or national security
- Private employers who provide certain security services (armored cars, security alarm systems, private guards, and so forth)
- Private employers that are involved in manufacturing, distributing, or dispensing controlled substances

Private employers, however, may administer polygraph tests to employees that are subjects of investigations regarding economic loss or injury suffered by the employer. For example, an employer may administer a polygraph to an employee suspected of theft, misappropriation of funds, embezzlement, and so forth.

This employer right is not without limitation. The employer must have a reasonable cause to believe that the employee was involved in the activity being investigated and had access to the lost, stolen, or damaged property. The employee does not have to take the polygraph and, if he or she elects to, may terminate the test at any time. The employer must provide the employee with a statement indicating why the test is requested and the questions that will be asked. The employer is prohibited from taking a personnel action based on the employee's refusal to take the test. Furthermore, the employer cannot use the polygraph test results as the sole determinant of a personnel action. There must be other evidence that the employee was involved in the alleged infraction.

Americans with Disabilities Act (1990)

This act, commonly referred to as ADA, is the major federal legislative act that prohibits employment discrimination against the disabled. Title I of the act prohibits discrimination in employment decisions against qualified individuals with a disability. This includes job application procedures, hiring, firing, promotion, compensation, selection for training and any other terms, conditions, or privileges of employment.

The act is enforced by the EEOC and covers employers that have 15 or more employees for 20 or more calendar weeks in the current of preceding year, employment agencies, labour unions with fifteen or more employees, state and local governments, and joint labour-management apprenticeship committees. These are the same employers covered by the Civil Rights Act of 1964.

For an employee to be covered by the act, the individual must be disabled and qualified for the job. After that is determined, the employer might have an obligation to engage in reasonable accommodation. These subjects are covered in the following sections.

Disability

The act covers a disabled individual that

- Has a physical or mental impairment that substantially limits one or more major life function
- Has a record of such impairment
- Is regarded or treated as having an impairment

The courts have also included into coverage under the act those that have an association or relationship with a disabled individual. For example, an employer could not fail to hire an individual who has a disabled child on the basis that that person might miss too much work in caring for the child.

Physical impairment refers to any physiological condition or loss of one or more body systems (neurological, respiratory, speech organs, cardiovascular, digestive, and so forth). Mental impairment encompasses such conditions as mental retardation, mental or emotional illness, and learning disabilities. The Supreme Court has ruled that correction or control of an impairment by medicine or medical device to the level of normal functioning may remove the individual from coverage under the act. For example, eyeglasses that restore vision to the normal range or medicine that controls blood pressure may return the employee to normal functional capacity, thus eliminating the limitation on a major life activity.

Major life functions include:

- Caring for oneself
- Reproduction
- Performing manual tasks
- Walking
- Seeing
- Hearing
- Speaking
- Breathing
- Learning
- Sitting or standing
- Lifting or reaching
- Thinking or concentrating
- Interacting with others

Case law is ever-changing in this area. The definitions of impairment and major life function are constantly evolving. However, certain conditions are specifically exempted from the definition of disability in the act. They are as follows:

- Homosexuality and bisexuality
- Sexual behaviour disorders (such as pedophilia and exhibitionism)
- Gender identity disorders not resulting from physical impairments
- Compulsive gambling
- Pyromania
- Kleptomania
- Current illegal use of drugs

Although illegal drug use is not covered under ADA, drug addiction itself might be if the employee has undergone or is undergoing drug rehabilitation and is not currently using illegal drugs. The same is true for alcohol addiction. An employee can be disciplined for on-the-job use of alcohol, but comes under the protection of the law if the individual is a recovering alcoholic.

Qualified Individual

A disabled person, to be a qualified individual, must be able to perform the essential functions of the job with or without accommodation. Job analysis is a critical process for determining those tasks that are essential for successfully performing in the job. A function is essential if the following conditions are true:

- It is the reason why the job exists. In other words, the job was created specifically to perform the function in question.
- The function cannot be assigned to another employee. If assignment of a particular task would disrupt the primary purpose of the job, it is not an essential function. For example, the primary job responsibility of the job is to load trucks with a forklift whereas a minor function is to perform periodic maintenance on the forklift, such as changing the tires. If the organization has a department that performs other maintenance on the forklifts, the function of changing tires could likely be easily reassigned to that department without disturbing the primary purpose of the job. Thus, changing tires would not be an essential function.
- The function requires a great deal of skill not found in employees in other job categories. The more skill required, the more difficult it is to assign the function to another employee and, consequently, the more likely that function would be considered an essential function.

Reasonable Accommodation

An employee or applicant that is disabled but qualified to perform the essential functions of the job is entitled to reasonable accommodations by the employer. The intent of the law is that this be an interactive process with the employee or applicant requesting the accommodation and the employer responding in an appropriate manner. However, it is good practice to be proactive in this area, particularly if it is obvious that accommodation is needed and the nature of the disability might prevent the employee from asking for the accommodation. The employer can require documentation for disabilities or requests for accommodation that are not obvious. Failure to do so relieves the employer from responsibility and the employee is not entitled to accommodation under the law.

Reasonable accommodation is the modification of the workplace or work requirements to permit the individual to perform the essential functions of the job unless those accommodations would create and undue hardship on the employer. There are no legislative rules that clearly define reasonable accommodation as opposed to undue hardship. Each situation must be determined individually. Often the determination is based on the resources available to the employer. A reasonable accommodation for a large corporation might very well be undue hardship for a smaller one. The EEOC has determined that there are three categories of accommodation. They are as follows:

- Job application process The job application and selection process must not be discriminatory. Accommodations such sign language interpreters, modification of testing procedures, applications in Braille, and so forth might be appropriate in certain circumstances.
- Work environment Accommodations in the work environment are virtually unlimited. Accommodations can be made to the physical layout itself such as making the restroom handicapped-accessible, widening aisles for wheelchair access, providing teletype phone capabilities, and so forth. The nature of the work and the work flow itself can be modified by eliminating nonessential job functions or assigning those tasks to another individual. Finally, the work schedule itself can be modified as an accommodation.

- Benefits and privileges of employment In some circumstances accommodations can be made to allow the employee to continue to work or to deal with the medical treatment associated with the disability. If the employee can no longer perform the essential function of the job, reassignment to another job is often preferable to termination. However, there is no obligation under the law to create a special position for the employee. In addition, leaves of absences to attend to medical issues might be appropriate.

ADA restricts the use of pre-employment medical examinations and medical inquiries. An employer cannot inquire into the medical conditions and medical history of an individual prior to employment. The employer, however, may ask whether the employee can perform the essential functions of the job. Pre-employment medical examinations are prohibited. However, medical examinations can be required after a conditional offer of employment is given to the applicant.

Medical examinations must be nondiscriminatory in that either all applicants or all applicants in a given job category can be required to have a pre-employment medical examination. Requiring medical examinations for only those whom the employer believes might be incapable of performing the job is a violation of the act. Medical examinations for current employees may be required if they are clearly job-related, required by law, required to determine whether a disability exists or a particular accommodation is required and, in limited circumstances, to determine whether the employee can perform the job (fitness for duty examinations).

After the employee has received a conditional job offer, medical information necessary for normal processing may be collected. For example, medical information needed for health and life insurance or by the occupational health nurse may be collected. The employer is responsible for maintaining the confidentiality of any medical information collected. Access to medical records must be restricted to those who need to know, and the records themselves must be kept separate from other employment-related records.

Drug tests are not medical examinations under ADA and they can be used in the employment prescreening process. Employment discrimination is not the only prohibition covered by the act. Title II of the act prohibits discrimination against the disabled in government programmes and public transportation. Title III requires access for the disabled to public and commercial facilities, and Title IV requires closed-captioning services in television broadcasts for those who are hearing impaired. Finally, the act prohibits retaliation against an employee for exercising any right provided by the act.

You most definitely will receive one or more questions regarding ADA. Remember that the individual must be disabled or thought to be disabled and qualified to perform the essential functions of the job. When that threshold is reached, the employer has an obligation to provide reasonable accommodations. You should know the definition of disability and when an individual is qualified under the act. In addition, you should be familiar with reasonable accommodations and undue hardship.

Civil Rights Act of 1991

The Civil Rights Act of 1991 is an amendment to the Civil Rights Act of 1964. It was passed largely to offset some conservative judicial decisions by the Supreme Court in the late 1980s, often called the Reagan Court. Major provisions of the act are as follows:

- Returned the burden of proof to the original standard. The Supreme Court had, in the late 1980s, issued a decision that placed the burden of proof on the employee to prove that the employer had engaged in illegal discrimination. The act changed the burden of proof back to the original standard. An employee has the burden to prove that he or she is a member of a protected class and that the employer's employment practices have resulted in adverse impact on members of the protected class. After passage of the act, the burden of proof then switches to the employer to prove that the adverse impact was not a result of illegal discrimination.

- Allowed for jury trials and compensatory and punitive damages. The Civil Rights Act of 1964 permits only actual damages. That is damages for lost wages, attorney fees, and court costs. The Civil Rights Act of 1866 provides for additional damages but only in specified situations. The Civil Rights Act of 1991 permits damages to compensate the employee for pain and suffering, mental anguish, and other intangible damages. It also permits the courts to award punitive damages designed to punish the employer for egregious instances of intentional discrimination.
- Prevents the use of a "mixed motive" defence. Prior to the act, employers could defend discriminatory action by proving that the action was justified in the absence of discriminatory intent. For example, the employer could argue that the employee's performance was so poor that termination would have occurred in any event. The act prohibits such defences and requires the plaintiff only to prove that protected class status was a factor in the decision to take an action.
- Prohibits the practice of race-norming. Many employers began the process of adjusting the scores of protected classes on tests used in the employment process either by adding to the score or establishing different passing scores for protected classes. The process was used to level the playing field when statistics revealed that certain protected classes scored lower on the particular test. The act prohibits such practices.
- Extended protection of the Civil Rights Act of 1964. Protection was extended to include certain federal and state government employees not previously covered

under the act. Protection was also granted to United States citizens working for United States organizations in foreign countries except where those rights conflict with local law or customs.

Table: Compensatory and Punitive Damage Limitations (Civil Rights Act of 1991)

Size of Organization	*Limit*
15–100 employees	$ 50,000
101–200 employees	$100,000
201–500 employees	$200,000
More than 500 employees	$300,000

Congressional Accountability Act (1995)

This act brought employees of the United States Congress under coverage of 11 major employee relations and employment-related laws. Those laws are as follows:

- Fair Labour Standards Act (1938)
- Civil Rights Act of 1964, as amended
- Age Discrimination in Employment Act (1967)
- Occupational Safety and Health Act of 1970
- Rehabilitation Act of 1973
- Civil Service Reform Act (1978)
- Employee Polygraph Protection Act (1988)
- Worker Adjustment and Retraining Notification Act of 1988
- Americans with Disabilities Act (1990)
- Family and Medical Leave Act (1993)
- Veterans Reemployment Act (1994)

Fair and Accurate Credit Transactions Act (2003)

This act, frequently referred to as FACTA, amended the Fair Credit Reporting Act discussed earlier. The act was passed largely in reaction to the increasing problem of identity theft.

It provides certain rights for consumers, such as the right to get a free copy of their credit report annually, and mandates a number of obligations for providers, resellers, and users of credit reports. As a user of credit reports and other third-party information, FACTA predominantly affects HR in two ways:

- Pre-investigation notification and consent are no longer required when contracting with a third party for certain types of investigations, such as allegations of employee misconduct, violations of law, or violations of employer policies. The post-investigatory notification requirements are still mandated.
- The employer cannot maintain credit reports on employees. After an employment decision is made, based in whole or in part on a credit report, the report must be removed from the files and disposed of.

Precedent Case Law

Court decisions regarding employment and antidiscrimination law are constantly interpreting and modifying the current statues. As discussed earlier, Supreme Court rulings become the law of the land. Where those rulings differ from the current intent of the legislative body, they can be overturned only by congressional action as in the case of the Civil Rights Act of 1991.

Griggs v. Duke Power (1971)

The Supreme Court decision in Griggs created the judicial concept of adverse impact and established two major points:

- Discrimination does not need to be overt or intentional to violate the Civil Rights Act of 1964. It is the outcome of the practices that is in question. If a practice results in differential effect (adverse impact), it is a potential violation of the law.
- The employer must prove that a practice is job-related as a business necessity if that practice creates adverse impact.

McDonnell-Douglas Corp. v. Green (1973)

This Supreme Court ruling established the concept of disparate treatment and created what is known as the McDonnell-Douglas test. Disparate treatment, by definition, is intentional discrimination. To establish a prima facie case of disparate treatment, the court set the following conditions:

- The person belongs to a protected class.
- The individual applied for a job and was qualified for the job for which the employer was seeking applicants.
- The individual was rejected for the job.
- After the rejection, the employer continued to seek applications from persons with the same or similar qualifications of the individual.

Abermarle Paper Company v. Moody (1975)

The Supreme Court decision in Abermarle expanded the guidance provided in Griggs by clarifying that employment tests, including performance evaluation systems, used to make employment decisions must not only be job-related but that they must also be valid predictors of performance on the job. The effect of the ruling was essentially to make the federal regulations contained in the Uniform Guidelines for Employee Selection Procedures take on the impact of law.

Chandler v. Roudebush (1976)

The Supreme Court ruled that federal employees have the same rights under federal employment discrimination statutes as private sector employees.

Washington v. Davis (1976)

The Supreme Court ruled in Washington that an employer practice, in this case a verbal skills test for police officers, can be job-related even if it creates adverse impact for a protected class. To be job-related, a practice must be a valid predictor of performance.

Regents of the University of California v. Bakke (1978)

The Supreme Court ruled that a medical school could legitimately consider race in its admission procedures but that race could not be the only factor considered.

United Steelworkers v. Weber (1979)

The Supreme Court ruled that voluntary affirmative action quotas agreed to by an employer and a union is legal. However, the court indicated that such agreements can be used within very narrow limitations so as to not trammel the interest of nonprotected groups.

Meritor Savings Bank v. Vinson (1986)

The Supreme Court ruled that a hostile work environment was a violation of Title VII even if there are no negative employment consequences and that an economic effect is not required for sexual discrimination to occur.

Johnson v. Santa Clara County Transportation Agency (1987)

The Supreme Court ruled that gender could be used as one factor in an employment decision if under-representation is shown and the affirmative action plan does not have firm quotas.

Martin v. Wilks (1988)

The Supreme Court ruled that reverse discrimination could occur if the nonprotected class is not consulted in the negotiations for a consent decree giving a protected class employment preference.

City of Richmond v. J. A. Croson Company (1989)

The Supreme Court ruled that rigid numerical quota systems were unconstitutional when past discrimination was not documented.

Taxman v. Board of Education of Piscataway (1993)

The United States Court of Appeals ruled that a nonremedial affirmative action plan cannot violate the nondiscrimination mandate of the Civil Rights Act of 1964.

Harris v. Forklift Systems, Inc. (1993)

The Supreme Court ruled that a "reasonable person" test must be used to determine the existence of a hostile work environment that violates Title VII.

Hopwood v. State of Texas (1996)

The United States Court of Appeals ruled that taking race into account, even as a means of achieving diversity, violates the Fourteenth Amendment guarantee of equal protection. The Supreme Court refused to hear this case on appeal.

Ocale v. Sundowner Offshore Services, Inc. (1998)

The Supreme Court ruled that Title VII prohibitions against discrimination based on sex includes same sex harassment.

Faragher v. City of Boca Raton (1998)

The Supreme Court ruled that the employer has vicarious, as opposed to strict, liability for the hostile environment created by a supervisor unless it establishes and clearly communicates procedures for handling sexual harassment complaints and the employee fails to follow those procedures. The Court further stated that if the harassment results in a tangible employment action, there is no defence and the employer is strictly liable.

Ellerth v. Burlington Northern (1998)

The Supreme Court defined a tangible employment action as a significant change in employment status such as hiring, firing, failing to promote, reassignment with significantly different responsibilities, or a decision causing a significant change in benefits.

Grutter v. Bollinger et al. (2003)

The Supreme Court ruled that narrowly tailored use of race in admission decisions to a law school does not violate the Fourteenth Amendment guarantee of equal protection when it is used to further a compelling governmental interest in the educational benefits that flow from a diverse student body. The Court ruled that the decision must be made based on a highly individualized review of each applicant; that no decision can be based automatically on one variable such as race; and that the process must ensure that all factors contributing to diversity are meaningfully considered.

Gratz et al. v. Bollinger et al. (2003)

The Supreme Court ruled that giving preference to minorities for admission to a college undergraduate programme serves a governmental interest in the educational benefits that result from a racially and ethnically diverse student body. However, the Court ruled that the procedures used in this case violated the Fourteenth Amendment guarantee of equal protection because they were not sufficiently narrowly tailored.

General Dynamics Land Systems, Inc. v. Cline (2004)

The Supreme Court ruled that the Age Discrimination in Employment Act does not protect younger workers who are over 40 years of age from employment decisions that favour older workers (reverse age discrimination).

EQUAL EMPLOYMENT OPPORTUNITY

Laws, regulations, and executive orders require various employers to engage in affirmative action to increase the applicant supply of individuals in protected classes that are under-represented. Employees that believe they are victims of illegal discrimination have the legal right to bring those complaints to the Equal Employment Opportunity Commission. These two important processes are discussed in the following section.

AFFIRMATIVE ACTION

Affirmative action is the process by which employers engage in employment practices designed to eliminate the present effects of past discrimination. Affirmative action can be voluntary or involuntary. Voluntary affirmative action is engaged in by organizations that realize that is good business practice and the right thing to do. These employers understand that diversity in the workforce often creates a positive image for the organization, which could result in improved organizational performance, increased customer loyalty, and improved employee recruitment and retention programmes. In these cases, a written formal affirmative action plan might or might not be developed.

Voluntary affirmative action plans can be a problem and result in complaints of reverse discrimination, particularly where there is no history of past discrimination in the organization. However, as discussed previously, many organizations are required to develop and implement, if indicated, formal affirmative action plans as required by Executive Order 11246, the Rehabilitation Act of 1973, and the Vietnam Era Veterans' Readjustment Act of 1974. In general, the following employers must develop and implement, if appropriate, written affirmative action plans (AAPs) and submit them to the Office of Federal Contract Compliance Programmes on an annual basis:

- Federal contractors and subcontractors with 50 or more employees and $50,000 in government contracts during any 12-month period
- Depositories of federal funds
- Issuing or paying agents for United States savings bonds and savings notes

In addition, certain other employers might also be required to submit written affirmative action plans. The courts can require employers in certain instances to prepare and implement AAPs. Also, employers might agree or be required to submit affirmative action plans as part of consent agreements negotiated under the auspices of state or federal courts.

The threshold for coverage under the Vietnam Veterans' Readjustment Act has been raised to employers that have contracts of at least $100,000. In November of 2000, the OFCCP issued new regulations designed to simplify the AAP development process. The new regulations require an organizational profile using either a workforce analysis or an organizational display, a job group analysis, an availability analysis, a utilization analysis, and goals and actions, if appropriate. These topics are discussed in the following sections, as are several judicial issues dealing with affirmative action.

Organizational Profile

An organizational profile displays information on the composition of the organization by gender and ethnicity. It provides an overall view of the composition of the organization. An organizational display is a graphical presentation by organizational unit. An organizational unit is defined as one that has one or more managers that have authority to make employment decisions such as hiring and firing. Each managerial/supervisory level is listed along with the gender and ethnicity of the manager(s)/supervisor(s). The numbers of employees supervised by each manager are listed along with each employee's gender and ethnicity. A workforce analysis was the required method of presenting the organizational profile prior to the new regulations in 2000. It provides the number of employees in an organizational unit by job title, ordered by rate of pay, and each employee's gender and ethnicity.

Job Group Analysis

A job group analysis aggregates the information from the organizational profile based on job titles, regardless of which organizational unit they are assigned to. Thus the job group analysis provides an overall picture of the organization by job title. The difference between the organizational profile and the job group analysis is often explained with the analogy that the workforce analysis provides a vertical slice of the organization by departmental unit, whereas the job group analysis provides a horizontal view by job groups.

Availability Analysis

An availability analysis is a two-factor examination in which the organization evaluates the availability of minority and women candidates potentially available for the job groups determined in the job group analysis. It is called a two-factor analysis because two distinct factors or sources of workers must be considered. The first factor is those internal employees that could be promoted or transferred to the job with appropriate training. The second factor is the availability of workers with appropriate skills from the relevant recruitment area. An availability analysis shows the candidate pool potentially available to fill jobs in each job group by gender and ethnicity.

Utilization Analysis

A utilization analysis compares the availability analysis for each job group with the job group analysis. The purpose of the comparison is to determine whether underutilization exists. Underutilization exists if a protected class constitutes a lesser percentage in the organization's workforce than it does in the availability analysis. Underutilization can be determined using a variety of methods, including

- Any difference rule in which underutilization is determined to exist any time the current workforce percentage for a protected class does not equal the availability analysis percentage in a particular job group
- The 4/5ths rule previously discussed in which the current workforce percentage of a protected class must be at least 4/5ths (80%) of the availability analysis percentage in a particular group
- The two standard deviations rule in which the current workforce percentage of a protected class cannot vary from the availability analysis percentage by more that two standard deviations

Goals and Actions

If underutilization is indicated in any protected class, goals must be set for bringing the utilization up to parity and action decided on to achieve those goals. In the case of multiple areas of underutilization, multiple goals are required. The issue of goals has gathered considerable controversy over the years. The regulations consider goals to be targets that the organization will make reasonable good-faith efforts to achieve. They are not to be mandatory quotas. However, many argue that goals are, in fact, de facto quotas.

The organization must develop action plans to achieve the goals, including appropriate programmatic activities. Activities typically include targeted recruiting and training and development programmes designed to increase the applicant supply pool of underutilized protected groups. The organization must develop internal auditing and reporting systems to monitor its progress toward achieving goals. After a goal is reached, affirmative action activities with respect to that goal must cease.

Judicial Issues and Affirmative Action

Three issues raised in the courts should be discussed: reverse discrimination, quotas, and the "glass ceiling." The issues are interrelated in that quotas create reverse discrimination. Case law is often conflicting and confusing, and is still evolving. As a general statement, current court decisions trend toward conservatism in the use of affirmative action programmes, limiting the situations in which such programmes can be engaged in largely to those in which past discrimination is evident.

Reverse discrimination occurs when an equally qualified or more qualified member of a nonprotected class (generally white male) is not hired or promoted in favour of a member of a protected class. Preferential treatment and quota systems can create situations in which reverse discrimination is created. Court decisions in this area tend to strongly support prohibitions against reverse discrimination and protect valid affirmative action initiatives. Obviously this is a gray area and dependent on the situation in each instance.

Quotas are created when all individuals that are not members of a targeted protected class are excluded from consideration for a position. In the absence of a valid bona fide occupational qualification, case law prohibits firm quotas in affirmative action plans. In general, law and the courts permit the consideration of protected class status as one factor in employment decisions if there is evidence of past discrimination. However, protected class status cannot be the only criteria except in very narrowly defined situations.

Nothing in affirmative action law and regulations requires organizations to hire unqualified candidates. Affirmative action activities where there is no underutilization or history of past discrimination are generally found to violate Title VII. Affirmative action plans and activities are designed to be temporary in nature. Affirmative action means that employers attempt to place protected class members in jobs in which the class is under-represented. Continuation of these activities after the goal is achieved is illegal.

Glass ceilings and glass walls (also referred to as glass elevators) are concepts associated with affirmative action and illegal discrimination. Whereas affirmative action activities might result in hiring members of under-represented protected classes, such actions do not guarantee that those individuals will rise to the highest levels of the organization. Glass ceilings is a concept that means that protected class individuals are promoted only so far in the organization and then reach a seemingly impenetrable barrier in which they can see the top of the organization but cannot achieve promotion to it. The Civil Rights Act of 1991 created a Glass Ceiling Commission to study barriers to the advancement of women and minorities in the workforce and to recommend means of overcoming those barriers.

Glass walls or glass elevators is the phenomenon that occurs when women and minorities are hired into nonrevenue-producing staff functions that do not normally lead to high-level executive positions and are prohibited from transferring into other occupations within the organization. Public relations, corporate communications, and HR are often given as examples of nonrevenue-producing functions.

Affirmative action plans, consequently, must be concerned not only with getting protected classes into the organization, but also with moving them up the organization. Activities such as mentor programmes, lateral transfers to revenue-producing departments, and developmental programmes are often implemented by organizations to improve the potential for promotion of members of protected classes to alleviate both glass ceilings and glass walls.

The courts are constantly wrestling with the issue of preferences for protected classes, quotas versus goals, and reverse discrimination. For example, following the series of reverse discrimination cases from Bakke to Gratz and Grutter provides a perspective as to the thinking of the Supreme Court. As new justices are appointed, that thinking might be modified or significantly changed.

EEOC Complaint Process

Following the discussion of the complaint process itself is a brief discussion regarding employer response to a complaint. The process has been amended several times by law or new regulations issued by the EEOC. The process can be summarized as follows:

- Initiation of the complaint What might seem simple can be a bit complex in that the complainant often is covered under two or more separate antidiscrimination laws. The basic rule is that an employer must file a complaint within 180 days of the alleged discrimination. However, the EEOC permits local and state equal employment opportunity agencies to process and attempt to settle federal discrimination complaints. In these cases, the local or state agency typically has exclusive jurisdiction for the first 60 days after complaint filing. If a state or local agency has jurisdiction, the individual has 300 days from the date of the alleged discriminatory action or 30 days from the date of receipt that the state or local agency has terminated its processing to file a charge with the EEOC, whichever is earlier.

Discriminatory acts that are continuing in nature, such as a hostile work environment, do not all have to occur within the stated time period (180 or 300 days). However, at least one of the acts must. When that occurs, acts outside the time period may be considered for determining employer liability. For simplicity and because state or local laws may differ, the following description of the complaint process addresses only EEOC procedures.

- Determination of jurisdiction The EEOC determines whether it has jurisdiction. If not, the complaint is rejected. For example, a complaint against an organization that has five employees is not covered under the Civil Rights Act of 1964.
- Initial acceptance and request for information If the EEOC has jurisdiction, it accepts the complaint and advises the employer that a complaint has been filed against it, generally within 10 days of receipt of the complaint. It simultaneously sends the organization a Request for Information form that the employer must complete and return.
- EEOC investigation The EEOC next determines the level of investigation that it wants to pursue base on a priority lists. Full investigations are normally conducted on charges that appear to involve matters that have been targeted as priorities. Lesser levels of investigation are required for complaints that appear to have some merit, but require additional information and little or no investigation might be done on complaints that appear to require dismissal.

Depending on the level of investigation, the EEOC requires the organization to produce certain records. In full investigations, the EEOC often requires the production of voluminous records. The organization, in addition to the records required, provides an explanation and its defence of the alleged violation. In complex or priority cases, an EEOC investigator might visit the organization to review records or talk to individuals having knowledge of the complaint.

If the investigation reveals that no discrimination has taken place, the EEOC issues a Dismissal and Notice of Rights Letter. The complainant may then pursue the case in the court system. If there appears to be reasonable cause to believe that illegal discrimination has occurred, the EEOC issues a Letter of Determination, also referred to as a cause letter.

- Conciliation After the Letter of Determination is issued, the EEOC attempts to get the organization and complainant to settle the case. This often involves continuing negotiation and conciliation efforts. The EEOC has begun a programme of offering the parties voluntary mediation ("Employee and Labour Relations") to speed up complaint processing and settlement.
- Final action If attempts at conciliation fail, the EEOC has two options. First it can initiate suit against the employer. As a practical matter, the EEOC is likely to undertake this action only when the complaint involves a number of employees. The second option is more likely and that is the issuance of a Right-to-Sue letter. This permits the complainant to purse the case in court.

Employer Response to a Complaint

On receipt of notification that a complaint has been filed with the EEOC, an organization should take the following steps:

- Review the complaint and the employment records of the complainant.
- Take no retaliatory action against the complainant.
- Conduct an internal investigation regarding the allegations contained in the complaint.

- Cooperate, to the extent possible, with the EEOC. EEOC investigations can be quite burdensome for the employer with massive and, sometimes, seemingly irrelevant requests for information and analysis. The scope of these requests can often be reduced through negotiation with the EEOC investigators.
- If the agency issues a cause letter, the organization must determine whether to settle or to fight the complaint in the court system. The decision is often a difficult one, taking into consideration the merits of the complaint, costs of defence, and ethical implications. An organization might elect to defend itself in court even though the costs of such a defence might run much more than the cost of settlement. The SPHR must lead the organization in these matters, attempting to determine the importance of the case to the organization and the message the decision will send to stakeholders and, most importantly, the employees.

GENDER DISCRIMINATION

Title VII of the Civil Rights Act of 1964 prohibits discrimination in employment based on sex. However, the definition of what defines discrimination has been the subject of much judicial interpretation. In this section, the following issues are discussed:

- Sexual harassment
- The broad scope of hostile environment
- Harassment prevention programmes and affirmative defence
- Sexual orientation issues

Sexual Harassment

Sexual harassment is a violation of Title VII. The EEOC first issued its Guidelines on Sex Discrimination in 1980 defining sexual harassment as a violation of Title VII prohibitions against discrimination based on sex. The EEOC defines sexual harassment as unwelcome sexual advances, requests for sexual favours, and other verbal or physical conduct of a sexual nature that takes place under any of the following conditions:

- Submission to such conduct is made either explicitly or implicitly a term or condition of employment.
- Submission to or rejection of such conduct by an individual is used as the basis for employment decision affecting the individual.
- Such conduct has the purpose or effect of unreasonably interfering with an individual's work performance or creating an intimidating, hostile, or offensive work environment.

For the employer to be held liable for sexual harassment, the individual making the claim must prove

- There was unwelcome conduct or communication of a sexual nature (harassment).
- The harassment was based on a person's sex.
- The harassment affected a term, condition, or privilege of the person's employment.
- The employer is legally responsible for the harassment.

Both the EEOC and the courts recognize two distinct types of sexual harassment: quid pro quo and hostile environment. They are discussed next.

Quid Pro Quo

Quid pro quo means this for that and occurs when an employee is forced to choose between submitting to sexual advances or forfeiting employment opportunities or benefits. It is harassment in which employment outcomes are linked to the granting of sexual favours. By definition, the harasser must be in a position or perceived to be in a position to, in fact, create the employment opportunities and tangible employments promised. Consequently, quid pro quo harassment must be perpetrated by a supervisor or manager. EEOC guidelines provide that the employer is strictly responsible for the actions of its supervisors, regardless of whether the employer knew or should have known of their occurrence. Nevertheless, it is possible for the employer to avoid legal liability in some cases of quid pro quo sexual harassment by using an affirmative defence. This issue is discussed later in this section.

Hostile Environment

The Supreme Court decision in Meritor Savings Bank established the concept of hostile workplace environment. A hostile workplace environment can violate Title VII even if there are no employment or economic effects if that environment unreasonably interferes with an individual's work or work performance or creates an intimidating, hostile, or offensive working environment.

As opposed to quid pro quo sexual harassment, the employer is liable only if it knew or should have known that the conditions existed. Also as opposed to quid pro quo, the harassers do not have to be supervisors for the organization to be found guilty. In fact, the harassers do not even have to be employees of the organization. Customers, suppliers, independent contractors, and so forth can all create a hostile work environment. Activities such as sexual or derogatory jokes or remarks, offensive physical contact, sexually oriented horseplay, posting of offensive or pornographic material, inappropriate emails, solicitation of sexual favours, and so forth might lead to hostile environment claims.

The courts have consistently ruled that such behaviours and activities must be severe or pervasive to be considered harassment. In its Harris decision, discussed earlier, the Supreme Court ruled that a "reasonable person" test must be used to determine whether harassment has occurred. This means that the environment must be one that a "reasonable person" would find abusive. Examples of environments that might be considered abusive are ones that

- Prevent advancement in one's career.
- Result in constructive discharge. Constructive discharge occurs when the work environment is so hostile that a reasonable person would quit.
- Affect the psychological well-being of the victim.
- Detract from the individual's work performance.

As stated before, the employer has strict liability in quid pro quo cases because that type of harassment must be perpetrated by an agent of the organization—a manager or supervisor. However, what happens if the hostile environment is a result of managerial behaviour? There are two Supreme Court decisions that together address the issue. Faragher v. City of Boca Raton provides the basis for an employer's defence of actions of its managers as long as a tangible employment action has not occurred. Ellerth v. Burlington Northern defines what types of actions are to be considered tangible employment actions.

The Broad Scope of Hostile Environment

In 1999, the EEOC provided new and comprehensive guidance on the subject of harassment and hostile environment. The guidance expands the concept of hostile environment from prohibition against sexual harassment to include prohibition against national origin harassment. EEOC defines actions that might include a hostile or abusive work environment based on national origin to include ethnic slurs, workplace graffiti, or other offensive conduct directed toward an individual's birthplace, ethnicity, culture, or foreign accent. The EEOC indicates that the following factors should be considered in determining whether the national origin harassment rises to the level of creating a hostile work environment.

- Whether the conduct was physically threatening or intimidating
- How frequently the conduct was repeated
- Whether the conduct was hostile and/or patently offensive

- The context in which the harassment occurred
- Whether management responded appropriately when it learned of the harassment

Harassment Prevention Programmes and Affirmative Defence

To defend itself against complaints of harassment, either quid pro quo or hostile environment, the organization must first have a proactive harassment prevention programme in place. Critical components of an effective programme are as follows:

- Establishment of a harassment policy covering all protected classes
- Executive-level support and commitment to the policy
- Training of managers on the policy
- Communication of the policy throughout the organization
- Providing a procedure for employees to bring issues of sexual or other types of harassment to the organization's attention
- Protection of complainants from retaliation
- Quick and thorough investigations of complaints
- Taking timely and effective action if indicated by the results of the investigation

If the organization has a viable harassment protection programme and can demonstrate that it took reasonable care to prevent harassment, it might be able to raise an affirmative defence against allegations of quid pro quo sexual harassment or national origin or sexual discrimination based on hostile environment. The critical issue in this defence is that the organization followed its procedures and policies as indicated in its harassment prevention policies. An affirmative defence must be based on two factors:

- The organization exercised reasonable care to prevent and promptly correct any harassing behaviour.
- The complainant unreasonably failed to take advantage of any preventive or corrective opportunities provided.

If the employee suffered no tangible employment action, an organization that has developed, implemented, and rigorously followed its harassment prevention plan might be able to avoid liability, even with respect to the actions of its managers, in a discrimination complaint. However, if a tangible employment action has occurred as part of the harassment, the organization has no viable defence.

Sexual Orientation Issues

Sexual orientation is not recognized or protected under Title VII. Although the Oncale v. Sundowner Offshore Services decision, discussed earlier, protects individuals from discrimination and harassment by the same sex, it does not provide protection based on sexual preference or orientation. However, many state and local laws and ordinances do prevent discrimination based on sexual preference.

TIME WORK ARRANGEMENTS

Feldman (1990) delineated five ways in which part-time work could be differentiated, two of which are examined in this research. Part time work can be permanent or temporary; and, sourced directly from an organization or indirectly through an employment agency.

Permanent part-timers work fewer than 35 hours per week on a continuous basis in the same organization, while temporary workers are hired for limited periods of time to deal with fluctuating worldoads or short-term personnel shortages. Part-timers can source their work directly from an organization and be paid by the same organization. Or, they could get their lob assignments through an employment agency, in which case they will be paid by the agency.

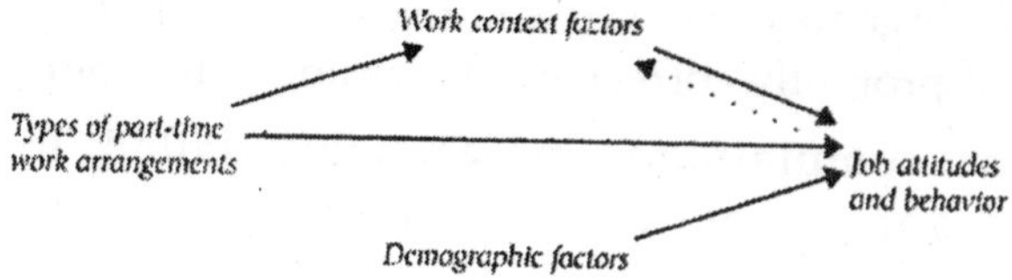

Fig. Proposed Framework for Research

Job attitudes and behaviours among part-timers differ across different part-time work arrangements. Generally, temporary part-timers display the poorest job attitudes and lowest commitment to their organizations. On the other hand, because of the sustained contributions they make to their employers, permanent part-timers are viewed as more valuable. They tend to get higher wages, more fringe benefits and greater job challenge and hence display better job attitudes. Therefore, we predicted that permanent part-timers experience higher levels of job satisfaction, work motivation, and lower level of intention to turnover compared to temporary part-timers.

Feldman (1990) suggested that it is unlikely for employment agencies to invest in training for part-timers who are on their payroll, while organizations are likely to do so. The short term nature of their job assignments makes it uneconomical for agencies to invest in training part-timers. On the other hand, organization-hired part-timers generally stay with the same employee for a longer period. It therefore makes sense for them to invest in training to improve the part-timers' skills and help them integrate into the work group. Feldman's suggestion regarding the contrasting attitudes of agencies and organizations toward training of part-timers certainly holds true in the Singapore context. As part-timers are likely to view training as beneficial to their career development, we hypothesized that organization-hired part-timers experience higher levels of job satisfaction, work motivation and lower level of intention to turnover compared to agency-hired part-timers.

Work Context Factors

Part-time work arrangements may also affect work context factors which are deemed to be important to such employees. Five such factors – scheduling flexibility, relation with co-workers, relation with supervisors, pay and fringe benefits packages – are examined in this research. The ability to integrate work life with personal demands – such as family commitment, leisure activities, school and friends – is a key concern for part-timers.

As such, part-timers who are given freedom in work scheduling are likely to have more positive job attitudes and are less likely to change their jobs. In this regard, it is interesting that permanent part-timers experience greater job scheduling conflict than temporary part-timers. It could be that in order to secure the more permanent temporary jobs – which typically offer higher pay, better fringe benefits and more challenging assignments – permanent part-timers have to trade-off some schedule flexibility. For instance, they may have to work on undesirable schedules which conflict with family demands. Hence we predicted that permanent part-timers experience greater conflict in job scheduling than temporary part-timers.

Agency-hired part-timers are likely to experience more scheduling conflict than organization-hired ones due to restrictions imposed by personal demands. Hence we predicted that agency-hired part-timers experience more conflict in job scheduling than organization-hired part-timers. Feldman (1990) proposed that permanent and organization-hired part-timers are most likely to receive adequate training opportunities. These training opportunities provide for social interaction, which translates into greater integration in the work groups. On the other hand, temporary and agency hired part-timers, realizing that they are usually the first to be displaced in an economic and organization downturn, are less likely to maintain close bonding with their colleagues. Hence we predicted that compared to their temporary and agency-hired counterparts, permanent and organization-hired part-timers enjoy better relation with co-workers.

The natures of their employment enable the permanent and organization hired part-timers to make a greater sustained contribution to the firm, thus enhancing their value to the organization. Recognizing this fact, supervisors are more likely to support and interact with these part-time employees. It has also been suggested that the supervisors' perception regarding the peripherality of employees influence the type of work assigned. For instance, if an employee is perceived to be marginal, less desirable tasks may be assigned. Both these factors would lead one to hypothesize that permanent and organization-hired part-timers should enjoy better work relations with supervisor compared to temporary and agency-hired part-timers.

Research indicated that permanent part-timers receive higher pay and fringe benefits than temporary part-timers. This suggests that organization-hired part-timers may also receive better pay and fringe benefits compared to agency-hired part-timers. Temporary employment holds great appeal for young workers who want flexible schedules to juggle between school and work. These young part-timers also tend to turn to employment agencies for their job placement to decrease their job search costs. As such, agency-hired part-timers, who usually are equipped with minimal work experience, are likely to receive lower pay and fringe benefits. Therefore, permanent part-time employees are likely to receive higher pay and more fringe benefits than temporary part-timers; likewise organization-hired part-timers are likely to receive higher pay and fringe benefits than their agency counterparts.

Impact of Employment Characteristics

Feldman and Doerpinghaus (1992b) found that from a set of employment characteristics (types of work arrangements, demographic factors, work context factors, frame of reference), work arrangements and demographic factors accounted for much of the variance in part-timers' job attitudes and behavioural intentions. However, they did not provide any theoretical considerations for the order of entry among the independent variables. In order to provide a renewed foundation for the explanation of the dependent variables, this study re-explored the nature of relationships that exist between the variables. Emphasis was placed on deriving a tighter framework for future research.

METHOD

Sample and Research Design

Responses were received from employment agencies, hotel, healthcare, travel, retailing, food and entertainment organizations. The final sample comprised part-timers from 7 employment agencies and 12 organizations. A strategy of purposeful variation among participants on the organization-hired versus agency-hired dimension ensured that these two sub-groups of part-timers could be adequately represented for statistical analyses. Questionnaires were distributed to the part-timers through the Recruitment/Human Resource Department in the participating employment agencies and organizations. Completed questionnaires were sealed and deposited in a box provided at the Recruitment/Human Resource Department. These were then collected by the researchers after two weeks.

In-depth personal interviews with six part-timers were conducted before the actual survey and feedback from these sessions was used to reduce ambiguity in the questionnaire. The cover letter was specially worded to encourage greater response and, last but not least, respondents were assured of complete and strict confidentiality.

Measurement Scales

Job satisfaction was assessed using a 15-item scale developed by Warr, Cook and Wall (1979). Representative items include, "How satisfied are you with your fellow workers?" and "How satisfied are you with the amount of responsibility you are given?" The 7-point Likert scale has responses ranging from 1. Work motivation was measured by a 6-item scale developed by Hackman and Oldham (1975). Representative questions include, "Most people on this job feel a great sense of personal satisfaction when they do the job well," and "Most people on this job feel bad or unhappy when they find they have performed the work poorly." Response options range from 1 to 7. Coefficient alpha of .79 and internal reliability of 0.71 were reported.

Intention to leave was measured using a 3-Item scale derived from Cammann et al. (1979). A representative question from the scale is, "I often think about quitting." Mean values were not cited in the source publication but the coefficient alpha was reported to be 0.83. Types of part-time work arrangement were assessed by two close-ended questions. Respondents were asked if their part-time assignment was temporary or permanent in nature and sourced directly from the organization or through an employment agency.

The Work Facilitation-Subordinate Relations sub-scale from the supervisor module of the Michigan Organizational Assessment Questionnaire was used to measure relation with supervisor. A representative item is, "My supervisor keeps subordinates informed about things that go on in the organization." The 7-items scale has 7 response options ranging from 1 to 7 and mean values across the items constitute the scale score. On a sample of more than 400 employees, authors of the scale found that the sub-scale yielded alpha coefficient of 0.93.

Relation with co-workers was assessed through the 3-item scale developed by Taylor and Bowers (1972). A representative item is, "Persons in my work group exchange opinions and ideas." The 7-point Likert scale had responses ranging from 1 to 7. In the source publication, the alpha coefficient was reported at 0.90.

Pay, fringe benefits, and scheduling flexibility were assessed through single-item measures. A list of fringe benefits was provided and respondents were asked to indicate the benefits that they currently received. Some of the fringe benefits listed were CPF contribution, paid sick leave, and paid holiday leave. Scheduling flexibility was assessed through the question: "How often do you experience outside-life conflict (e.g. family, friends, school, leisure) in working at your current part-time job?".

Descriptive Statistics

Of the 745 questionnaires distributed, 379 part-time workers from 7 employment agencies and 12 organizations responded; 17 questionnaires were found to be incomplete and thus excluded, bringing the number of usable questionnaires to 362. The effective response rate turned out to be 48.6%.

Table given below shows that the sample comprised 68.1% females and 31.9% males. These respondents were predominantly single (66.6%), Chinese (85.8%), students (56.5%). More than half of them attained secondary school qualification and below, with 63.2% between 15-24 years of age. The sample characteristics are somewhat different from the national sample which has more married (63.4%) and older (more than 50% between the ages of 30 to 49) part-timers. Two events could have accounted for this occurrence.

First of all, this research was carried out during the June school holidays which is a popular period for school students to Join the part-time workforce. Hence more of them were surveyed. Secondly, more organizations which participated in the research were from service rather than the manufacturing sector. As the service sector tend to employ younger part-timers, the current sample ended up with a bigger proportion of younger part-timers. Conclusions drawn from this research should be seen in the light of these factors.

Table: Profile of Respondents

Variable Gender	*Valid Percentage (%)*
Male	31.9 %
Female	68.1 %
Marital Status	
Single	66.6 %
Married	32.3 %
Others	1.1 %

Race	
Chinese	85.8 %
Malay	8.9 %
Indian/Others	5.3 %
Education	
PSLE level/'N' Level	23.8 %
'0' level/NTC	45.6 %
'A' level	12.9%
Diploma and above	17.8 %
Age	
15 - 24 years	63.2 %
25 - 34 years	10.3%
35 - 44 years	14.6%
45 - 54 years	7.8 %
55 years and above	4.1%
Student status	
Yes 56.5 %	
No 43.5%	
Wages	
$4 and below	14.9%
$4 - $4.99	16.6%
$5 - $5.99	40.4%

Table: Profile of Respondents

Variable Gender	*Valid Percentage (%)*
$6 - $6.99	10.4%
$7 - $7.99	6.2%
$8 and above	11.5%
Tenure	
less than 6 months	56.9 %
6 to 12 months	11.9 %
13 to 24 months	6.3%
2 to 5 years	11.9%
more than 5 years	13.0 %

Types of part-time work arrangements	
(i) Organization-hired	55.8 %
Agency-hired	44.2 %
(ii) Permanent	32.7 %
Temporary	67.3 %

Note: N = 362; Missing values have been excluded.

Factor and Reliability Analyses

All multi-item scales were factor analyzed to ascertain their dimensionality. Factor analysis performed on the job satisfaction scale showed that the two newly included items (fringe benefits offered and flexibility of job schedule) both displayed strong factor loadings of 0.60 and above. These results confirmed their inclusion in the job satisfaction scale.

The fourth item on the work motivation scale was discarded as it yielded a factor loading of only 0.19 (well below the cutoff point of 0.50). The reliability of the scale improved significantly from .62 to .76 when this item was deleted. Being a reverse-scored item, it could have caused some confusion to the respondents.

Items belonging to the intention to turnover, work relations with supervisor and co-workers scales all loaded into the hypothesized factor structure; all factor loadings were at least .60.

Evidence for reliability of the measurement scales was provided by high Cronbach's alphas. The Pearson correlation matrix also shows that correlations between these established measurement scales were significantly high, thus confirming the validity of these constructs.

Job satisfaction and work motivation were positively and significantly correlated ($r = 0.46$, $p < .001$). Furthermore, intention to turnover was negatively and significantly correlated with these two attitudinal scales ($r = -0.46$ and $r = -0.18$ respectively; $p < .001$).

Table: Means, Standard Deviation, Reliabilities and Correlations

Variables	*Mean*	*SD*	*1*	*2*	*3*	*4*	*5*
1. Supervisor	4.71	1.07	(.88)				
2. Co-workers	4.71	1.13	.44***	(.85)			
3. Job Satisfaction	78.68	15.17	.55***	.46***	(.91)		
4. Work Motivation	5.20	.90	.33***	.33***	.46***	(.76)	
5. Intention to Turnover	3.69	1.56	.27***	.22***	.46***	.18***	(.74)

*** $p < .001$ $N = 358$ Figures on the diagonals are the reliabilities

Supervisor: Relation wtih supervisor; Co-workers: Relation with co-workers

Results in Table support the hypothesis that permanent part-timers expressed significantly higher levels of job satisfaction ($t = 5.32$, $p < .001$), work motivation ($t = 1.76$, $p < .05$), and are less likely to quit or leave their current assignments ($t = -6.45$, $p < .001$). Likewise, organization-hired part-timers reported higher levels of job satisfaction ($t = 5.94$, $p < .001$), work motivation ($t = 3.21$, $p < .001$), and less intent to turnover ($t = -8.27$, $p < .001$).

Table: Comparison of Job Attitudes and Turnover Intention between Permanent/Temporary and Organization-hired/ Agency-hired Part-Timers

Variable	*Job Satisfaction*	*Work Motivation*	*Intention to Turnover*
Permanent	84.54	75.41	5.32***
Temporary	5.32	5.14	1.76
t - Value	2.97	4.06	-6.45***
Organization hired	82.52	73.19	5.94***
Agency hired	5.33	5.03	3.21***
t-Value	3.14	4.40	8.27***

*** $p < .001$ ** $p < .01$

Results from Table show that permanent part-timers enjoy better relation with supervisor and fringe benefits than temporary part-timers (t = 4.19, p < .001 and t = 10.89, p < .001, respectively). No significant differences were detected in their response to the other work context factors. Interestingly, part-timers contrasted on source of employment show more significant differences. Results supported most of the hypotheses, suggesting that organization-hired part-timers do experience more favourable work conditions than agency-hired ones. These employees experience less scheduling conflict (t = -1.37, p < .1), enjoy better relations with co-workers, (t = 2.48, p < .01) and supervisor (t 4.68, p < .001), and finally, receive significantly more fringe benefits (t = 12.11, p < .001).

Table: Sample Sizers, Means and t-values by Work Context Factors

Work-Context Factors	*Perma-nent (N)*	*Tempo-rary (N)*	*t - value*	*Organization-hired (N)*	*Agency-hired (N)*	*t - value*
Scheduling Flexibility	4.10 (114)	4.04 (235)	0.61	3.99 (200)	4.13 (160)	-1.37*
Co-workers	4.75 (114)	4.68 (235)	0.53	4.84 (202)	4.54 (160)	2.48**
Supervisor	5.04 (114)	4.53 (235)	4.19***	4.93 (202)	4.42 (160)	4.68***
Pay	3.14 (113)	3.15 (233)	-0.02	3.22 (196)	3.08 (160)	0.88
Fringe Benefits	3.07 (114)	1.30 (235)	10.89***	2.57 (202)	0.97 (160)	12.11***

Tests of Multicollinearity

Tolerance and variance inflation factor (VIF) measures were used to help detect the presence of collinear variables (Tabachnick & Fidell, 1989). DIagnostics accompanying the regression results for intention to turnover show that age and marital status were highly correlated. The low tolerances (age = .24 and marital status = .22) and high VIF's (age = 4.24 and marital status = 4.56) is expected, since there is a natural relationship between these two variables. Bivariate correlation data revealed that the correlation between these 2 variables is

.87 ($p < .01$). This multicollinearlty problem was eliminated by deleting the marital status variable from the regression analyses.

Stepwise Regression Analyses

Results from the regression analyses, shown in Table below, revealed that variance in job satisfaction were explained by work context factors and type of work arrangement ($R^2 = .40$, $p < .001$). The bulk of the variance - 39% out of a total of 40% - were explained by relations with supervisor and co-workers, and fringe benefits. Variance in work motivation was significantly explained by relations with supervisor and co-workers, and age ($R^2 = .21$, $p < .001$). The most significant predictors, once again, were the work context factors. Variance in intention to turnover were significantly predicted by source of employment, age and relations with supervisor and co-worker accounted significantly for the ($R^2 = .24$, $p < .001$). The first three variables contributed most to the variance in intention to turnover, with the subsequent addition of co-worker relation contributing merely an additional 1% ($p < .01$).

Table: Statistical Stepwise Regression Analysis of Employment Characteristics with Job Satisfaction, Work Motivation and Intention to Turnover

Dependent Variables	*Independent Variables*	R^2	R^2 *Change*
Job Satisfaction	Supervisor	.29***	.29***
	Supervisor, Co-workers	.35***	.06***
	Supervisor, Co-workers, Fringe Benefits	.39***	.04***
	Supervisor, Co-workers, Benefits, Work Arrangement	.40***	.01**
Work Motivation	Co-worker	.11***	.11***
	Co-worker, Age	.15***	.04***
	Co-worker, Age, Supervisor	.18***	.03**
Intention to Turnover	Employment source	.16***	.16***

Employment source, Age	.19***	.03***
Employment source, Age, Supervisor	.23***	.04*
Employment source, Age, Supervisor, Co-worker	.24***	.01*

Note: N = 361; ***p < .001 ** p < .01 * p < .05

Discussion

The results of this research highlight the importance of part-time work arrangements, demographic, and work context factors in understanding the job attitudes of part-timers. In line with Feldman and Doerpinghaus (1992b), the findings show that permanent and organization-hired part-timers expressed significantly greater job satisfaction, work motivation and less intention to turnover compared to their temporary and agency-hired counterparts.

Contrary to Feldman and Doerpinghaus (1992a), there is no significant difference in scheduling conflict between permanent and temporary part-timers. On the other hand, agency-hired part-timers did experience significantly more outside-life conflict compared to organization-hired ones. This difference could be accounted for by the fact that agency-hired part-timers, many of whom are in their teens, might have more personal commitments than their older organization-hired counterparts.

Besides their family, friends, school and leisure, this group of part-timers must also submit time-sheets on a regular basis to their employment agencies or report to the agencies to collect their pay cheques. Having to integrate such demands into their life probably generate the greater level of conflict. Another contributing factor could be the way companies manage their core workers and "buffer" group of part-timers. Firms usually turn to agency-hired part-timers to fill temporary positions in the undesirable weekend and holiday shifts during peak periods. Being stuck with these work schedules could have affected their ability to integrate their work life with personal demands.

The results indicated that permanent and temporary part-timers do not differ significantly in relation with co-workers. However, organization-hired part-timers do enjoy better work relation with co-workers. Training opportunities offered by the organizations could have provided such part-timers greater interaction opportunities which in turn allow them to be integrated into their work groups. Such opportunities are often not given to agency-hired part-timers. The short-term nature of their work contract means that it does not make economic sense for agencies to train them.

In contrast with Feldman and Doerpinghaus (1992a), this research found that permanent and organization-hired part-timers do enjoy better relation with supervisor compared to temporary and agency-hired part-timers. There seems to be greater work facilitation by supervisors which in turn engenders better supervisor-subordinate relations between the two parties. The supervisors' investment of time and effort in these categories of part-timers is understandable since they remain in the same company for a longer period of time.

In contrast to Feldman and Doerpinghaus (1992a), this research does not support the claim that permanent part-timers receive higher pay than temporary part-timers. The same result was obtained with reference to part-timers contrasted on the source of employment. However, both permanent and organization-hired part-timers received more fringe benefits than their temporary and agency-hired counterparts. The findings indicate that employers are inclined to use fringe benefits rather than pay as the "carrot" to retain part-timers. As a case in point, extending equitable benefits to both part-time and full-time employees has helped JVC Electronics in Singapore to retain their staff and reduce turnover.

The regression analyses show that almost all employment characteristics significantly explained the variances in the part-timers' job satisfaction, work motivation and intention to turnover, though the list of predictors are not identical to that in Feldman and Doerpinghaus (1992b). In line with extensive literature in this area, work context factors accounted for most variance in job satisfaction. The permanent/temporary job dimension also contributed significantly to the model, thus suggesting that favourable work conditions accompanying permanent part-time work arrangements (e.g., better work relations with supervisors and fringe benefits given) could have led job incumbents to experience higher level of job satisfaction.

As for work motivation, relation with supervisor accounted for most of the variance. Being motivated usually entail the presence of the three psychological states of knowing results, experiencing responsibility and meaningfulness on the job. Relation with the supervisor is directly linked to these states. If a supervisor provides support and facilitation on the job, the employee is likely to be assigned greater task responsibilities and accumulate learning experiences. Much of the variance in intention to turnover was accounted for by the organization-hired/agency-hired dimension. The other significant predictors in the regression were age and relations with both supervisor and co-workers. This suggests that work arrangements, demographic and work context factors exert collective effects in influencing the turnover intention of part-timers.

To maintain a high level of performance and ensure desired behavioural outcomes, organizations and employment agencies must integrate these relevant factors into their management plans and policies. Agency-hired part-timers paled in comparison with organization-hired ones. The source of these differences lies mainly in training opportunities offered by organizations. However, the lack of training of part-timers by agencies may become a thing of the past. As competition intensifies in the employment services industry, one may see agencies assuming the entire burden of the training costs in order to entice part-timers.

The agencies' role in the functioning of the part-time work system in Singapore may also change as they consider taking on not just the training but the entire contingent staffing function. This is a step in the positive direction as it ensures that part-timers are well matched with the job requirements in organizations. An example in Singapore is PF1, a partnership between ECCO (an employment agency) and IBM, which assumed the role of the human resource department to take care of IBM's entire contingent staffing needs. It is a win-win situation for both IBM Singapore and ECCO as PF1 ensures a better alignment of recruitment efforts with organizational needs.

According equal opportunities and benefits, in terms of wage increments, training, etc., to all staff, regardless of employment status is another direction which organization should take. This strategy has helped JVC Electronics to retain staff and curb turnover Singapore. Besides attracting and motivating part-timers to stay on their assignments, it negates the possible resentment between full-time and part-time employees.

In short, there is need for employment agencies as well as organizations to provide conducive working conditions to all categories of part-timers in order to instil positive attitudes and curb premature turnover. In this regard, it is important for management to note the paradigm shift in employment patterns and take a proactive approach to integrate it into their human resource plans. As Feldman and Doerpinghaus (1992b) noted, employers who view part-time work as merely full-time work with shorter work hours, may miss the most important human resource issues involved in managing part-time employees.

A methodological trade-off may be present in using self-reported questionnaires. Respondents could be subjected to social desirability effect, though this limitation was partly addressed by the assurance of confidentiality. Only two out of the five relevant job dimensions suggested by Feldman (1990) were examined here. Future research could examine other dimensions such as voluntary/involuntary, sole-employment jobs/moonlighting jobs, and year-round/seasonal part-time employment.

Amongst these dimensions, sole-employment/ moonlighting jobs have not been the subject of any empirical research. In addition, future studies could also investigate whether the various blocks of independent factors exert direct or indirect effects on part-timers' job attitudes. Regression analyses employed in this study have provided an initial but useful idea concerning the critical independent variables involved. A final related avenue to pursue is to examine the existence of reciprocal causality among the key variables in Feldman's (1990) model.

Chapter 3

Job Evaluation

JOB ANALYSIS AND JOB DESCRIPTION

Job analysis is the systematic process of gathering information regarding the duties required of a job and the human characteristics necessary to successfully perform those duties. The work products of job analysis are job descriptions, which describe the job, and job specifications, which describe what kind of person to hire for the job. Job analysis can be described as the foundation of human resource management because it the basis for so many HR programmatic activities. Job analysis is used for

- *Recruitment:* Provides information about the nature of the job to guide recruitment activities
- *Selection:* Provides information on the knowledge, skills, and abilities required of persons that can successfully perform the job
- *Training Provides:* information regarding the tasks to be performed and the skills and knowledge required in order to guide the development of training programmes
- *Performance Evaluation:* Provides information on the level of proficiency of various tasks that are required in order to develop performance standards

- *Compensation:* Provides information necessary to evaluate the internal worth of the job to the organization and to compare it with jobs in the relevant job market in order to determine appropriate wage and benefit levels
- *EEO compliance:* Forms the basis for determining whether employment practices and decisions are job-related

The SPHR should be familiar with a number of concepts regarding the process of job analysis. Discussed in the following sections are

- Job analysis process
- Job analysis information requirements
- Data collection methods
- Writing job descriptions and job specifications
- Competencies and the future of job analysis

THE JOB ANALYSIS PROCESS

Job analysis can be described as a six-step process as follows:

1. *Determine the purpose for conducting job analysis:* The purpose should be clearly linked to organizational success and the organizational strategic plan. A frequent reason for conducting job analysis projects is that jobs are much more dynamic than ever before. Technology and the demands of a competitive environment frequently change the nature of the job requiring reevaluation. Rapid organizational growth often means new types of jobs requiring job descriptions. High turnover or low job satisfaction might be other indicators of the need for job analysis projects. High turnover might indicate that jobs are not properly priced in relation to the external job market. Because job analysis drives compensation decisions, old job analysis results might need to be updated. Low job satisfaction is often the result of

boring or repetitive jobs. Job analysis can identify new ways to design jobs to make them more interesting and challenging.

2. *Identify the jobs to be analyzed:* After the purpose is identified, it provides some indication as to which jobs should be included in the job analysis. Often, however, time and resource constraints limit the total number of jobs that can be included in the process. For example, if the organization as a whole is experiencing turnover, that data should be analyzed to determine the particular departments in which the problem seems to be the worst. That analysis indicates the direction for the project. The same is true if the organization is growing or experiencing significant change in only certain areas. Those are the jobs that are most appropriate for job analysis.

   When a large number of employees encumber the same job, a determination must be made as to how many of the positions will be included in the project. Statistical sampling might be appropriate if the number is large.

   This is also the time in the project in which communication with both employees and managers begins to take place. They should be advised as to the purpose of the project and provided a general overview of the process.

3. *Review relevant background data:* Efficient and effective job analysis often builds from previous work and data that are already corrected. A review of current job descriptions and organizational charts provides basic information with which to begin the project. Analysis of workflow assists in understanding the responsibilities of the job and how it fits into the total work process.

4. *Plan and execute the job analysis project:* Planning is the key to successful projects. The appropriate data-gathering methodologies must be determined and an

action plan developed as to project activities and milestones. Data collection methods are covered in the next section.

5. *Write the job description and job specifications:* After the data are collected and analyzed, they must be turned into the written work outputs, job descriptions, and job specifications. Before these documents are finalized, they should be reviewed with a representative sample of both the affected employees and their managers. If modifications to the documents are required, they should be made and the appropriate final approvals obtained.
6. *Periodic review:* It is good HR practice to engage in a planned process of periodic review of job descriptions and job specifications. Many organizations use a revolving process, reviewing a portion of the organization each year so that the entire organization is reviewed in a cycle—usually three, four, or five years. During the review, managers in that portion of the organization under review are required to verify the accuracy of the job descriptions and job specifications. If managers indicate job descriptions are out of date, those descriptions are included in the job analysis review. In addition, a random sample of jobs is also included for review.

Job Analysis Information Requirements

The job analysis process requires the collection of sufficient information to fully understand the job, its functions, and how it fits in both the workflow and organizational structure of the organization to produce the job description and job specifications. The following information is representative of the types of data collected during the job analysis process:

- *Work activities:* Information must be collected on the tasks performed by the job and what is to be accomplished (work outputs). The data should include how, why, and when the activity is performed.

- *Worker activities:* These data include worker behaviours such as decision-making, communicating, and performing physical actions such as lifting heavy weights.
- *Machines, tools, and equipment:* Data here include information regarding the types of equipment that are used in the job. This might include computers, safety equipment, machines, and other devices that facilitate accomplishment of the work.
- *Job-related tangible and intangibles:* Information is required on the types of materials used and the products made or services rendered. In addition, information is needed on the type of knowledge dealt with (chemistry or accounting, for example).
- *Performance standards:* Information is needed about requirements for productivity and quality required for successful performance of the job. Work standards, production records, and so forth are collected.
- *Job context:* A wide variety of information is collected here. Examples include reporting relationships, type of employees supervised (if any), working conditions, financial incentives, and types of contacts the job has with other jobs and the purposes of those contacts.
- *Human requirements:* These include job-related knowledge and skills such as education, training, credentials, and work experience. In addition, information is needed on required personal attributes such as aptitudes, physical characteristics, and personality.

Data Collection Methods

Information regarding the tasks performed and the human characteristics needed to successfully perform them can be gathered in many ways. The most common are as follows:

1. *Observation:* The observer watches the individual that is performing the job and takes notes as to what is occurring. The advantage of such an approach is that

the individual doing the job analysis sees for him or herself exactly what is being done. However, there are several disadvantages. The first is that this method might be appropriate only for what are referred to as short-cycle jobs; that is, those that are repetitive in nature and in which the full range of job responsibilities is repeated at relatively short intervals. Otherwise, the observer is liable to miss some of the tasks that are essential to the job. Observation cannot really capture work that is not observable, such as decision-making, thinking, and analysis. Another issue is time. Observation methods are very time-consuming, and, thus, expensive to do. Some types of observation methods are

- *Time and motion studies:* These are normally performed by industrial engineers and involve determining the most efficient way to perform a particular task and the normal time required to do so. Time and motion studies can be used to not only develop job descriptions and job specifications, but also to develop piece rate compensation programmes.
- *Work sampling:* This process involves statistically sampling what is being done by the worker during random periods of the day. These are recorded and analyzed. This method is typically more efficient than continuous observation and is most appropriate for repetitive jobs.
- *Critical incidents:* Critical incidents are the recordation of positive and negative job performance. Critical incidents can be used to develop the job description and job specifications and also to develop the associated performance standards.
- *Employee logs:* The employee can observe him or herself by completing a diary or log, recording exactly what is being done at periodic intervals during the day. In addition to the obvious interruption of work, other issues associated with this method are that the

employee might often forget to record activities and might indicate what he or she thinks should be done as opposed to exactly what is being done.

2. *Interviews:* The job analyst can interview the employee inquiring as exactly what activities are engaged and what knowledge, skills, and abilities are required. To cover all aspects of the job and provide a basis for analysis, good practice is to develop a standardized and structured interview protocol that is used in all interviews. Interviews provide in-depth information and might be appropriate when there are only a few persons occupying the job or when the data can be used to develop a survey instrument to be given to a larger number of employees. The disadvantage of using interviews is that they are very staff-intensive and can be costly.
3. *Questionnaires and checklists:* Surveys can be developed and given to a large number of employees. This is an efficient way of gathering data when a large number of individuals occupy the same job and when the employees are widely dispersed geographically. In addition, data gathered in this method can often be statistically analyzed.

   However, questionnaires are only as good as the questions they ask. Poorly developed questionnaires do not yield the data required to accurately prepare job descriptions and specifications. In addition, some employees might not have the literacy skills to properly complete the questionnaire, and others might purposefully answer the questions inaccurately. There are numerous off-the-shelf questionnaires and checklists that can be purchased from vendors or that are available from governmental agencies. Some of the more frequently used ones are:

   - *Position analysis questionnaire:* This is a specialized checklist, usually referred to as PAQ, which analyzes the job in six dimensions based on responses to nearly 200 questions. It can be used both for job analysis and job evaluation. The dimensions analyzed are

- Information input
- Mental processes
- Work output
- Relationships with other persons
- Job context
- Other job characteristics

- *Function job analysis:* Referred to as FJA, this is a comprehensive approach to job analysis that incorporates the goals of the organization, what workers do to achieve those goals, level and orientation of what the workers do, performance standards, and training content. The FJA evaluates the function of the job in three classifications: data, people, and things.
- *Management position description questionnaire:* This instrument is similar to the PAQ, but has been developed specifically to describe managerial jobs.
- *O Net Online:* This is a resource provided by the Department of Labour. It is a huge database, providing standardized job descriptions for a large number of jobs and incorporates the DOL's Dictionary of Occupational Titles.
- *Computer-based systems:* A huge number of computer-based job analysis systems can be obtained from a variety of vendors. These systems frequently contain large databases of descriptive statements that can be used to describe various tasks, based on responses to questions. These systems can often dramatically decrease the time required for job analysis and can facilitate decentralization of the process to management.

- *Multiple methods:* It is often good practice to use multiple methods of data collection. For example, interviews can often be used to develop a basic understanding of the jcb under evaluation and can be used to develop a questionnaire used to capture data from many employees. The data can then be analyzed and entered into another system prior to developing the job descriptions and job specifications. This often provides a deeper understanding of the job and more defensible job description and job specifications should either be an issue in a complaint process being heard before a third party.

  Job analysis data collection is extremely important in regard to compliance with the Americans with Disabilities Act. Analysis of the data must reveal what the essential functions (as opposed to marginal functions) of the job are. The essential functions, as previously discussed, are those that a disabled individual must be able to perform to be considered qualified for the job. Disqualification of an individual based on an inaccurate determination of the essential functions of the job might be a violation of the ADA.

Job Descriptions and Job Specifications

Job descriptions are written documents that describe the functions and working conditions of a job. Job specifications are the human characteristics necessary to successfully perform the job. Job specifications are typically a subsection of a job description. In general, federal law does not require job descriptions. One exception is employees that handle or dispose of certain types of hazardous chemicals. However, job descriptions are desirable for a number of reasons:

- They assist employers in complying with the Americans with Disabilities Act and Fair Labour Standards Act as discussed earlier.

- They assist in compliance with antidiscrimination laws that require employment practices and decisions be job-related as they define the job.
- They assign work and document work assignments.
- They help clarify the mission through the types of work assigned.
- They provide the basis for developing training and performance evaluation programmes.

Job descriptions should use action verbs to specifically describe the essential functions and duties. These descriptions should be logical, concise, and specific as to exactly what is to be done by the employee. It contains the following components, which are typically included in job descriptions:

- Identification section This section provides general information regarding the job including the job title, where the position is located in terms of geography, the department in which the job is located, whether the job is exempt or nonexempt under the Fair Labour Standards Act, the pay grade of classification of the job, the EEOC classification required for the EEO-1 report, and whether the job is included in the bargaining unit. In addition, this section often includes a job code or other identifying number used for identification in the human resource information system (HRIS). The HRIS might permit or require the entry of skill codes that identify the type of skills used in the job. If so, those codes are often placed in the identification section. Finally, the section might include information regarding the name of the individual that wrote the job description and job specifications and the name of the manager that approved them. The amount of information placed in this section depends on the needs of the organization and might range from merely identifying the job to a rather extensive section with large amounts of identifying information.

- Position summary This section is a concise statement indicating what the job does, why it exists, and what makes it different from other jobs. The statement is generally only one or two sentences.
- Essential functions This section is the meat of the job description and specifies clearly what the major functions of the job are. This is the most important section of the job description and the most difficult and time-consuming to write.
- Nonessential functions This section lists other duties of the job that are minor in nature. For the purposes of the ADA, these are the duties that could potentially be assigned elsewhere in the organization as a reasonable accommodation.
- Job specifications As previously stated, job specifications are normally included within the job description. This section should list the knowledge, skills, and abilities that a job incumbent should possess to perform the job successfully. Such characteristics as experience, education, and physical abilities are included in this section if they are requirements of the job. For example, "B.S. degree in biology," "two years of directly related experience," and "able to lift 100 pounds above the shoulders" are examples of explanatory statements that might be used in this section.
- Working conditions This section describes the environment in which the work is performed. Such issues as exposure to weather, fumes, heat or cold, noise, and so forth should be described in this section. If the job is not performed in a difficult environment, the conditions under which the work is performed should still be described. For example, "the work is performed in an office environment with no disagreeable conditions" might be appropriate in those situations.

- Disclaimers Many organizations put a variety of disclaimers in this section. These statements often include information that the management reserves the right to change the nature of the job and that the job description does not describe all tasks and responsibilities of the job. The purpose of these statements is to clarify that the employee might be required by management to perform other tasks. Often employers include this concept in a statement under the functions section using the terminology "other duties as assigned." However, the courts find this a bit problematic, especially if placed in the essential functions section, because the essential functions have to be clearly defined. A disclaimer section at the end of the job description is preferable. A final disclaimer often used is a statement to the effect that the job description does not constitute a contract for employment and may be changed at the discretion of the employer.

A common error in writing job descriptions and job specifications is to base them on the person currently doing the job as opposed to what the actual requirements of the job are in terms of duties and human abilities. Incumbents often take on additional responsibilities and bring special skills to the job, neither of which is a requirement.

Future of Job Analysis

Job analysis, job specifications, and job descriptions meet the needs of organizations experiencing stable environments and stable markets. The process allows the organization to describe its jobs in relation to its mission and specify exactly what tasks must be performed to facilitate achievement of organizational goals. These processes are recognized by the court systems, which provide guidance through case law as to the characteristics of legally defensible activities. However, more and more frequently organizations are affected by a dynamic and volatile environment with rapidly changing technology, increased competition, and fluctuating customer demands. This has led to the "dejobbing of America."

Dejobbing refers to the fact that jobs often change every day and cannot be specifically described in the traditional ways. Increased competition has often resulted in a flattening of the traditional hierarchy, removing multiple layers of management. When this occurs, employees at the bottom of the organization often are required to manage themselves and are empowered to make decisions. To be quickly adaptive to the market and customer wants, employees must be able to make instantaneous decisions and engage in a variety of new and innovative behaviours. The nature of work has often become one of teams, projects, and task forces, requiring new skills and ever-changing job responsibilities.

Many organizations engage in the practice of enriching jobs by increasing the skill variety, task identity, task significance, autonomy, and feedback. This practice makes the jobs more flexible and increases responsibilities for planning and decision-making. High-performance work systems and employee involvement programmes provide for more employee input into their jobs and more flexibility as to how jobs are performed. To deal with these new dynamics, many organizations are beginning the transition or have already transitioned to using competencies rather than tasks, duties, and responsibilities. Rather than task-based, job analysis has become competency-based. Competencies and competency-based job analysis are discussed in the sections that follow.

Competencies

Competencies are personal or organizational capabilities that are linked to successful performance outcomes. For the individual, competencies can be defined as characteristics of the person that enable performance. Competencies also consider how the knowledge, skills, and abilities are used. No single definition of competency has emerged as the standard because this is a relatively new area of study and practice. However, competencies include knowledge, skills, and abilities but are more than that. There is a component of behaviour, performance outcomes, motivation, and attitude included in the concept. Many organizations believe that the use of competencies is a more strategic approach and better aligns employee behaviour with the organization's mission and values than do description of tasks and functions.

Competencies can be categorized as technical, general, and leadership. Technical competencies apply to the particular job being analyzed. General (also called behavioural) competencies are required in varying amounts throughout the workforce. Leadership competencies are required by supervisors, managers, and others that have leadership responsibilities. Table below provides some commonly used competencies.

Table: Competencies

Developing subordinates	*Resolving conflicts*
Focusing on customer satisfaction	Working creatively
Communicating effectively	Leading decisively
Working with others	Thinking
Listening	Understanding technology

Competency-based analysis follows essentially the same process as described previously, but its purpose is to determine competencies needed to successfully perform the job rather than the functions performed in the job. There is a difference in emphasis between the two processes: Traditional or task-based job analysis focuses on the job and what is actually being done, whereas competency-based analysis focuses on the person and how the job outcomes are to be accomplished.

Focusing on the "how" and the person is problematical. Discrimination law and associated case law is based on "what" is being done and the job itself. As discussed previously, one of the basic concepts is that of job-relatedness. There is very little case law on competencies at this point in time.

A transition to competency-based job analysis has implications for many other programmes. If the jobs descriptions describe the work in terms of competencies it means that associated training plans, performance management systems, compensation strategies, and so forth must be aligned.

RECRUITMENT [M H]

The outcome of the workforce strategic-planning process provides the organization with information as to how many employees and what types will be needed in the future. One of the possibilities is that fewer employees will be needed. That process is often referred to as decruitment. It is also possible, and frequently likely, that the organization might need additional employees but that the current workforce does not have and is not likely to be able to develop the skills needed. In that case, the organization might be involved in both recruitment and decruitment at the same time. Decruitment strategies and actions are discussed later, in the "Organizational Exit" section.

Recruitment is the process of attracting qualified applicants for the organization to consider when filling its positions. Two strategic determinations must be made initially before the process begins. The first is whether the organizations want to do its own recruiting or to contract it out. Organizations lacking internal expertise might want to have an outside vendor do the recruiting for them. The vendor might be used for all recruiting or only for specified jobs. Some organizations find that it is cost-effective to outsource all recruiting gaining access to expertise and efficiencies of scale. Other organizations find that using vendors to recruit for specific jobs is most effective and efficient.

There are several scenarios in which having a vendor perform the recruiting and initial screening might be advantageous to the organization. The first scenario involves hard-to-fill jobs. Recruitment firms often specialize in filling specific positions, such as CEO or research scientist. In these cases, outside vendors may be in a better position that the organization to attract qualified candidates. The second scenario deals with entry-level workers. Organizations often find it cost-effective to deal with employment and temporary agencies to find these types of workers.

The second strategic issue is "make or buy." The organization must decide whether to engage in a practice of internal promotions and transfers (make) to fill its positions or to go to the external labour market (buy) to fill them. The decision is driven by the outcome of the strategic workforce-planning process, which evaluates the availability and skill levels of internal applicants. It is the SPHR's responsibility to ensure that the recruitment strategy is in alignment with organizational goals and objectives.

For example, an emerging organization in a highly technical field might engage in predominantly external recruitment because it does not have the time or capability to develop expertise internally and because the technical skills required are constantly changing. However, an organization operating in a relatively stable environment and attempting to compete based on cost-leadership and efficiency might find that internal recruitment is more in alignment. Also, organizations are often constrained by labour agreements that require an internal process prior to looking for applicants externally. The decision, in practice, is not an either/or choice. Organizations often pursue both strategies, frequently simultaneously.

The concept of employer branding is increasingly being discussed in relation to recruitment. Branding is a marketing concept that refers to customer perceptions of an organization or its products that differentiate it from it competitors. In a recruitment context, branding is the process by which an employer becomes the employer of choice in its relevant labour markets. Employer branding is tied to the perception and popularity of the organization and its products or services. Recruitment activities can leverage that image to facilitate attracting applicants.

To be effective, the recruitment strategy must be in alignment with the brand. If the organization has innovative products and a creative culture, the recruitment strategies should be a bit innovative and "out of the box." For example, recruitment strategies for Yahoo! would be considerably different than those for Wells Fargo bank in order to align themselves with the organizational and product image. A critical issue in employee branding is the selection and training of recruiters.

Recruiters must not only have the appropriate skills and attitude, but they must also reflect the culture and image of the organization. Continuing with the preceding example, a recruiter for Yahoo! should act, dress and, in general, reflect a different attitude than one from Wells Fargo.

If the organization decides to not contract out recruitment, it must determine what types of recruitment activities to engage in and it must evaluate the effectiveness of those activities. The following sections discuss the potential methods that an organization can use to recruit both internally and externally. Also discussed are recruitment metrics used to evaluate recruitment activities.

Internal Recruiting

Internal recruiting involves recruiting current or former employees for job openings in the organization along with soliciting referrals from current employees. Various methods are discussed in this section.

HRM INFORMATION SYSTEM

Sophisticated HRISs and employee databases are excellent sources of applicants. Many of these systems include data on employee training, education, and skills. In addition, some systems also include information on employee career goals and employee performance ratings. The system is able to match the requirements of a job with the characteristics and career goals of an employee to instantaneously create a potential applicant list. These employees can then be contacted, often by an automated email system, regarding their interest in a job opening.

Job Posting

Job posting is the process of advertising and publicizing job openings to employees. This might be accomplished by physically posting the opening on bulletin boards or by electronically posting them on the company's intranet or Internet. It is then up to the employee to actually apply for the position.

Job Bidding

Job bidding is similar to job posting and is more common in unionized environments. Job bidding permits an employee to apply for a position even if no openings exist. The employee's application is then held for a period of time, usually for a year, and the employee receives automatic consideration should the position come open. The process is often referred to as automatic consideration. Job bidding might be more efficient when openings for a job come open quite frequently. The employer can go to the job bid list without having to post each opening separately.

Former Employees

Former employees are often a good source of applicants. Former employees include three categories:

- Employees that have temporarily dropped out of the workforce For example, individuals that have elected to stay home with their young children. Often these former employees are ready to come back to the workforce or are willing to accept part-time employment.
- Retirees that might be willing to come back to the employer on a consultant or contract basis.
- Employees that have left the organization for work in another organization.

Assuming that these employees were good performers prior to their exit from the organization, they are likely to be good performers on their return. Many organizations have alumni and retiree clubs and groups to keep in touch with former employees. This frequently provides a rich base from which to recruit. Often employees leave thinking that a new organization provides a better working environment, better pay, or more challenging work, only to be disappointed. They often can be enticed back to the organization.

Former Applicants

Applicants that previously applied for positions with the organization are to some extent known quantities, depending on how far they got in the selection process. Good applicants should be reconsidered. Many organizations keep files on excellent candidates that were not selected for prior openings and re-recruit them for current positions. This method is both efficient and effective. Much of the screening might have already been done and, if the applicants were previously interviewed, they might have already been judged as acceptable.

Keeping in touch with prior applicants and making them feel good about the recruitment and selection process is good practice and an extension of the branding process discussed earlier. Applicants should be kept informed of their status throughout the hiring process and given feedback.

Employee Referrals

Many organizations have active formal employee referral programmes, particularly in tight job markets or where the employer has difficult-to-fill or high-turnover positions. These programmes reward employees for referring applicants to the organization. Other organizations have less formal programmes and encourage employees to refer potential applicants, but do not provide an incentive for doing so.

Experience and research show considerable benefit to the employee referral type of recruitment. First, employees are not likely to refer applicants that would not be good employees. They do not want to be embarrassed by the performance or conduct of their referral. Also, candidates that are referred by employees typically already have begun the orientation process and have somewhat of a realistic job preview via their relationship with the current employee. Finally, there is a positive correlation between employee referral and employee retention of those hired as a result.

There is, however, one potential problem that can associated with employee referrals. Employees tend to refer their relative and friends, who most likely are of the same ethnicity or sex as themselves. Therefore, this type of recruitment does not normally facilitate the achievement of diversity and affirmative action plan goals and can create adverse impact. This is particularly true if the organization has a past practice of discrimination.

External Recruiting

External recruiting involves obtaining applications from individual external to the organization. A threshold strategic issue for the SPHR is the determination of the appropriate external labour market from which to recruit. For lower-level jobs, the appropriate market is most likely to be the local labour market—defined as the geographical area from which most people are willing to commute.

However, a sufficient applicant pool might not be available in the local labour market for many jobs. For certain types of jobs, particularly professional jobs, the appropriate labour market is determined in terms of the profession. Recruiting is often most effective when performed inside the profession, using professional organizations and professional journals for example. For mid-level types of positions, a regional labour market might produce a better applicant pool, whereas many top-level and highly specialized jobs require recruiting nationally and even internationally.

Of course, use of the Internet, which is discussed later, facilitates a broader recruiting area. However, Internet recruiting often is not appropriate, effective, or efficient for many jobs and the critical decision affecting the success of a recruitment effort remains in the selection of the appropriate labour market from which to recruit. External recruiting can involve many methods, the most common of which are discussed in this section.

Media Advertising

Media advertising refers to recruitment using radio, television, newspapers, and so forth. This is a technical area requiring expertise not normally available within the HR function. Writing effective advertisements frequently calls for professionals in the field. Professionally done media advertising can be an extremely effective and cost-efficient recruitment method. It allows the organization to reach a large number of potential applicants, often resulting in significant savings in hiring costs. By use of appropriate outlets targeted protected groups can be reached, which facilitates diversity and affirmative action efforts. However, when poorly done media advertising can be extremely expensive.

College and School Recruiting

College and university recruiting is a good source of entry- and mid-level managers and professionals. In general, college recruiting requires a continuing relationship with the organization and its placement office, and a history of hiring the college's graduates. These together tend to put the organization at the front of the referral queue. However, this is often an expensive proposition requiring expenditure of both staff and financial resources. Sponsoring professional clubs and providing scholarships and internships can be expensive if the organization never hires individuals from the college. Many organizations have scaled down their college recruiting efforts to focus on a few schools where they can maintain a continuing presence and hire excellent candidates in a cost-effective manner.

Two-year colleges (junior and community colleges) and technical schools can be good sources for entry-level, para-technical, and para-professional positions. The strategies associated with recruiting at these institutions are the same as for higher-level institutions—only the type of positions being recruited for is different.

High schools are a good source of blue-collar, clerical, and retail entry-level positions. Many organizations do not realize the potential of recruiting at this level, often assuming that graduates will pursue higher education. Good relationships with school counselors and athletic departments often facilitate this type of recruitment.

Labour Unions

Labour union hiring halls are often a good, and sometimes the only, source of applicants. This is particularly true in the construction trades.

Employment Agencies

As mentioned earlier in the discussion of outsourced recruitment, employment agencies and job search firms often are good sources of job candidates. First, all states have unemployment offices, displaced worker units, or similar agencies performing the same function. These are often sources of applicants.

Private employment agencies can be viable sources of applicants. These firms most frequently charge the organization a fee for referral of candidates, either on a contingency or retainer basis.

Contingency-based firms receive the fee only if the applicant is hired, whereas retainer-based firms receive a fee for engaging in the search even if no one is hired. Employment agencies normally prescreen the applicants for the organization and refer only those that are qualified. The agencies often have contacts and relationships that the organization does not, and might be able to locate excellent candidates for higher-level managerial and hard-to-fill technical and professional positions.

Although using employment agencies and search firms might be cost-effective and yield results that the organization could not achieve on its own, doing so can be extremely expensive. Costs for using these types of firms often run 25–30% of the yearly salary for the position being recruited.

Temporary Employment Agencies

Many private employment agencies provide temporary, part-time, or just-in-time workers. These employees are paid by the temporary agency and are not employees of the organization. Temporary agencies screen these workers and often provide training. These agencies have traditionally provided lower-level blue-collar and clerical workers, but that is no longer the case. There are now temporary employment agencies that specialize in providing technical, professional, and managerial temporary workers. There are even agencies that specialize in temporary executives up to and including CEOs.

The advantage of these agencies is in their flexibility. The employer has no continuing obligation to the employee and can, within limits, rotate them in and out of the organization. This is especially important to firms than have frequent variations in demand or are seasonal in nature. Employers pay a fee to the temporary agency and do not have to worry about employee benefits or employment taxes. In addition, organizations often use the temporary employment as a probationary period. The temporary agency permits the organization to hire these temporary workers as permanent employees for a fee.

Customers

Loyal customers are pleased with the organization's product or services. To some extent they have made a commitment to the organization, and might be familiar with the culture, the responsibilities of some of the jobs, and the working conditions. In other words, they have a realistic job preview. Many organizations have found customers to be an excellent source of candidates. They frequently recruit actively in their retail establishments, taking job applications on the spot and providing easy access to employment information and application procedures on their websites.

Suppliers and Competitors

Employees of suppliers and competitors are often good sources of applicants. They are familiar with the industry and frequently familiar with the organization itself.

Professional and Trade Associations

Virtually all professional and trade associations provide placement services for their members and allow employers to post job openings on their website, typically for a fee. In addition, these associations normally publish newsletters or journals in which the organization can place recruiting advertisements. Most associations also have annual meetings or conventions that provide additional opportunities for the organization to recruit in person. Organizations have found professional and trade associations to be excellent sources of applicants, particularly for specialized types of jobs such as banking, finance, human resource management, and so forth. Some associations are organized around gender or ethnicity. They are good sources of candidates for organizations engaging in diversity or affirmative action initiatives.

Walk-Ins

Many organizations accept applications from individuals that visit the organization for the express purpose of inquiring about job opportunities. Walk-ins have been found to be good sources of entry-level employees. The mere fact that they have taken the time and effort to visit the organization shows some level of interest and commitment.

Job Fairs and Special Events

Job fairs held by other organizations—for example, the local chamber of commerce—tend to attract a wide variety of applicants and might provide the organization with numerous recruiting leads and applicants. However, many organizations have found that some individuals attending these types of events are merely shopping and are not really interested in changing jobs. In addition, many of the individuals tend to have low skills and might be largely unemployable. That being said, job fairs held by organizations such as professional associations (for example, the Society for Human Resource Management) can be an excellent source of candidates.

Internally held job fairs have proven to be an effective means of recruitment, particularly for entry-level blue-collar and clerical employees. Organizations often open up their facilities during the evening or on the weekend and provide free food and prizes as an incentive for potential applicants to visit. Actually visiting the work site begins the realistic job preview process and might result in better retention of applicants who are actually hired. Organizations have also found that using special events as a recruiting tool has proven effective. A booth or kiosk at sporting and civic events could produce viable candidates.

Internet

The Internet has opened up all sorts of possibilities and associated challenges in recruiting. It provides access to a worldwide population of potential applicants. There are essentially three major sources of applicants using e-recruiting: commercial job boards, professional/trade association websites, and the employer's website.

Many organizations have successfully used commercial job boards such as Monster.com and Hotjobs.com where, for a fee, employers can post job opportunities. Job boards have been found to provide access to a large number of qualified candidates. However, because of ease of access many of the candidates often are not seriously looking for a new job but are merely testing their competitiveness in the job market or trying to determine current compensation rates.

As discussed previously, many professional and trade associations publish job openings on their website. These can provide viable candidates for specialized positions. Most larger employers now provide employment information on their websites. They typically find this to be an effective and efficient means of generating applications. To be effective, access to job information must be easy. Most employers provide a button on the home page that leads prospective applicant to the information. Effectiveness is increased if the web page for employment information continues the same format and theme as the home page and is consistent with the organization's image and culture. This is an important continuation of the employer branding previously discussed.

Internet recruiting can save time because the application forms and/or resumes are readily available. Applicants can be immediately contacted via email. Internet recruiting is typically much less expensive than media advertising or onsite recruiting initiatives. Internet recruiting expands the relevant job market to the globe and has the potential to generate a large number of qualified candidates.

However, the ease of application in Internet recruiting and the wide exposure of job opening information often generate applications from those that are not qualified or that are not seriously looking for work. In fact, Internet recruiting might generate too many applications that must be screened and applicants that must be contacted, thus increasing the workload on HR. Fortunately, there are now software packages that can largely automate many of these processes.

Internet recruiting poses problems for the tracking of applicant flow data. However, recent rulings by both the EEOC and OFCCP have clarified the issue somewhat. As a general overview of that guidance, employers have to consider applications received on the Internet as applicants for applicant flow data only if the organization actually considers the applicant for an open position, if the applicant maintains continued interest and follows the organization's standard application process, and if the applicant expresses interest and is basically qualified for a particular position.

A final concern about Internet recruiting is the potential for adverse impact caused by what is known as the digital divide. Although access to the Internet has increased dramatically, certain minority groups might have less access than other groups.

Outplacement Firms

Many organizations have formed alliances with outplacement firms. These firms provide placement assistance to individuals, many of whom have been involuntarily separated from their former employer through no fault of their own. These individuals are often excellent candidates.

Evaluating Recruitment Effectiveness

Efficiency evaluation is largely operational in nature, whereas effectiveness evaluation is strategic. Unfortunately, organizations tend to do a rather good job at developing efficiency metrics, but a poor job of developing effectiveness measures. The efficiency metrics provide information regarding the accomplishments of short-term objectives. However, the critical issue is the long-term strategic impact of recruitment activities on the success of the organization (effectiveness metrics).

Typical efficiency metrics are as follows:

- Quantity of applications This is a gross measure of the effect of recruitment activities with the philosophy that the more applications an organizations gets, the more likely it is to fill its openings with highly qualified individuals. Quantities can be evaluated by source, giving a gross estimate of the cost-effectiveness of television versus newspaper advertising, for example.
- Quality of applications Organizations might want to evaluate the percentage of applications that were considered qualified for the job or that were actually offered an interview. Again, this is a gross measure of the impact of the recruitment programme and can be analyzed by the source of the application.
- Time to fill Most organizations evaluate the time it takes to fill a position, typically in terms of the number of days from the date the request is received in the HR department until new employee actually reports onboard. These data are then compared against goals,

historical averages, and benchmarks to evaluate recruitment efficiency.

- Yield rates Yield rates were discussed earlier. Recruitment is often evaluated in terms of yield rates from one stage of the process to another. For example, the organization needs to know what percentage of applicants were actually considered to be qualified for the job, what percentage that were qualified passed the initial screening, what percentage passing the initial screening also passed the pre-employment tests, what percentage passing the pre-employment test were offered in-person interviews, and so forth. This provides an additional measure of efficiency in that higher yield ratios reduce wasted staff effort and produce more viable candidates for the organization to consider.
- Cost per hire Many organizations track the average cost to hire employees, typically by dividing all recruitment-related expenses by the number of actual hires. The measure provides an indication of the efficiency of the recruitment programme in terms of costs, but yields little information regarding effectiveness. Also, the calculation of recruitment costs is often difficult.
- Selection rates Selection rate provide some indication of efficiency because they evaluate the number of new hires against the total number of applicants. For example, if 50 hires were made from an application pool of 100, the selection rate is 50%.

  However, one cannot really necessarily evaluate that metric in terms of effectiveness. Presumably, the higher the selection rate, the more efficient and effective recruitment process. But are selections being made using the "any warm body" philosophy because positions must be filled with any applicant that is minimally qualified? Selection rates along with other measures of efficiency do not give the organization any indication of the actual performance of an individual after being hired, nor do they tell the organization anything about employee retention.

- Acceptance rates Some organizations track selection rates, which are typically evaluated as the number of applicants that accept the position divided by the number of applicants that were offered the position. The higher the ratio, the more efficient the recruitment programme is considered to be. However, acceptance rates can be significantly affected by outside influences that have nothing to do with the quality of recruitment efforts. For example, acceptance rates could be expected to be appreciably higher during periods of high unemployment.

This metric is frequently used to evaluate both individual recruiter and recruitment sources. When evaluating individual recruiters, the interest is in how effective the recruiter is in actually convincing the applicant to accept the job. This might be a critical issue, especially with higher-level jobs where the costs of recruiting are substantial. The organization is also interested in knowing whether the acceptance rate differs among the various recruitment methods so that it can adjust its strategies.

Effectiveness measures are those that evaluate the long-term strategic impact of the recruitment programme. As discussed, "Human Resource Development," in the context of evaluation of training and development there is often an inverse relationship between the value of data and analysis and its difficulty. However, this is the value added by the SPHR. The SPHR must develop metrics that strategically evaluate recruitment efforts in terms of their impact on organizational effectiveness and strategic success.

An effectiveness measure frequently overlooked is that of customer satisfaction with the recruitment process and results. In this case, customers can be defined in a number of ways. First, management satisfaction should be evaluated. Managers should be questioned as to their overall satisfaction with the recruitment process and the timeliness of actions and the quality of recruits in particular. Because managers at different levels often have different expectations, satisfaction should be surveyed at multiple levels in the organization. The second, and probably more important, customer group is the actual recruits themselves. This includes both those who were hired and those who were rejected for employment. They should be questioned about their perspectives regarding the various stages of the recruitment and selection process. These data often provide valuable information regarding recruitment effectiveness and identify areas that might need improvement.

The effectiveness of recruitment efforts should be evaluated in terms of eventual employee performance and retention. Therefore, the SPHR should lead the HR function in engaging in longitudinal studies in these areas. In the press of current requirements historical research is often ignored. Yet these data are the ones that allow the organization to fine-tune current operations. Organizations that have effective recruitment evaluation programmes periodically (usually yearly) evaluate a sample of hires from previous years, correlating retention, promotion rates, and performance data with recruitment sources, selection tests, and other employment practices. Evaluation of individual recruiters can also be done using the same process. These data provide rich information as to the long-term effectiveness of recruitment programmes. The potential value of these types of evaluations is, however, moderated by the nature of the organizational environment and the organizational strategies. These data have the greatest impact in planning and engaging in activities to improve the recruitment programme when the environment is relatively stable.

CONTINGENT WORKFORCE

The contingent workforce is composed of those individuals who work for an organization but are not permanent full-time employees. Use of a contingent workforce is increasing and it is estimated that contingent workers represent more than 20% of the total United States workforce.

The dynamics of today's organizational and business environment often drive employers to use contingent workers to achieve a strategic advantage. These drivers of change are discussed and in others, but a brief summary is appropriate.

Increased competition and the need for cost-efficiency require that employers have flexibility in adjusting employment levels and employment costs to demand for its product or services and in relationship to its level of operations, both of which might be constantly changing and volatile. A permanent full-time workforce does not permit that. The changing psychological contract encourages lack of permanency of relationships, both in employee and employer expectations.

Contingent workers are in alignment with those expectations. Changing technology often requires new skills that permanent full-time employees might not have and might not be capable of developing. Downsizing and rightsizing could result in the loss of organizational capability, which can be augmented with the use of contingent workers. The increasing difficulty of compliance with the complexity of employment laws and the cost associated with them can be largely avoided by having workers that are employees of other organizations. Finally, significant cost savings can often accrue from outsourcing the organization's work to organizations located in foreign countries in which the wage rates are low.

However, the use of contingent workers does not come without some organizational concerns and disadvantages. Increased flexibility often brings about loss of control. The employer might be able to control only the outcome of work, not the means used to obtain it. Use of some types of contingent workers might, in the long run, be more expensive than permanent employees because the source of those workers must not only be reimbursed for compensation and benefit costs but must also be paid a fee in addition.

There is a concern regarding the loyalty of employees that are not employed on a full-time basis. Will the employee act in the best interest of the organization or of the actual employer? Another issue of substantial concern is the impact of this strategy on the remaining permanent full-time workforce. Does the practice lower overall morale and induce stress and concern among the remaining workers who might become worried about their own job security?

A final issue is one of ethics and social responsibility. The SPHR must lead the organization in balancing its obligations to its employees, the community or communities in which it operates, and society as a whole against the organization's legitimate desire to maximize its profits for stockholders. The advantages and disadvantages of use of the contingent workforce are summarized in Table below.

Table: Advantages and Disadvantages of Using the Contingent Workforce

Advantages	*Disadvantages*
Flexibility.	Perceived lack of loyalty
Savings in the cost of taxes and benefits	Lack of knowledge of the organization's culture, policies, and procedures
Access to expertise not internally available.	Potential for overall higher costs, depending on the situation
Potential savings in overall compensation costs.	Concern with disclosure of organizational proprietary information
	Impact on morale of permanent workforce
	Loss of internal capabilities
	Potential for increased training costs when contingent workers must be trained on unique or unusual processes or procedures used by the organization.

A contingent workforce can be composed of many types of workers. Employers often use several sources simultaneously. Common types or sources of contingent workers include the following:

- Part-time workers Part-time workers can be obtained from a temporary employment agency, in which case flexibility is maximized and the organization avoids liability for taxes and benefits. Part-time workers can be employees of the organization. Although that arrangement might be somewhat permanent in nature and of limited flexibility, organizations often provide no or a limited range of benefits, resulting in cost savings.
- Temporary workers Traditional temporary workers are obtained from employment agencies that specialize in providing these types of workers. However, the employer can also hire temporary workers internally.

The employer that hires temporary workers must do so based on some rational basis such as temporary or seasonal increases in operations, the need to replace workers during the peak vacation period, and so forth. The temporary workers should be terminated when the temporary demand for additional workforce ceases. Continued employment of temporary workers for extended amounts of time might negate their temporary status and obligate the employer to provide expensive benefits. Microsoft Corporation paid a 97-million dollar settlement to workers that it had mischaracterized as temporary workers.

Hiring temporary labour from a temporary employment agency can also pose potential legal problems for the employer. If the organization exercises control over the temporary employees, provides training, negotiates compensation, or engages in other employment-related practices, the temporary employee is likely to be considered by the courts as an employee of both the organization and the temporary employment agency (referred to as dual employment).

In such cases the organization might be obligated to provide certain benefits. In addition, as a dual employer, the organization must comply with all employment laws in its relationship with the temporary workers. For example, the organization might have an obligation to provide reasonable accommodation to a temporary worker under the Americans with Disabilities Act and can be found liable for illegal discrimination or harassment under the Civil Rights Act of 1964.

Temporary employees in many situations have the right to join unions that are the certified bargaining agent either of the temporary employment agency or of the organization.

- Consultants: Often consultants are contracted with to provide expertise not currently available to the organization and not needed on a permanent and continuing basis.
- Contract workers: Contract workers are often hired on a project basis. After the project is complete, the organization has no further obligation to the individual.
- Outsourcing: Outsourcing is the process of contracting for services or products with external vendors rather than producing them internally. Frequently outsourcing results in substantial compensation savings because of the economies of scale that are created when an organization specializes in a particular type of work and/or employs specialized software. Outsourcing often permits access to specialize expertise not available internally to the organization.
- Offshoring: Offshoring refers to hiring workers in foreign countries to perform tasks previously done in the United States. Oftentimes, substantial cost savings can be realized because of the lower compensation rates in those countries.
- Leasing: Leasing typically involves a contract with a professional employer organization (PEO). A PEO is an organization that assumes the employer rights and responsibilities for employees that it provides to its clients. An employer wanting to lease its currently

employees signs a contract with a PEO and the PEO hires the employees. The organization then leases them back, with the PEO assuming the responsibilities of an employer. Employee leasing tends to be particularly suited for small employers that do not have internal expertise to comply with the complexities of today's employment laws. Also, because the PEO has a much larger workforce, it might be able to provide the former organizational employees with much better benefit packages. Obviously these services do not come without a cost, and it is estimated that leasing raises total labour costs by about 5%. For many employers this is additional money well spent.

CONCEPT, SCOPE AND LIMITATION

Corporate financial success and a healthful organizational environment have been long viewed as juxtaposed concepts. The conventional paradigm dictates that if resources are devoted to worker well-being, fewer resources will be available to contribute to corporate profit. At the managerial level, work and health are often interpreted as a choice between productive work practices and those practices which are safe and healthy. However, statistics reveal the cost burden that the lack of worker health imposes on the United States economy. Evanoff & Rosenstock (1994) reported that estimates of the annual direct and indirect medical costs associated with occupational stress in the United States have ranged from $80 billion to $150 billion. These estimates do not include the additional costs incurred from lost productivity.

Furthermore, research in recent years has begun to recognize the significant role of employee health in the performance of the organization as a whole. Sauter et al. (1996) acknowledged that organizational performance and worker well-being are mutually reinforcing and introduced a model developed by the National Institute of Occupational Safety and Health (NIOSH) for use in their investigation of "healthy" work organizations. Zink (2002) asserted that human resources are the most relevant enabler of success of a company. Rapid changes in the organization of work due to the indoctrination of work improvement efforts in corporate cultures (e.g., lean manufacturing, six sigma), together with the new demographics of the American work population (e.g., increasing numbers of women, minorities, and aging workers) have far outpaced the knowledge regarding the implications of these changes on the quality of working life.

As such, this area has been established as one of the 21 priority research items under the National Occupational Research Agenda (NORA). While the physical and mental demands form the job content of the overall work-system model, the organizational environment together with the physical environment form the context in which work tasks are executed. However, an organizational environment model which aims to optimize work outcomes (i.e., productivity, quality) while seeking to optimize the quality of life of the work-system participants has received little attention in the scientific research arena. Furthermore, the set of parameters, which constitute the organizational environment as well as the concepts underlying a model's development, have been the subject of vigorous debate and terminological confusion.

The objective of this article was to develop a model for organizational health assessment to address the subsystems of factors, which interact to form the culture (the shared meanings and values) and climate (the work practices) within the totality of the work environment. Preliminary evidence suggests both positive and negative effects of changing organizational practices on the safety and health of workers. As a result of these conflicting findings, NIOSH suggests that an important focus of research should be the clarification of circumstances (for whom and under what conditions) in which these practices protect or increase the risk of harm to workers.

To address this need, a model of the organizational work system, these factors and their interrelationships must be developed. Although several recent efforts have documented correlations between various work factors and individual/organizational well-being measures, a comprehensive organizational-systems model from which to empirically define pathways to promote health is required. This article aims to fill this need. However, prior to describing the Organizational Health Model, the evolution of the organizational health concept will be reviewed.

Evolution of the Organizational Health Construct

In the many years American businesses enjoyed in the absence of global competition, a healthy corporation was simply a by-product of an environment with a lack of obvious physical or chemical hazards. The Occupational Health and Safety Act, effective in 1971, was enacted to ensure safe and healthful working conditions. As a result, the Occupational Safety and Health Administration (OSHA) establishes and monitors compliance to safety and health standards. In the occupational-health perspective at this time, a healthful organization constituted one that did not violate the enacted standards.

The roots of the organizational health concept in the United States began in the 1960s, presented through the humanistic researchers' concerns regarding how employees were treated in the work organization. Their work linked job content to individual well-being in the context of the effective organization. Argyris (1958, 1964) questioned the ability of an organization to meet the needs of its employees while remaining competitive. McGregor's (1960) descriptions of Theory X (authoritarian management) and Theory Y (democratic management) asserted that the role of the organizational environment is critical in determining effectiveness as well as utilizing worker potential. Herzberg et al. (1959), Maslow (1965), Porter and Lawler (1968), and Vroom (1964) explored the interactions between individual motivation and performance. These theories formed the basis for numerous intervention efforts aimed at improving various aspects of organizational health.

What is organizational health? In the aftermath of several popular corporate improvement programmes such as the total quality management (TQM) and downsizing, the term "organizational health" has emerged in both the occupational health and mainstream business literature, heralding a blending of the traditionally paradoxical values of productivity versus health and safety. Effectiveness, a universal organizational goal, can be regarded as a composite of the following factors: product quality, customer service, flexibility, initiative taken by employees, and capacity to meet deadlines. Jaffe (1995) characterized organizational health as implying an expanded notion of organizational effectiveness.

He offered a contextual definition of organizational health stating that a company can be healthy for (a) its own livelihood by growing and being efficient, adaptable, and coherent; (b) stockholders by increasing the value of stock; (c) employees, offering a healthy work environment as well as meeting their highest growth needs for meaning and participation; (d) suppliers and customers by offering good products and services; and (e) the community by assuming concern for its viability as well as for the environment. Jaffe added that the needs of all the benefactors of organizational health must be balanced to ensure success. Rosen (1991) described a healthy company as one that holds a core set of humanistic values: commitment to self-knowledge and development, firm belief in decency, respect for individual differences, spirit of partnership, high priority for health and well-being, appreciation for flexibility and resilience, and passion for products and process.

Although these descriptions provide an ideology for and list of benefactors of organizational health, they fail to define the components of an organization that interact to create its level of well-being. Williams (1994) cited the four elements of organizational health as environmental factors, physical health, mental (psychological) health, and social health; the details of interventions describe a holistic approach to employee health. Yet, he myopically equated the health of the employee to the health of the organization. To effectively assess organizational conditions for healthy work, other aspects of the work system—physical job demands, mental job demands, and physical environment demands as well as individual characteristics—must be considered simultaneously.

However, little research has been devoted directly to the concept of organizational health, especially in the United States. In the strictest sense, most work-improvement efforts are only tangentially related to the organizational health construct in that the majority of these approaches are aimed primarily at optimizing performance (improving effectiveness) rather than the quality of work life for all participants. Conversely, job-stress research has considered individual and job characteristics as they relate to individual measures of health (e.g., physical symptoms).

Overall, previous efforts to address human effectiveness in conjunction with consideration for worker well-being can be classified into three categories according to the variable identified for intervention: the individual, the job, and the organizational framework. Notably absent from this classification is the process-based orientation. Numerous contemporary work-improvement efforts, such as statistical process control, lean manufacturing, reengineering, and six sigma, regard the optimization of the process as paramount. However, these methods, focused on the pursuit of effectiveness, have failed to consider the effects of process improvements on the quality of working life for work participants.

Work improvement strategies can be classified according to these three orientations. Although no organizational health interventions can be classified as process-based, this category is included in the model for completeness. In this model, strategy boundaries are diffuse due to the likely overlap between classifications. The large circle (organization) circumscribes the smaller circles (individual, job, and process), as the intervention in the larger circle is broader in scope and therefore affects the intervention in the smaller circle. For example, organizational interventions such as restructuring a manufacturing area into an autonomous work group can alter both the scope of a job as well as the individual's role.

The orientation of the United States' research on workplace health has been overwhelmingly individual-focused, not surprisingly congruent to its cultural ideology. This orientation implicitly assumes that the aggregation of individual physically and psychologically healthy workers equals a healthy company. The majority of empirical research advancing the development of organizational health concepts in the United States has primarily resulted as an outgrowth of job stress studies. Overall, these studies have focused on individual health as affected by workplace demands.

Historically, in the occupational stress research tradition, wellness strategies were exclusively aimed at the individual's physical and mental health. Consequently, the most common interventions recommend development of individual coping strategies such as stress-management training and employee-assistance programmes. Common elements of workplace health promotion include smoking cessation, hypertension screening and control, stress management, nutrition and weight control, exercise and fitness, and drug and alcohol programmes. However, wellness promoting strategies also must refer to the improvement of intrinsic job factors and therefore serve a dual purpose of attempting to better work life on both the individual as well as organizational planes.

Wellness-promotion strategies seek to bolster individual and organizational resilience by increasing inherent capability. On the individual level, capability may be developed through the practice of conflict-resolution skills or support networks. On the organizational level, work may be designed such that self-determination, social interaction, and professional responsibility are central concepts cited job characteristic criteria as well as strategies for good work organization, such as mastery of work, management of change processes, support of employees by occupational health services, and emphasis on career stage and future perspectives. Inclusion of wellness-promoting strategies must emphasize the prerequisite for active job content and work-setting design in creating a robust organization. In this manner, the traditional paradigm of healthy work as that in which stress and harm are absent is expanded. Another individual-based orientation emphasizes the leader's importance in the formation of a healthy company.

This perspective largely attributes the creation and existence of an organization to its founders or leaders. Thus, the leader's personal characteristics and management style are viewed as the primary catalysts for organizational well-being. Gardell (1987) cautioned against focusing preventative strategies primarily on the individual as this emphasis translates a larger organizational problem into a private one.

Job redesign also has been used as a means for improving health. Job characteristics that support healthful work conditions are defined, and then the job is modified to possess these characteristics. Generally, the job is considered as an independent entity, in isolation from the organizational context. In this perspective, the job is used as the medium thorough which to affect individual motivation. For example, Hackman and Lawler (1971) defined five job characteristics for meaningful work: skill variety, task identity, task significance, autonomy, and feedback. The Job Diagnostic Survey was developed to assess jobs based on the five aforementioned job characteristics.

The job characteristics defined by Hackman and Lawler (1971) provided a set of variables that could be manipulated to increase job meaning and therefore worker motivation. Job enrichment adds complexity often by allowing greater worker autonomy. Techniques such as job enlargement (expanding the scope of the job by adding more task variety) and job rotation (alternating task assignments) are additional examples of job-based interventions. Job-based approaches use task redesign as the means to affect individual worker satisfaction. Critics of this orientation argue that these efforts may not succeed as psychological differences between individuals are not addressed.

Efforts focused primarily on the improvement of work life through organizational variables began in Scandinavia around the mid-1960s, and soon thereafter social science research and health research united in the investigation to improve quality of work life. The orientation in Scandinavian countries as well as Finland has tended to focus more on the resources and structure of the work environment itself rather than the individual worker or job process. In the organizational orientation, interventions such as the establishment of autonomous production groups are used to incorporate considerations of job demands, individuals' self-determination, resources (technical, organizational, social, personal), and autonomy. Collective control allows groups to create their own distinctive adaptive strategies. The importance of these efforts to improve quality of work life has been further emphasized in the Swedish Work Environment Act, effective since 1977, which states that "jobs shall be designed so that the employees themselves can influence their work situation" and "working conditions shall be adapted to the mental and physical capacity of human beings."

Organization-based interventions redesign the "job" by changing its overall structure within the context of the work organization. In their terminology, "job redesign" has been enlarged to "work reform." Conceptually, this approach emerged from socio-technical design theory, which advocates that work should be organized in groups that have control over decision making and are responsible for a complete work cycle. To encourage autonomy and social support, interdependent autonomous work groups were implemented, therefore magnifying the individual's role within the context of the work environment. Several advantages of autonomous work groups are cited in Gardell (1981):

- Within a group setting, the individual can expand his or her possibilities for attaining some amount of freedom and competence at work;
- The possibilities for learning, variation, and all-around use of human resources will be improved;

- The individual and the group will be able to achieve wider control over the work system and work methods; and
- Human contact and solidarity between people will be more likely.

Karasek and Theorell (1990) later formulated a model using three factors to characterize work: job demands, job control, and social support. They concluded that high-demand- low-control jobs resulted in higher incidence of health problems than jobs that are high demand-high control, thus validating Gardell's (1982) previous experiments on work-place autonomy and participation on which his interventions were based. Critics of the socio-technical approach argue that this orientation does not go far enough to affect organizational change in that it does not address the employees' beliefs regarding organizational goals, priorities, and behaviours, except in regard to job content and social relationships.

Recent efforts to describe the environment for organizational health suggest debate among research communities over the emphasis of worker or process, and individual level factors versus structural, organizational level factors. Lindstrom (1994), of the Finnish Institute of Occupational Health, cites job characteristics such as optimal quantitative and qualitative workload, opportunities for control at work, clarified work balanced by other roles, and supportive social interactions as the psychosocial criteria for good work organization, and also cites organizational strategies to support these criteria. Sauter et al. (1996), of NIOSH, presented a model which wholly ignores job-level factors (e.g., work- load, autonomy, role stress) and shifted all emphasis to "macro-organizational" characteristics (e.g., climate,, values).

Lack of attention to all four variables (individual, job, process, and organization) in intervention strategies can result in a failure to improve the level of work performance as well as quality of work life. Cox and Cox (1993) explained that health problems may arise because jobs, technology, and work environments have not been systematically de- signed with workers in mind due to management practices, organizational culture, or failure to develop workers' knowledge skills and attitudes. For example, extended work hours due to staff reductions may increase the risk of physical injury. Frankenhauser (1991) recommended that individual-oriented programmes need to be supplemented by organization- wide changes that may involve altering the conditions under which people work, the tasks they perform, and the rewards they obtain. Gardell (1987) concluded that "preventative psychosocial work" must proceed on both the individual as well as the organizational planes. This strategy, calling for the collaboration of orientations, marks the starting point for the organizational model's development.

Organizational Health Model Development

With the recent emergence of the concept of organizational health, researchers have acknowledged the significance of the role of worker well-being in the establishment of a healthy as well as effective workplace. Several areas of study have fed the idea's germination, notably the humanistic organizational research and the job-stress research traditions. However, the concept suffers from the lack of a holistic approach on two levels. First, current descriptions of organizational health must be enlarged to include all components of the work system (e.g., physical, mental, organizational, environmental) as well as their interactions.

Second, although some researchers identified criteria for good work organization, this work has not yet been integrated within a systemic framework that lends itself to practical industrial application. Analogous to biological health, the determination of healthy work is based on a system of interrelated components functioning together, seeking balance. To assess organizational health, the resulting work-system equilibrium must be quantified.

The company's values and organizational goals drive the establishment of work practices and policies. Processes dictate the job content, that is, the mental, physical, and environmental demands on the worker. Resources act to encourage worker well-being (e.g., meaningful job characteristics, mentoring, training, advancement opportunities) act to offset the negative effects of the demands on workers (e.g., fatigue, boredom) and consequently, simultaneously encourage successful achievement of organizational goals.

The interrelationships between work-system components ultimately determine the state of the organization's health. Culture is the premise upon which the climate, the everyday operations, is based. These daily practices (climate), in turn, affect the culture. The model is predicated upon the occurrence of two outcomes: effectiveness in achieving the desired goal and the wellness as described by the quality of work life of the members. Therefore, the definition of organizational health blends the historically paradoxical objectives of optimizing performance and overall well-being. This section details the model's components and explains their interrelationships.

References to organizational culture abound in both scholarly and mainstream literature. Culture can be casually defined as "how things are done around here". Organizational culture is a relatively new area of study that has experienced recent popularity through business self-help books, which target work culture as a variable for manipulation in the pursuit of effectiveness. Much academic work has been devoted to the definition and description of the concept; however, little effort has focused on the empirical study of culture in the contemporary work organization. Although comprehensive book-length explications of the concept have been accomplished, there has been little research on methodology for practical application or reported experience substantiating the theoretical views in industry. The concept of organizational culture has suffered from the lack of a focus, causing theoretical efforts to remain inaccessible to the industrial work environment.

The problem of defining organizational culture is based on the fact that the concept of the organization is itself ambiguous. The many definitions of culture are divergent in scope, overlap with other concepts (notably, climate), and sometimes contradict other definitions; however, most include reference to both beliefs (values) and actions (behaviour). However, to evaluate the complex interrelationships of the work system, the interactions that form the context through which individuals interpret their experiences must be evaluated. Culture constitutes a significant variable in the model of organizational life. For the purposes of this study, culture will be defined as the shared values (what is important) and beliefs (the why behind what happens) which guide the behaviour of its members.

Values are common to nearly all of the varied definitions in the culture literature. Values central to an organization's being can be revealed in two ways. First, they may be enacted as ideologies represented in the way business is conducted. Second, central values may be espoused through formal means of communication (i.e., written company literature, speeches). If values are enacted without being stated, they must be deciphered by organization's members. Therefore, espoused values provide a clearer declaration. When well defined and continually expressed, central values serve as the precepts which structure behaviour. Many researchers have fallen victim to the trap of advocating a prescribed set of values as a recipe for corporate success.

Many mainstream business books, although written from the perspective of the corporate environment, tend to offer generic "quick fixes," often proposing that their exists a model culture for effectiveness and suggesting that any organization's current culture is malleable enough to achieve the prescribed ideal. Furthermore, these mainstream writings generally lack scientific credibility in that they are based on anecdotal evidence, use a relatively small sample size, and ignore psychometric issues such as data reliability and validity.

However, while convenient to assume, central values, like personal values, cannot be dictated or imposed. Central values result from the genesis of a company's history, emerging from the organization's leaders and members. As the company grows, articulation of the central values is essential for reinforcement in incumbent members and instilling in new members. Collins and Porras (1994) reported that visionary companies usually possess between three and six central values. Some examples of well-known, visionary companies and their central values are: Wal-Mart–customer service, Procter and Gamble– product quality and honest business, and Hewlett-Packard–respect and concern for the individual.

The work culture is further shaped by an organization's goals. Organizational goals are the specific actions the company strives to accomplish. Consequently, they function as the impetus for the company's strategic plans. To be authentic and deserving of full commitment from the organization's members, organizational goals should reinforce the central values held. For example, General Electric's goal of training every employee in six sigma methodology and basing promotional consideration on the completion of training reflects their espoused high regard for quality. Goals that conflict with an organization's central values are likely to result in dissent among its members, therefore hindering the potential for achievement.

Organizational goals in conjunction with central values constitute the organization's strategic intent. The attainment of the strategic intent, while influenced by many factors (i.e., resources, market, competition), is initially fueled by its clear communication and strength of the bond between the central values and organizational goals. These elements describe the medium of culture that influences the constitution of the climate. For organizational goals to be realized, effective work processes must be designed and maintained. Processes, in turn, must be enacted by individuals who perform various jobs in support of the process goals. Figure 3 illustrates how the four orientations (i.e., individual, job, process, and organizational) influence organizational health.

Organizational climate, colloquially defined as "the way things are done around here", is a multidimensional concept which has experienced a long, prolific history in the research literature. Although more advanced a concept than organizational culture in terms of practical application and empirical inquiry, organizational climate also has been subject to controversy regarding its definition and has assumed varying levels of focus in terms of the content it includes. Organizational climate, a concept indigenous to the field of organizational psychology, has functioned as an instrument for quantifying environmental influences on individual motivation, satisfaction, and workplace behaviour through the summary of perceptions.

From the beginning of the concept's explication, data collection and empirical analysis have been key components of the majority of studies. The breadth of the organizational climate topic results in a limitless set of elements that constitute the work environment. Thus, organizational climate as a general concept for study can include a myriad of potential dimensions for assessment. As a result, content critical for assessment may be ignored or the list of dimensions may grow so large that assessment is impossible. Schneider (1990) noted that the representation of climate as an abstract construct lacks a strategic focus. Climate without reference to a specific outcome (i.e., safety, quality, creativity) Organizational health across four orientations has no content boundaries as well as no definitive purpose for assessment and therefore lacks practical utility. Thus, it is essential to assess climate within the context of organizational, process, individual, and job goals.

In recent years, numerous researchers have directed their efforts toward developing assessments to measure climates for a specific type of environment. Several studies have demonstrated the utility of this focus through industrial application. Zohar (1980) tested an assessment measure of a safety climate. Other measures available for the assessment of a specific climate or work outcome include conflict resolution, motivation and leadership, job satisfaction, and organizational performance.

As the purpose of this article was to develop a model for the assessment of organizational health, a practical and clear definition is needed which recognizes all variables in the determination of organizational climate. Therefore, the definition presented by Schneider and Cunnarson (1991) stating that organizational climate refers to "the themes that employees believe describe their organization based on the practices, procedures and rewarded behaviours that employees see happening to them as well as around them" will be used in this article.

For the purpose of work-system assessment, climate is more fully characterized by inclusion of job demands and resources. Job demands encompass the physical and mental task requirements as well as environmental conditions the worker may be exposed to (e.g., noise, vibration). Resources are factors in the work climate that act to encourage the worker to achieve job goals and job satisfaction. In the work system, resources may be individual based (e.g., smoking-cessation programmes), job based (e.g., expansion of task content), process based (e.g., improved work techniques), or organization based (restructuring of departments).

The relationship between culture and climate has caused much confusion and has been the subject of a multitude of debates in the research literature. While some researchers have described one concept in terms of that it is not the other, many culture researchers have wholly ignored organizational climate in their work. These two concepts, which obviously interlock in practical application, have been developed academically in parallel.

However, several researchers have acknowledged that culture and climate are distinct. Some have attempted to describe the relationship between culture and climate by stating that culture includes climate. However, this explanation fails to establish an area of demarcation between the two concepts. With greater clarity, Schneider (1985, 1987) described culture and climate as complimentary topics, and explained that climate research focuses on the what and how organizational activities and behaviours are rewarded while culture focuses on the underlying reasons why the activities and behaviours happen. In this way, culture "informs" climate by helping individuals define what is important and structure their experiences. Hence, climate can be viewed as a manifestation of culture.

Organizational climate, although subject to some debate regarding definition and details of operationalization issues, has proved a viable instrument for characterization of the work environment, especially for those work settings with a specific theme. However, the full potential of the climate concept can be realized best through its coupling with the organizational culture concept. While progress has been made in clarifying the relationship between the two, work to integrate the concepts has not progressed beyond theoretical discussions.

As these two concepts when paired are capable of wholly describing the context for behaviour in the work setting, it is essential that both be considered in the characterization of the organizational environment. This study will utilize the concepts of culture and climate in a model to describe the organizational environment to develop an analysis framework and methodology for the promotion of organizational health in the industrial work environment.

In the Organizational Health Model, culture explicitly drives the climatic conditions. Therefore, the climate represents how the culture is operationalized on a surface level. In this model, the factors selected to describe climate are those relevant to the two outcomes of interest: effectiveness as related to specific performance goals and organizational wellness as related to the quality of working life. Culture, as the essential values upon which an organization is based, provides a deep-rooted structure from which everyday policies, practices, and goals can be grounded.

When this progression occurs, the organization's values are enacted, reinforced, and clarified through its practices. In a study at a U.S. manufacturing company, values and organizational climate were found to influence organizational effectiveness while work practices were found to influence worker satisfaction and stress. Although the distinction between "climate" and "practices" was not clarified in this research, this effort provides evidence of the significance of these work-system components in the determination of organizational health.

Furthermore, numerous researchers have noted the positive effects of the congruence between cultural values, organizational goals, and daily practices. Morgan (1986) argued that a healthy organization requires its culture to be consistent with its structure, policies, and procedures. Schneider et al. (1996) proposed that what people believe is the culture and experience is the climate ultimately determines whether sustained change is accomplished. Collins and Porras (1994), in their study of the distinguishing characteristics of visionary, high-performing companies, found that organizational alignment so that members receive a consistent set of signals to reinforce the desired behaviour and achieve de- sired progress was perhaps the key finding of their 5-year research. In evaluating a proposed practice, Collins and Porras asserted that the key question is not "Is the practice good?" but "Is this appropriate for us—does it fit with our ideology and ambitions?"

Recently, rapid changes in the organization of work precipitated by work process improvement initiatives, coupled with changes in worker demographics, have necessitated the need to assess the impact of these changes on long-term work performance. Contemporary work-improvement strategies such as lean manufacturing and six sigma have focused their efforts to optimize process performance while largely ignoring the effects of these new work practices on workers. However, human performance plays an integral role in the determination of organizational effectiveness. The organizational health assessment model introduced in this article proposes a new paradigm for optimizing work in which the individual's health, safety, and satisfaction is viewed as the precursor of process and organizational effectiveness.

Work system interventions can be crafted only from data-driven evidence of the safety, performance, and health consequences currently faced by workers in the contemporary work environment. The Organizational Health Model introduced here provides a frame- work for health surveillance in industries with contemporary organizational practices (e.g., lean manufacturing, six sigma) and changing worker demographics (e.g., increasing numbers of women, ethnic minorities, and aging workers).

In the Organizational Health Model, culture – represented by an organization's values and goals – constitutes a company's strategic intent. Climate driven and reaffirmed by the culture establishes the context for behaviour (performance) and state of being (wellness) in the work setting. Further development of this model will serve to structure the gathering of empirical data, thus fostering the process of designing both healthy and competitive enterprises.

Chapter 4

Selection and Recruitment

SELECTION

Selection is the commonly used term, but probably a misnomer for what the organization attempts to accomplish during this stage of the employment process. Selection is the process used to choose individuals with the right qualifications to fill job openings in the organization. The more strategic term is placement, which means the process of ensuring that the right person is placed in the right job. Placement includes two separate but integrated concepts:

- Person-job fit This is the process of ensuring that the knowledge, skills, and abilities of the individual match the requirements of the essential functions of the job.
- Person-organization fit This is the process of ensuring that the personality and value system of the individual match the culture and objectives of the organization.

Person-job fit is especially critical when jobs and organizations are stable and the emphasis is on quality, productivity, and efficiency. However organizations and jobs are often not stable in today's dynamic and volatile world. If the nature of the job is constantly changing and the goals of the organization are flexible and fluid, person-job fit does not provide the workforce flexibility needed. In such situations, person-organization fit becomes increasingly important and facilitates creativity, innovation, and organizational and workforce flexibility and adaptability. In reality, both are important and the relative importance of each in the placement process depends on the situation.

The selection process follows a relatively consistent pattern in most organizations, although the complexity and number of steps vary based on the sophistication and needs of the organization. However, prior to the start of the selection process, a determination must be made as to the basis on which selection and placement is to be made. To do this, the organization must develop selection criteria that link those criteria to on-the-job performance. Finally, the organization must evaluate its selection processes. These topics are discussed in the following sections:

- Development of selection criteria
- The selection process
- Evaluation of the selection process

DEVELOPMENT OF SELECTION CRITERIA

As previously discussed, the selection process and all its components are tests in terms of the Uniform Guidelines for Employee Selection Procedures. Criteria used for selection must be both job-related and valid. The question then becomes how to achieve compliance with the law, avoid adverse impact on protected classes, and develop a process that accurately predicts on-the-job performance.

As discussed earlier, the process begins with quality job analysis. Job analysis provides information necessary to determine what the critical elements of performance are with respect to the job. Those elements can be defined in terms of quality of work, quantity of work, and so forth. In general, the selection process cannot directly measure job performance because the individual would have to actually be in the position, often for an extended period of time, to be able to measure that individual's performance. However, the organization can develop selection criteria that are believed to be correlated with the job performance elements. Criteria are often defined in terms of characteristics that the individual must possess such as knowledge, motivation, ability, intelligence, interpersonal skills, and so forth.

Unfortunately, selection criteria are not often directly observable, so the organization must develop predictors that can be used to evaluate whether the desired criteria are present in the individual. Predictors are such items as experience, education, certifications, test scores, references, background checks, past performance, interview results, and so forth. The predictors are used in the selection process. Predictors are those items used to determine the presence of desired attributes (selection criteria) in an individual because those selection criteria are directly correlated with job performance. Each step in this linkage must be a valid predictor of the next step.

The selection process should be designed to make correct decision and avoid incorrect ones. Appropriate selection and validation of predictors, selection criteria, and job performance elements facilitates the acceptance of qualified candidates and the rejection of unqualified ones, but also prevents the acceptance of unqualified candidates and the rejection of those that are qualified.

The Selection Process

A threshold question in designing the selection process is determining how the applicant should proceed through the process. Two options are most frequently used:

- Multiple hurdle approach In a multiple hurdle approach, the applicant must pass each step in the selection process. Failure at any step disqualifies the applicant from further consideration.
- Compensatory approach In the compensatory approach, applicants complete the whole selection process and their scores in each stage are added up to determine final ranking.

There are advantages and disadvantages to both approaches. The multiple hurdle approach is efficient, eliminating candidates at each step of the process. However, it might result in the elimination of outstanding candidates who are excellent in all areas except for one. The compensatory approach allows for a fuller examination of every candidate and enables a candidate to compensate for a weakness or poor performance in one stage. However, it is more time-consuming and expensive. The ultimate decision as to which type of approach to use likely revolves around the importance of the job, the availability of candidates, and organizational time and resource constraints. Most organizations use the multiple hurdle approach.

A typical selection process that includes

- Initial applicant contact
- Prescreening
- Application forms
- Applicant testing
- Interviews
- Background and reference checking
- Conditional job offer
- Medical/drug testing
- Offer and acceptance

Each stage in the process is discussed in the following sections.

Initial Applicant Contact

Recruitment methods were discussed earlier. Often candidates express interest by showing up at the employer (such candidates are called walk-ins) or by telephoning and inquiring as to current or potential job openings. Other candidates might mail or fax unsolicited resumes. These types of inquiries must be handled appropriately by the organization. Employer branding concerns require that these inquiries or submissions be handled in a professional and courteous manner. Yet the requirements for applicant flow tracking make additional clerical work. Many employers do not accept unsolicited resumes and require all applicants to follow standard application procedures, accepting applications only when openings are currently available.

Prescreening

Prescreening is the process of determining whether candidates meet the basic qualifications for the position. Many employers prescreen applicants prior to the application process. For example, if the employer accepts walk-in applications, it might determine at that time whether the candidate is qualified for its jobs. If not, the walk-in is not provided with a job application. In that way, the employer does not incur the time and expense of processing the application and can avoid the need to track the candidate for applicant flow purposes.

Other organizations prescreen on receipt of the application. They then reject those candidates that do not meet the minimum qualification standards for the job.

Application Forms

Application forms serve multiple purposes:

- Provides a record of interest in employment
- Provides information to determine the qualifications of the individual
- Provides information that can be used in the employment interview
- Provides the basic data needed for initial preparation of the personnel file
- Clearly puts the employee on notice regarding the selection process and the nature of the employment relationship in that it typically contains one or more of the following notices:
  - That employment is at-will and either the employee or employer may terminate the relationship for any legal reason at any time
  - Notifies the applicant that falsification of information on the application is grounds for immediate termination

- Notifies the applicant of any tests, including medical and drug tests, that will be required during the selection process
- Advises the applicant that references will be checked

Application forms are tests and must not be discriminatory. Unless there is a business necessity or bona fide occupational qualification applications must yield information that would permit the identification of the applicant's protected class status.

It is possible to use applications to rank order applicants in terms of qualifications for the job. This type of applications is called a weighted or biodata application form. Scores are assigned to specific answers on the application form. Those scores are then added together to come up with an overall score that can be used to rank candidates. These processes often can be done by computer software that scans the application for key words and assigns points when they appear. Although these types of systems are efficient, they must be valid predictors of performance and job related to avoid adverse impact issues.

Employers must make a determination as to whether to accept resumes as applications. Even though resumes could contain rich data about the candidate, they might also contain information such as age, race, or religion—information that the selecting official should not know. Frequently, candidates attach pictures to their resumes, again providing information that cannot legally be used in most selection processes. Good HR practice, if resumes are to be accepted, is to

- Redact (black out) information that cannot be used in the selection process.
- Require the applicant to also complete an application. In that way, the candidate is provided with the notifications described earlier and the organization is assured of getting the required information necessary to consider the qualifications of the individual.

APPLICANT TESTING

Many organizations use a variety of types of tests to improve the validity of the selection process. Valid tests that are job-related can be powerful predictors of subsequent on-the-job performance. Types of tests used in the selection process are discussed in the following sections.

Cognitive Ability Tests

These types of tests measure an individual's mental abilities and acquired knowledge. Examples of cognitive ability tests are those that test memory, analytical ability, verbal capabilities, mathematical ability, and reasoning.

Physical Ability Tests

These test measure an individual's physical skills and mobility. They are often important indicators of the ability to perform manual types of jobs, such as work on assembly lines. Examples of physical ability tests are those that measure strength, flexibility, balance, and stamina.

Work Simulation Tests

These tests require the applicant to perform a representative sample of the tasks that are part of the responsibility of the job. To the extent that the test is representative of the actual job, these types of test can be excellent predictors of future performance.

Personality Tests

Certain personality traits can be specifically correlated with performance on the job. If predictive validity has been proven, these tests are excellent tools.

Assessment Centres

Assessment centres are processes not places. They consist of a variety of tests and exercises that are scored, often by multiple raters. Assessment centres can be used as developmental tools or in the selection process. Because of the expense involved, they are frequently used only for selection and development of higher-level positions.

Honesty / Integrity Tests

Although polygraph tests are generally prohibited as pre-employment tests in the private sector, honesty and integrity tests are not. They are particularly useful in the selection process when individuals will have access to money, such as retail cashiers and bank tellers. The downside to using such tests is that they send the message to the applicant that he or she is not trusted.

Drug Tests

Drug tests can be used as a pre-employment test. Many employers elect to wait until a conditional offer of employment is made. Drug testing is discussed in the following section on post-offer employment practices.

INTERVIEWS

Organizations might use one or more interviews in the selection process. The purpose of interviews is to determine both person-job and person-organization fit, and to clarify information found on the application or gathered throughout the application process. If an organizations uses more than one interview, the first interview is normally used as a screen early in the selection process. HR is frequently responsible for performing the initial interview, and it is used to screen out those candidates who are obviously unsuitable for the position for which they applied. Subsequent interviews are conducted at higher levels of the organization, usually with management participation. They are used to evaluate the potential of viable candidates.

The interview is a traditional mainstay in the selection process. However, its validity is questionable. Yet few managers feel comfortable in selecting individuals without an interview. To maximize validity, interviews should be structured, directive, behavioural, or situational, and conducted by more than one interviewer. There are numerous common problems in the interview process that could lead to incorrect determinations. Also there are certain types of questions that either do not elicit the responses required to evaluate the candidate or should not be asked because they might create the potential for adverse impact and EEO complaints. These issues are discussed in the following sections.

Types of Interviews

There are numerous types of interviews that can be used in the selection process. It is up to the SPHR to guide the organization in selecting the type(s) of interview that best allows it to make a determination as to the potential of candidates to perform on the job. Types of interviews include the following.

Structured Interview

Structured interviews are those that include prescripted questions that are asked of all candidates. Interview structure runs on a continuum from highly structured to unstructured. At the far end of the structured interview continuum, the interview is totally scripted and the interviewer is not free to divert from the script. In addition, potential answers to each of the mandatory questions are often evaluated and given a score. The interviewer then must determine which of the potential answers is most like the one that the interviewee gave and assign it the predetermined score.

At the other end of the continuum, the interviewer is free to ask any questions that come to mind. In practice, structured interviews tend to be less restrictive than the example given, but still require that a number of prescripted questions be asked. A structured interview is more valid and defensible than other interview types when making selection decisions because all candidates are asked the same questions and comparisons can be made between the answers given.

Directive Interview

An analogous but somewhat different concept to structured interviews is the concept of directive interviews. Directive interviews are those in which the interviewer maintains control of the flow of the questioning. It also is on a continuum from strict control by the interviewer to a nondirective approach at the other end, which is essentially a free-flowing conversation with little or no direction. In this situation, the interviewer essentially relinquishes control of the interview to the interviewee. Obviously, there is some correlation between the concepts of directive and structured interviews. A structured interview must also be directive.

Behavioural Interview

Although the term behavioural interview is commonly used, the term behavioural refers more to the type of questions than to the type of interview. For example, a behavioural interview might be structured and directive, using behavioural questions. Behavioural questions are those that ask the individual how the individual handled a particular situation in the past. For example, a candidate for a managerial position could be asked how he or she handled a situation in the past when an employee was habitually late for work. The concept behind behavioural questioning is that past behaviour is the best indicator of future behaviour in the same or similar situation. The weakness in this approach is that behavioural questions do not take into account any learning that might have occurred after the situation.

Situational Interview

Situational interviews, like behavioural interviews, also refer to the type of questions being asked. Situational interviews ask candidates to explain how they would handle a particular situation when confronted with it on the job. The concept behind situational questions is that answers to these types of theoretical scenarios are good predictors of future performance. The weakness in this approach is that candidates can often fake it by giving the answer they believe the interviewer wants.

Stress Interview

Stress interviews are appropriate when the essential functions of the job are performed under demanding conditions that require quick thinking and control of one's emotions. A stress interview is one designed to create anxiety and place pressure on the interviewees to determine how they respond. Stress interviews are appropriate for certain types of jobs such as public safety and customer complaint-handling. The risk in this type of interview is the negative image that the interviewees might get about the organization, leading them to withdraw from consideration or refuse a subsequent offer of employment.

Mass Interview

A mass interview is one in which more than one interviewee is interviewed at the same time. The mass interview is infrequently used, but when used, often involves some sort of problem-solving exercise that is given to the interviewees to work through. Each candidate is evaluated on characteristics such as leadership, interpersonal skills, and teamwork.

360° Interview

A 360° interview is one that is conducted by a panel of interviewers representing various constituencies in order to get a broad perspective in the evaluation of the candidate. For example, this type of interview might include the supervisor, a peer, a customer, and a subordinate if the interview is for a supervisory position. The concept behind the 360° interview is that the candidate is evaluated from a broad perspective. The potential problem with this concept is that each of the stakeholders might come to the interview with a different perspective as to the characteristic needed to do the job effectively.

Panel Interview

A panel interview is one in which more than one interviewer conducts the interview. Panel interviews are generally considered to be more valid than other types because more than one perspective is included in the evaluation process.

Problem with Interviews

There are common problems in perception that occur in interview that might cause the interviewer to make an incorrect determination of the candidate's potential. Interviewers receive training regarding these errors so that they can avoid them in the interview process. Common perceptual errors include the following:

- Snap judgments: Interviewers often make up their minds regarding a candidate in the first few minutes of the interview. Such a quick decision precludes a full evaluation of the candidate's characteristics.
- Stereotyping: Stereotyping involves evaluating persons based on their demographic characteristics rather than their individual capabilities.
- Similar to me: The candidate is evaluated based on having a similar characteristic to the interviewer. For example, candidates from the same college as the interviewer are evaluated higher than those from other colleges.
- Negative emphasis: Unfortunately, in the culture of the United States negative information is given more credence than positive information. One negative piece of information often precludes selection for the position and cannot be offset by many positive characteristics.
- Halo/horn effect: Frequently all the candidate's characteristics are evaluated based on an evaluation of only one characteristic or trait. A positive evaluation is referred to as the halo effect, whereas a negative evaluation on all traits based on a negative evaluation of one trait is referred to as the horn effect.
- Contrast error: It is important that candidates be evaluated against objective criteria related to job performance (predictors). However, interviewers frequently evaluate candidates against the prior candidate rather than the objective criteria. This can

cause errors in the evaluation. For example, an average candidate interviewed after a poor candidate might be evaluated higher than average.

Interview Questions

Questions used in interviews should be designed to gather information need to make a determination as to whether to offer the individual a position. Questions that are poorly formulated do not assist in that endeavor. Questions that lead to answers that would identify the protected class of an individual, in the absence of BFOQ or business necessity, are illegal and should be avoided. The following types of questions do not lead to responses that facilitate evaluation of the candidate:

- Questions that are not job-related: Questions not directly related to the job decrease the validity of the interview and do not assist in gather information regarding the candidate.
- Bipolar questions: Bipolar questions are those that can be answered with yes or no. They provide little or no definitive information.
- Leading questions: Leading questions guide the respondent to the answer. The interviewer then does not know whether or not the answer is truthful.
- Illegal questions: Questions that would identify protected class status are illegal. The following areas of questioning should be avoided unless they constitute a BFOQ for the specific job or are directly job-related:
  - Age
  - Sex
  - Race
  - National origin
  - Disability
  - Ancestry
  - Number of children

- – Marital status
- – Arrests
- – Height and weight
- – Date of college degree or high school graduation
- – Religious holidays observed
- – Birthplace
- – Medical history

BACKGROUND INVESTIGATIONS

Background investigations are frequently the last step in the selection process prior to making a job offer or conditional job offer to the applicant. Background investigations serve two purposes. First they provide accurate information on the individual that is needed to make a final decision regarding employment. Second they provide evidence that the employer conducted due diligence in its hiring practices, which could be beneficial in the event the organization is sued for negligent hiring. A side benefit of background investigations is that candidates are less likely to apply or to falsify applications when they know background checks will be done. Background investigations incorporate one of more of the following processes:

- Reference checks: Employers typically attempt to get information from prior employers regarding the nature of the applicant's prior employment. Former employers frequently are reluctant to provide any derogatory information on prior employees because of fear of litigation for defamation of character, libel, and slander. Checking of personal references is also usually done, but is unlikely to reveal information of value.
- Criminal record checks: Limited criminal background checks are available through local or state law enforcement agencies. Decisions based on criminal record checks must be job-related because certain protected classes have disproportionately higher criminal conviction rates and decisions that are clearly not job-related might create adverse impact.

- Credit checks: Credit checks should be performed when the nature of the job involves responsibilities of a financial nature (payroll, accounts receivable, and so forth) or handling money (cashiers, bank tellers, and so forth). As is the case with criminal record checks, certain protective classes have higher incidences of bad credit than others.
- Third-party background checks: Many organizations elect to have reference, criminal history, and credit checks done by third parties.

Remember that the provisions of the Fair Credit Reporting Act are applicable when the organization conducts credit checks. The act also covers most types of background checks if the organization contracts with a third party to perform them.

Conditional Job Offers, Medical Exams/Drug Testing, and Offers and Acceptance

These issues are discussed in the section on post-offer employment practices. In addition, medical examinations and drug testing were discussed in relation to the provisions of the Americans with Disability Act earlier.

Evaluation of the Selection Process

Strategies and methods used to evaluate the selection process are essentially the same as those used to evaluate the recruitment process, and is repeated here. The selection process should be continually evaluated in terms of its impact on protected classes. The Uniform Guidelines on Employee Selection Procedures calls for a bottom-up approach to evaluation. If adverse impact is indicated at the end of the selection process, the whole process must be dissected into its various stages to determine at what level or levels adverse impact occurs.

The organization should evaluate its selection process effectiveness in terms of the performance and retention of individuals hired. Predictors and criteria should be consistently evaluated for validity and predictive capacity.

Two issues are allied with selection and are important determinants of the ultimate effectiveness of the process. The first is realistic job previews, which were discussed previously. There are multiple opportunities throughout the selection process to provide the applicant with accurate information as to the exact nature of the job and the characteristics of the organization. The other issue is orientation. The selection process is an opportunity to begin the orientation process by providing the individual information on the terms, conditions, and benefits of employment with the organization. The accuracy and quality of both realistic job previews and employee orientation are positively correlated with employee retention.

POST-OFFER EMPLOYMENT PRACTICES

There are several commons employment practices that the organization might want to use after a determination has been made to hire an individual. First is the employment offer itself. Next the organization must decide whether it is in its best interest to formalize the employment relationship with a formal employment contract. In addition, the organization must determine its employment practice with respect to medical examinations and, finally, whether to offer relocation benefits. Each of these practices is discussed in the sections that follow.

EMPLOYMENT OFFERS

Often the hiring process is a long and intensive process frequently characterized by considerable stress, particularly on the part of the employee. This can lead to miscommunication and misunderstandings as to the parametres of the proposed employment relationship. Therefore, many organizations consider it good practice to place their employment offers, often referred to as job offers, in writing. It is recommended that employment offer letters be reviewed by legal counsel to ensure that the organization does not create a legal obligation that it did not intend. The offer should clearly delineate the terms and conditions of employment. Care should be taken to avoid vague language that might be interpreted by the employee to promise any future benefit such as job security, pay raises or bonuses, particular work schedules, and so forth. Especially important is a clear identification that the employment relationship is "at-will", and can be terminated by either party at any time for any legal reason.

The employee should be required to sign one copy of the offer and return it to the employer prior to or simultaneously with reporting for work. The signed offer should be retained in the employee's personnel file.

If the employee is to be paid by the hour or by some type of piece-rate or commission basis, the employment offer should clearly delineate how the employee is to be compensated. However, if the employee is to be paid by salary, it is good practice to for the employment offer to align the salary offer with the current compensation payment practice. In other words, whether the employer pays weekly, biweekly, or monthly, the offer should be for the gross amount to be paid during a pay period. Some courts have interpreted employment offers that quote annual salaries as creating an implied contract for that amount of compensation.

Employment Contracts

The legal concepts associated with contracts are discussed in additional depth. Organizations might want to negotiate a formal contract with employees that goes beyond the normal employment offer or agreement and clearly identifies additional terms and conditions of employment. Employment contracts are often used to negate the employment-at-will condition of employment and to establish fixed terms and conditions of employment—including length of employment and restrictions on employee activities should they leave the organization. Employment contracts provide protection, rights, and obligations for both the organization and the employee.

Medical Tests

Medical tests can be administered after a conditional offer of employment. The subject of medical tests is covered in depth earlier as part of the discussion of the Americans with Disabilities Act.

An allied issue is the emerging and somewhat complex issue of genetic testing. Genetics is a branch of biology that studies the transmission of hereditary characteristic from parents to offspring. Medical tests are now available that can identify the genetic markers for certain debilitating diseases. Employers could use these test results to discriminate against individuals that have an increased potential for developing serious illnesses that might require expensive medical treatment and, ultimately, affect the employer's health insurance costs. On the other hand, this information could be valuable to the employee. The employee could be advised of the potential for certain diseases and take preventative measures. In addition, the employer might be able to place the employee in certain jobs that would lessen the potential for certain types of diseases. For example, the employee could be placed in a job that does not come into contact with certain types of hazardous chemicals.

As stated before, this issue is emerging as the genetic technology improves. Taking employment-related actions based on genetic information that negatively affects the employee should not be done. The SPHR can expect legislation and additional case law in this area.

Relocation

Many employers provide some assistance with the expenses of moving should the employee be relocating from a different geographical area to accept employment. Relocation benefits often involve issues of taxability and real estate law. For those reasons, many organizations elect to outsource this programme.

ORGANIZATIONAL EXIT

It is up to the SPHR to strategically manage organizational exit so that it is, to the extent possible, controllable, involuntary, and functional. Organizational exit is controllable when it is the employer that determines when employees leave the organization. It is involuntary when employees leave the organization because of organizational mandates, not the employees' desire to do so. Voluntary organizational exit (also called turnover) is frequently a significant problem in organizations, and often it is the best employees that leave. Involuntary organization exit involves termination for poor performance or layoffs or termination of excess employees when they are no longer needed by the organization. Functional organizational exit means that the organization is more efficient and/or effective after the exit occurs. Dysfunctional organizational exit results in a decrease in the human capital of the organization and decreased organizational capacity.

Organizational exit is the process of managing the conditions under which employees leave the organization and is often referred to as decruitment. An employee might be required to leave the organization because of his or her own actions, or the exit might be mandated based on organizational strategy that is beyond the control of the individual. Layoffs are discussed in the first section, along with strategies that can be employed to either avert the layoff or lessen its impact on the employee. After that, discussion moves on to involuntary terminations based on employee performance or conduct. If organizational exit is to be controllable, involuntary, and functional, the organization must know why exit occurs, particularly voluntary exit. One of the ways of determining this is by conducting exit interviews. Strategies and practices associated with exit interviews are discussed. Finally, this section addresses the issue of wrongful terminations.

Layoffs

There are a number of reasons why an employer might desire to reduce the total number of employees. Some of the more common reasons include the following:

- Downturns in overall operations caused by economic conditions or drop in product or service demand; commonly referred to as downsizing
- Concentrating on core competencies; commonly referred to as rightsizing
- Mergers or acquisitions that create redundant or duplicate positions
- Increases in production or introduction of new technology requiring fewer employees
- Competitive decisions, such as movement of plants to lower cost labour areas domestically or internationally (offshoring)
- Competitive decisions to outsource work currently being done internally

Any of these reasons might result in a decruitment situation in which the employer has a surplus of employees and must reduce the overall size of its workforce or must change the composition of its workforce in terms of employee capabilities.

Decisions to terminate or lay off employees have significant organizational implications. First the organization should evaluate the impact of layoffs on its diversity programmes and the potential for creating adverse impact. Although seniority is generally considered to be a defence in adverse impact situations, the organization might be able to craft a layoff scenario that avoids adverse impact. Next the organization must consider the impact of layoffs on its important stakeholders. Layoffs send a mixed message to customers and investors. Even though the process might be perceived by these constituencies as prudent business decision-making, there is equal likelihood that it could be considered a sign of organizational, product, or service weakness, impacting demand and access to capital. The organization must consider the impact that such activities might have on the communities in which it operates, balancing business goals with social responsibilities. Finally, and most importantly, organizations should consider the impact of layoffs both on those employees directly affected and those who remain.

Because of these factors, the SPHR must be able to lead the organization in the development of programmes that might permit the organization to avoid layoffs entirely or reduce the total number of employees that are laid off and programmes that lessen the impact personal impact if an employee is in fact laid off. They are discussed the following sections.

It is not only the employees that are laid off that are affected, but also those who remain. Often they have to endure increased workloads, having to both perform their current duties and assume the duties of those who have left. The remaining employees often are affected by increased stress based on concerns for their future in the organization and a bit of guilt associated with still being employed while their former coworkers have been laid off. The organization can lessen these impacts by communicating honestly with employees as to organizational plans and providing programmes such as counseling to assist in development to the new condition.

Layoffs by definition imply that the employee is to be returned to work. This might or might not occur. It is good practice to advise employees in writing that the layoff is considered permanent and end in a termination at the end of a specified period of time.

Remember requirements under the WARN, discussed earlier, when implementing layoffs and plant shutdowns.

Strategies to Avoid Layoffs

Even though the organization has decided to reduce the total size of the workforce, there are many strategies for accomplishing this goal without involuntarily laying off or terminating employees. These strategies frequently take some time to have impact; consequently, they might not be feasible if the immediacy of action is critical. However, in other situations the strategies discussed in the following section might avoid it totally or reduce the number of layoffs required.

Early Retirement Incentives

Many workers are willing to retire early if provided with the right incentives. Early retirement options that provide added benefits and that do not violate the Older Workers Benefit Protection Act, can facilitate reductions in workforce levels. However, a major concern with this strategy is that it is often the best workers that are attracted by the offer. They are those who have additional options, such as second careers.

Part-time Work and Job Sharing

Many employees are interested in reducing the total number of hours worked, either through part-time work or job-sharing arrangements. This strategy can often accommodate family lifestyle needs and reduce total compensation costs.

Leaves of Absence

Organizations have had surprising success with offering unpaid leaves of absence. If the conditions requiring reductions in workforce levels are projected to be temporary, offering leaves of absence might assist in avoiding the need to involuntarily lay off employees.

Attrition and Hiring Freezes

Attrition is the reduction of workforce levels caused by the normal processes of retirement, resignation, termination, and so forth. Hiring freezes prohibit the hiring of new and additional employees and the replacement of current employees that leave the organization.

Voluntary Resignation Programmes

Employers might offer bonuses for employees that want to leave the organization voluntarily. Many employees might have other options available to them, but are not eligible for early retirement. Some sort of bonus might be sufficient to motivate them to leave the organization voluntarily. As with early retirements, these types of programmes must be crafted to avoid the loss of critical individuals and serious impact on critical departments.

STRATEGIES TO MINIMIZE THE IMPACT OF LAYOFFS ON INDIVIDUALS

Two common strategies that can be used to minimize the impact of layoffs on individuals are severance pay and outplacement services. They are discussed in the following sections.

Severance Pay

There is no federal legal requirement for severance pay. However, many organizations offer this benefit to provide former employees with income continuation in the event of involuntary termination. Severance pay is either a one-time lump sum payment or a temporary continuation of salary provided by the employer to terminated workers. Calculations of the total amount to be received are typically based on length of service, and frequently involve one week's pay for every year of service. Severance pay often makes good business sense because it serves both a humanitarian and public relations purpose.

Outplacement Services

Outplacement services are provided to assist terminated individuals in obtaining new employment. Services provided frequently include employment counseling, assistance with resume preparation, training in job search skills, training to improve interviewing skills, and job referral assistance. Generally, these services are outsourced to vendors that specialize in this area. As discussed earlier, outsourcing vendors are often good sources of external recruits.

EXIT INTERVIEWS

Many, in fact most, employers use exit interviews, which are conducted in an attempt to determine why individuals are leaving the organization. The objective is to determine what is good and what is bad about the organization in order to provide management with information that assists in developing or modifying programmes to improve organizational performance.

These interviews are typically conducted by the HR function. There is an assumption that the individual has no reasons to guard his or her remarks and is forthright in observations about the organization when leaving. However, recent research has revealed that changes in the psychological contract may be modifying that paradigm. In today's environment, employees often do not consider their termination of the employment relationship to be permanent and might want to retain their option to return at some future date. In these situations they are not likely to be totally forthright in evaluating the organization and its programmes. To overcome this reluctance current exit interview practice often involves delaying the interview for about 30 days after termination and conducting it via phone, guaranteeing anonymity.

Wrongful Termination

Wrongful termination occurs when the termination violates statutory or common law. Wrongful termination actions can be pursued as tort actions in court or under the provisions of the applicable employment law, but generally not both. Three types of wrongful terminations are discussed in this section: terminations that violate law, constructive discharge, and retaliatory discharge.

Constructive Discharge

Constructive discharge occurs when employer actions make the employment relationship so untenable that a reasonable person would have no obligation but to resign. In this case, the resignation is coerced and the employee might have recourse under either common law or certain employment laws. Recourse under common law is typically limited to situations in which the individual gives up a legal property interest in the employment relationship, such as when the individual has an employment contract. Constructive discharge might be another form of illegal discrimination under various employment laws.

Retaliatory Discharge

Retaliatory discharge occurs when the employer terminates the employee for exercising right or obligations under the law. This typically occurs under one of two scenarios:

- The employee is terminated for filing a complaint or otherwise exercising rights guaranteed under employment legislation. Examples are filing an EEO complaint, reporting OSHA violations, and so forth.
- The employee is terminated for fulfilling obligations under the law, such as testifying against the employer when summoned to do so in a court of law or reporting employer violations of law.

The employer can avoid allegations of wrongful termination actions by engaging in good HR practice such as the following:

- Providing internal complaint resolution processes and grievance procedures
- Training all managers on employment law
- Thoroughly documenting the reasons for all terminations
- Evaluating employment practices for adverse impact
- Engaging in the workplace strategies discussed earlier to avoid the necessity for involuntary termination

MANAGEMENT OF EMPLOYMENT RECORDS

To a large extent, the management of employment records is part of the administrative role of HR and an in-depth discussion of this issue is more appropriate in preparation for the PHR examination. A threshold issue is the determination as to whether the law requiring employment record retention actually applies to the organization. Various laws might apply only if the organization has a stated number of employees and/or federal contracts of more than certain dollar amounts. The information as to which organizations are covered by a law is contained in the discussion of that law and others. It is not repeated in this section.

It is not unusual for the same record to have different record retention requirements in different laws. In that case, the retention period for that particular record should be the one corresponding to the longest period. It is often prudent, and in some instances required, to keep records longer than mandatory retention period. If, for example, the records in question are part of litigation or a proceeding in front of a third party, such as the EEOC or OSHA, the records must be retained until final disposition of the complaint or lawsuit. In addition, it often is prudent to keep employment records until the statute of limitations for filing a complaint or lawsuit has expired if there is some potential that the employee might do so.

Table: Summary of Employment Record Retention Requirements

Law	*Record Retention Requirements*
Age Discrimination in Employment Act (ADEA)	Payroll records—3 years. Employment records (promotions, applications, layoff, recall, terminations and so forth)—1 year.
Americans with Disabilities Act (ADA)	Employment records (applications, requests for reasonable accommodations, promotions, selections for training, terminations and so forth)—1 year from record creation or taking of the action.
Title VII of the Civil Rights Act of 1964	Employment records (applications, promotions, transfers, layoffs, terminations and so forth)—1 year from record creation of taking of the action. A copy of the current EEO-1 Report must be kept in the files.

Consolidated Omnibus Budget Reconciliation Act (COBRA)	Notices, payroll actions, and so forth – 6 years.* -*COBRA does not mandate retention requirements, per se. However, COBRA amends ERISA and its retention requirements apply.
Davis-Bacon, Service Contract, and Walsh-Healy Public Contract Acts	Employment and payroll records – 3 years from end of the contract.
Employee Retirement Income Security Act (ERISA)	Annual reports, summary plan descriptions, plan changes, required reports to the Department of Labour and the Pension Benefit Guarantee Corporation, along with related materials to prepare such reports – 6 years.
	Information necessary to determine benefits for participants – As long as they are relevant.
Employee Polygraph Protection Act	Test results and reason for administration – 3 years.
Equal Pay Act	Payroll records – 3 years.
Executive Order 11246	Affirmative action plans – 2 years.
Fair and Accurate Credit Transactions Act (FACTA)	Documents containing information from credit reports – Must be shredded on completion of action/ determination.
Fair Labour Standards Act (FLSA)	Payroll records – 3 years.
Family and Medical Leave Act (FMLA)	Employment records, payroll records, leave records, employee notices, and so forth – 3 years.
Federal Insurance Contribution Act (FICA Federal Unemployment	Employment and payroll records – 4 years from the

Tax Act) (FUTA) Internal Revenue Code (Federal Income Tax Withholding)	date the tax is due or the tax is paid, whichever is later.
Immigration Reform and Control Act	Form I-9—3 years from date of hire or 1 year from date of termination, whichever is later.
Occupational Safety and Health Act (OSHA)	Logs and reports—5 years.
	Medical records and records of exposure to toxic substances for each employee—30 years from the date the employee leaves employment with the organization.
Rehabilitation Act of 1973	Employment and payroll records—2 years.
	A copy of the current affirmative action plan developed under the act must be kept in the files.
Uniform Guidelines on Employee Selection Procedures (UGESP)	Recruitment and selection documents, including the analysis of adverse selection based on these documents—2 years after the adverse impact is eliminated where analysis indicated adverse impact.
Vietnam Era Readjustment Assistance Act	Employment and payroll records—2 years
	A copy of the current affirmative action plan must be kept in the file.
	A copy of the current VETS-100 must be retained.

State laws might impose additional requirements regarding retention of certain employment records beyond that required by federal law and regulations.

GROUP SELECTION PROCEDURE

Employers have typically viewed the interview as an essential part of the employee selection process. Anyone who has been hired for employment has most likely experienced the selection interview. A wide range of interview formats is possible. Two main forms can be delineated: the non-structured interview and the structured interview. In its purest form, the non-structured interview is an open-ended, individualised, conversational dialogue between the employer and the applicant. The structured interview is a formal, test-like, question and answer session in which the employer assesses the applicant's specific credentials in a predesigned, organised manner. We will examine the positive and negative features of each type of selection interview. Then we will advocate an integrated format that draws on the strengths of the two interview formats, while avoiding their limitations.

THE PERSONNEL SELECTION INTERVIEW

The unstructured, personnel interview is probably the most commonly used selection tool in North America arid Western Europe, and the sole selection device in many other countries. The personnel interview has at least five advantages, which may explain its popularity among business and personnel managers.

1. The "personal touch". An employer or manager may wish to evaluate the prospective employee personally. The employer can ask questions that an indirect resource could not pose, and can obtain a personal feel for whether or not the applicant would be suitable for the position and would fit into the social context of the company.
2. Facility of operation. With a small number of applicants, interviews are relatively easy to operate. They can be given at any time or place, and do not need special materials for their execution.
3. Perceived inexpensiveness. The interview appears to be a low- budget operation (again, when the number

of candidates is small). No money needs to be spent on purchasing special tests or hiring test administrators.

4. Face validity. The interview has high face validity. Interviewing seems to be the most natural method of selection because the impressions we form of others in everyday life also come from speaking and interacting with people.
5. Flexibility. The interview is adaptable and is capable of serving multiple purposes. Interviews can be used at several stages of personnel management, including recruitment, screening, selection and negotiation. The interview is a way to introduce an applicant to the organisation in a warm, personal way. In addition, it gives the applicant the opportunity to satisfy his or her own questions about the company, and to get a feel for the group of people they might be working for.

Problems with the Non-structured Personnel Interview

Psychologists researching the non-structured personnel interview have examined its pros and cons. The prevailing view among researchers for many years was that an open-ended interview is very problematic, and that managers would do best if they assigned zero or a very low weight to the interview results. Conclusions drawn by Mayfield in his 1964 review are typical of the views of others who wrote about the non-structured personnel interview until the mid-1980s:

- Consensus (interrater reliability) among interviewers is low,
- Behaviour domains are not covered in a consistent way,
- Unfavourable information influences interviewers more than favourable information,
- Interviewers make their decision quite early in the interview and spend the rest of the interview justifying (for themselves) this decision.

- Interviewers' ratings are affected by a variety of cognitive biases (eg primacy-recency effect, first impressions, contrast effect, halo effect and social stereotypes).
- The interview has low predictive validity; performance during an interview does riot predict future job performance well.

Yet for those who use personalised selection interviews, the face- to-face format provides a sense of being informed and in control that they find hard to relinquish. And indeed, as described earlier, there are some benefits to an unstructured interview. Therefore, the goal should be to improve the interviewing process, and not to drop it or even to modify it to the point where it is no longer really an interview.

THE STRUCTURED INTERVIEW

The instrument that has recently emerged as a proposed solution for the problems inherent in the personnel interview is the structured interview. This device combines the features of a personnel interview and the features of a standardised selection device.

Designing a Structured Interview

The proper design of the structured interview entails several phases that must be followed. The first of these steps is the determination of the particular dimensions that are to be covered during the interview. The employer must decide on the abilities, traits, attitudes and values that are believed to be necessary for success in both the particular organisation and the particular position that is being offered. The best process for this objective is job analysis. Comprehensive and accurate job analysis has been shown to improve the validity of a structured interview. Job analysis is also necessary from a legal standpoint; the Uniform Guidelines for Employee Selection in the United States require that job analysis be performed as part of the development, application, and validation of employee selection devices. Data from the job analysis should be used in the development of interview rating scales. In order to add structure to the interview, the predetermined dimensions must be "translated" into specific interview questions. The interviewer must be able to elicit information that will satisfy the criteria of the required dimensions.

In the second phase of the design, standardised ratings must be developed to systematise the scoring and interpretation of the interview. This process is what really makes the instrument "structured". Scoring codes, accompanied by good examples and illustrations, allow for a uniform method of judgement by different raters, and across different applicants. These codes also determine the relative values of applicants' abilities and accomplishments, ie how important the various attributes are for being hired.

In the third phase of the design, several interview conditions should be controlled and standardised in order to ensure reliable results. First is the physical location of the interview. An office or similar room should be used for all interviews. Second, proper interview training is essential. Interviewers should be trained in a way that will enhance the uniformity and fairness of the interview. Moreover, interviewers should be made aware of potential biases and how to avoid them. Third, interviewees should be given the same questions in the same word order and question order. Fourth, a single panel for rating the applicants against each other has been found to increase both the reliability and validity of the selection process.

Table: A Comparison Between the Features of Structured and Non-Structured Selection Interviews

Feature	*Structured Interview*	*Non-Structured Interview*
Defining the specific dimensions to be covered by the interview.	Viewed as essential for the selection process. Specification of dimensions are guided by proper job analysis.	Not always viewed as necessary. Sometimes an assessment of "the quality and normality" of the interviewee is presented as the goal of the interview.

Questions presented to the interviewee.	For every dimension, a pool of predetermined questions is prepared. Questions during the interview are taken from these pools.	Questions differ from one interview to another depending on the dynamics of the interview.
Rating of the interviewee.	Rating is systematic. It is based on rating codes, anchored examples, and illustrations.	Rating either does not exist, or is performed by the interviewer intuitively.
Standardisation of the physical conditions of the interview setting.	Viewed as essentia	Viewed as advantageous but not essential.
Single vs. Panel of interviewers.	Panel of interviewers is preferred.	Single interviewer is preferred.
Training of interviewers.	Viewed as essential both methods.	

A highly structured interview will carry all five features presented under the "structured interview" title. A highly non-structured interview will carry the other five features, each one of them to its extreme.

Recent meta-analyses show that the structured interview has moderate predictive validity. Table presents the validities of structured and unstructured interviews, according to three most recent meta-analytical reports. Each of these three meta-analyses combines findings from several dozens of empirical "primary researches". The figures in the table express, via correlational scale, the strength of the relation between selection interview ratings.

1. This study has been corrected (observed validities) for range restriction and criteria unreliability.
2. This study has been corrected (observed reliabilities) for criteria unreliability only.

3. This figure was reported by Hunter and Hunter (1984). It was employed by Wright, Lichtenfels and Pursell (1989) as a basis for comparison.

Similarly, some recent individual studies that employed a structured interview for selection purposes found moderate predictive validity. For example, Campion, Pursell and Brown (1988) reported a corrected validity of r = .56 in a study of entry level production employees; and corrected validities of r = .42 and r = .61 for two samples of sales clerks were reported by Arvey, Miller, Gould and Burch (1987).

In the light of all of the structuredness characteristics, it seems appropriate to view the structured-unstructured quality of an interview as a continuum rather than as a dichotomy. Unfortunately, it has not yet been established which features of the structured interview are essential in terms of enhancing the reliability and validity.

Problems with the Structured Interview

Although the structured interview provides some advantages over the unstructured interview, problems still remain. Structuring the interview may have a sterilising effect on the procedure. That is, the interview becomes less spontaneous and the interviewer may Jose track of potentially important follow-up information. In other words, there is a loss of flexibility that results from the inclusion of external loci of control (ie predetermined questions). Another dehumanising effect is the "cold" atmosphere that results from structuring. This effect may influence interviewees to be less open during the interview and it may discourage applicants from pursuing an employment position with an "impersonal organisation", even if it is offered to them at a later stage. Interviewers and applicants tend to value an atmosphere where they can be spontaneous and direct.

Additionally, the introduction of structure brings an opportunity for applicants to "beat the system". The use of standard questions and a fixed-response rating code in the structured interview can be dangerous because lists of popular interview questions are widely circulated and applicants are often well-prepared for typical questions.

The Two-Step Selection Interview

Here, we propose a specific type of interview that offers "the best of both worlds". This "integrated" or "combined" interview consists of two parts. Part I is highly structured. In this part, the interviewer adheres to the format prepared beforehand. The interviewer presents a standard set of questions verbatim and in a predetermined order. Ratings are based on a standard rating guide. The probable duration of Part I is 20-40 minutes.

Part II is open-ended, flexible and unstructured. In Part II, the interviewer uses his or her training and experience to follow-up on important issues mentioned by the applicant. The interviewee is encouraged to bring up issues that he or she thinks are relevant to the hiring decision. This is done in a free-style, warm manner. The interviewer acts more as a clinical psychologist than as a personnel manager. The interviewer has to listen with his/her "inner ear" to any sign of pathology, personality disorder, difficulty in interaction with other people, behavioural disorders under stress, and so on. The score of the interviewee on Part II is based on the subjective, impressionistic judgements of the interviewer. Interviews ranging from 15—30 minutes are typical.

An experienced interviewer moves smoothly and in a natural style from the formal, structured part of the interview to the non-structured, more personal part of the interview. Weights for each part are determined ahead of time. For example, a decision may be made that the weight of the Part II score is 20% of the total score, and the weight of Part I is 809k. Knowing this ahead of time lessens the likelihood that interviewers will assign special weights to their "clinical" judgements. This tendency is a source of bias, and is considered to be one of the reasons for the low predictive validities of non-structured selection interviews. Therefore, once the relative weights of the parts are determined, interviewers should be consistent and fair across applicants.

The recent developments in selection interviewing research indicate that both structured interviews and personalised, unstructured interviews have advantages and disadvantages. The contribution of a structured design to the selection interview is a considerable boost in reliability, and more importantly, validity. Also, organisations are receiving greater scrutiny from many sources (eg government, unions), which has put pressure on them to objectify and standardise previously subjective procedures for hiring personnel. As a result, well-documented procedures for designing and improving the selection interview are now being utilised.

However, if too many constraints and regulations are placed on structured interviews, there is a risk that managers will revert to extremely unstructured procedures. Also, there is some likelihood that significant personal applicant information will remain hidden.

Thus, current research and reports from human resource professionals support the two-step interview process for personnel selection. Further research is needed to test and refine this approach. However, the value of a two-step selection interview seems clear based on experience and research to date.

Chapter 5

Motivation

THEORIES OF MOTIVATION

To retain good staff and to encourage them to give of their best while at work requires attention to the financial and psychological and even physiological rewards offered by the organization as a continuous exercise.

Basic financial rewards and conditions of service (e.g. working hours per week) are determined externally (by national bargaining or government minimum wage legislation) in many occupations but as much as 50 per cent of the gross pay of manual workers is often the result of local negotiations and details (e.g. which particular hours shall be worked) of conditions of service are often more important than the basics. Hence there is scope for financial and other motivations to be used at local levels.

As staffing needs will vary with the productivity of the workforce (and the industrial peace achieved) so good personnel policies are desirable. The latter can depend upon other factors (like environment, welfare, employee benefits, etc.) but unless the wage packet is accepted as 'fair and just' there will be no motivation.

Hence while the technicalities of payment and other systems may be the concern of others, the outcome of them is a matter of great concern to human resource management.

Increasingly the influence of behavioural science discoveries are becoming important not merely because of the widely-acknowledged limitations of money as a motivator, but because of the changing mix and nature of tasks (e.g. more service and professional jobs and far fewer unskilled and repetitive production jobs).

The former demand better-educated, mobile and multi-skilled employees much more likely to be influenced by things like job satisfaction, involvement, participation, etc. than the economically dependent employees of yesteryear.

Hence human resource management must act as a source of information about and a source of inspiration for the application of the findings of behavioural science. It may be a matter of drawing the attention of senior managers to what is being achieved elsewhere and the gradual education of middle managers to new points of view on job design, work organization and worker autonomy.

The current human resources shortage in the health sector - mainly of sub-Saharan African countries - threatens the realization of plans for scaling up interventions to control the spread of diseases such as HIV/AIDS, malaria and tuberculosis. The World development report 2004 states it clearly: Without improvements to the human resources situation, the health-related Millennium Development Goals cannot be achieved. The problems are multiple, the most serious being staff shortages, particularly in rural and remote areas. In many countries, the effects of insufficient capacity development in the health system are aggravated by migration and a mounting burden of disease. The World health report 2006 gathers ample evidence of the human resource challenges, but also provides ways forward to address the problems.

With respect to existing human resources, the low level of health worker motivation has often been identified as a central problem in health service delivery. For example, the results from a survey undertaken by the Gesellschaft für Technische Zusammenarbeit (German Technical Cooperation, GTZ) among representatives of ministries of health and GTZ staff from 29 countries showed that low motivation is seen as the second most important health workforce problem after staff shortages. From the perspective of health professionals, the challenges include lack of equipment, frequent shortages of supplies and a mounting workload – all these exacerbated in small and rural facilities. Furthermore, despite decentralization efforts, key functions of human resource management (recruitment, overall staff distribution, remuneration, promotion and transfers) remain highly centralized.

Despite interest in the issue of human resources for health, human resource management and the question of what can be done to strengthen health worker motivation in developing countries has so far not received as much attention as the subject merits.

There is a small but growing body of qualitative studies looking at motivation of health workers in developing countries that indicate the limitations of financial incentives on motivation and that reveal the importance of non-financial incentives. A study in South Africa on the effects of a newly introduced, so-called "rural allowance" showed the limited impact on retention and motivation. Similarly, analysing the role of wages in health worker migration, Vujicic et al. conclude that what they call non-wage instruments may be more effective in reducing migration flows, as portrayed in a WHO report. The study of Kingma, while undertaken in developed countries, also provides important insights on the limited effect of financial incentives on nurses and instead points at the relevance of non-financial incentives for nurses' job satisfaction and self-esteem.

In their study on health workers' motivation and performance in Benin, Alihonou et al. suggest introducing non-financial incentives while also improving structural conditions. Stilwell shows, by reference to Zimbabwe, that health workers based in remote areas, despite lack of financial incentives and hard working conditions, frequently exhibited a high level of motivation to perform well. She traces this motivation to good leadership and supportive management, among other factors. Her analysis suggests that certain non-financial incentives can have a beneficial effect on motivation, even under adverse conditions of insufficient pay and equipment, understaffing, etc. In a review of theories and empirical evidence of health workers motivation, Dolea and Adams equally stress the importance of non-financial incentives.

Low motivation has a negative impact on the performance of individual health workers, facilities and the health system as a whole. Moreover, it adds to the push factors for migration of health workers, both from rural areas to the cities and out of the country. It is therefore an important goal of human resources management in the health sector to strengthen the motivation of health workers, from heads of health facilities to auxiliary staff.

Financial incentives are important, and the problem of low salaries must be addressed, especially in situations where income is insufficient to meet even the most basic needs of health professionals and their families. But the evidence suggests that increased salaries are by no means sufficient to solve the problem of low motivation. More money does not automatically imply higher motivation. We therefore suggest that any comprehensive strategy to maximize health worker motivation in a developing country context has to involve a mix of financial and non-financial incentives.

To support the development of effective strategies for human resources management and the improvement of health worker motivation, the German Technical Cooperation (GTZ) has assessed motivation and motivational determinants in rural districts of Benin, Kenya, El Salvador and Nicaragua. The study aims at determining the role of non-financial incentives for motivation. This paper here presents the findings from the Benin and Kenya case studies.

The next section outlines the conceptual framework used, followed by a description of the methodology. The fourth section focuses on health workers' feelings, views and perceptions and opens the black box of the motivational process. The paper then analyses the current problems and potentials of selected HRM tools with respect to their motivational effect on health workers. The final section offers conclusions and recommendations for the way forward.

This paper will show that health workers overall are strongly guided by their professional conscience and similar aspects related to professional ethos that keep them going. Many health workers are demotivated and frustrated precisely because they are unable to satisfy their professional conscience and impeded in the pursuit of their vocation due to lack of means and supplies at work and due to inadequate or inappropriately applied human resources management (HRM) tools. The paper also indicates that the way HRM tools are applied is characterized by severe pitfalls affecting the motivation of health workers.

Motivation can be defined as "the willingness to exert and maintain an effort towards organizational goals". Motivation develops in each individual as a result of the interaction between individual, organizational and cultural determinants. Some of these factors are of more distal nature, such as cultural norms and values and individual personality, hence they lie outside the scope of human resources management.

Kanfer identifies two aspects of the internal motivation process: The "will-do" aspect concerns the establishment of congruence between personal goals and the goals of the organization (goal setting). Questions that characterize this psychological process are: "What is the personal value of devoting more of my resources to the job?" or "What is the personal value of achieving higher job performance?"

The "can-do" aspect concerns motivational effectiveness, the extent of individual resources that are mobilized to accomplish adopted goals (goal achievement). The related question is: "How likely is it to achieve the desired level of job performance?".

The "will-do" and the "can-do" component can be distinguished for analytic purposes but the line between the two is blurred, as the findings of this study will show. Efforts to strengthen the motivation of doctors and nurses have to influence one or both of these components. Kanfer and Franco et al. do not explicitly mention a cross-impact between the "will-do" and "can-do" components, but the empirical findings of this study strongly suggest that there may be such an effect, which is indicated by the two crossing arrows. The result of this psychological process can be observed as motivational consequences with impact on the behaviour (job performance), affection (job satisfaction) and cognitive aspects (work attachment) of health workers.

Kanfer's model offers a framework for the assessment of motivational determinants and the motivational process in greater detail, thereby going beyond the common and simpler distinction between motivators and satisfiers, as presented by Herzberg et al.

In this study, we assess the impact of organizational determinants on the motivational process, specifically of HRM tools and non-financial incentives as part thereof. We define an incentive as an available means applied with the intention to influence the willingness of physicians and nurses to exert and maintain an effort towards attaining organizational goals. This is borrowed from Buchan et al., who define an incentive as "one particular form of payment that is intended to achieve some specific change in behaviour".

The most common understanding of financial incentives is a transfer of monetary values or equivalents, such as wage increases, allowances, performance-related bonuses or housing. Adams/Hicks also include the basic salary, allowance schemes, health insurance premiums, housing or housing allowances in this category. Obviously, in practice it may be difficult to differentiate between the basic salary package and additional financial incentives. Non-financial incentives are by contrast those incentives that involve no direct transfers of monetary values or equivalents to an individual or group. This includes, for example, granting unpaid holidays, token awards or recreational facilities, as well as recognition and supervision.

Human resources management (HRM) is the management of people in an organization. HRM tools comprise the policies, practices and activities at the disposal of managers to obtain, develop, use, evaluate, maintain and retain the appropriate number, skill mix and motivation of employees to accomplish the organisation's objectives. There is a huge body of literature on HRM and tools, which cannot be captured here. But as the commentary on "what difference does ("good") HRM make?" by Buchan shows, good HRM determines performance and motivation. In other words, tools and techniques applied as part of HRM also function as non-financial incentives to strengthen motivation in line with the above definition. The following list, derived from EFQM (European Foundation of Quality Management) criteria, contains some of the core HRM tools that may affect motivation. These aspects are similarly assessed in the World health report 2006.

- Supervision schemes
- Recognition schemes
- Performance management
- Training and professional development
- Leadership
- Participation mechanisms
- Intra-organizational communication processes.

The organizational culture influences all these aspects, but changes in these aspects may also modify the organizational culture. Furthermore, work conditions constitute an important motivational determinant. Comprehensive HRM therefore also needs to look at and optimize the work conditions.

The in-depth study design entailed (semi-) structured qualitative interviews with doctors and nurses from public, private and NGO facilities in rural areas. The questionnaire contained mainly open-ended questions. The interviews took about 60 to 90 minutes. Results from individual interviews were backed up with information from focus group discussions. For further contextual information, interviews with civil servants in the Ministry of Health and at the district level were held.

The qualitative interviews with health workers covered the following topics: prevailing practice; experience and views of health workers on core HRM/QM tools, such as training, supervision, performance assessments, participation, leadership, working environment, personal and career plans; and implicitly their effect on motivation. Some of the questions were not applicable for health workers who own a private clinic; these questions were therefore left out.

The last part of the interview focused explicitly on motivation and motivational determinants, yet the word "motivation" was avoided, except for two direct questions - "How do health workers define motivation?" and later "How do they assess their level of motivation?" - based on a given definition.

The study assesses motivational determinants and is concerned only indirectly with motivational consequences, to the extent that health workers report about these. An action research setting would have been required to assess motivational changes over time, triggered by the introduction or change of specific HRM/QM tools and (non-) financial incentives.

Before prospective respondents agreed to participate in the study, the interviewer informed them about the overall subject of the questions: their experiences and views of certain HRM tools and needs around their work environment. The actual research question on the role and relevance of non-financial incentives was not unveiled in order to avoid "socially desired behaviour" responses. The questionnaires were translated into French in a one-round de-centring process and then pretested. In each country, interviews were carried out by a consultant taking notes, rather than tape-recording. Qualitative data were coded centrally, thus avoiding inter-rater reliability concerns. The SPSS (Statistical Product and Service Solutions (formerly Statistical Package for the Social Sciences)) software package was used for the analysis of the quantitative and the coded qualitative data.

The sampling for the study was layered: The selection of districts was purposive in that it focused on GTZ-supported project areas, giving easy access to regional and district authorities. Facilities within a district were randomly selected on the basis of the district's facility list, except for the district hospital, which was always included. As the selection of facilities was based on the district's facility list, informal, non-registered private clinics were not part of the sampling process.

Random sampling on the basis of a staff list proved difficult. It was hard to arrange appointments prior to the interview, due to insufficient means of communication as well as staff absences. Ultimately, staff for the interviews were selected on the spot in cooperation with those in charge. Given the low numbers of doctors in rural facilities, every available doctor was interviewed.

A target of 50 interviews per country was set. Due to resource constraints, only 37 interviews could be held in Kenya. The Benin counterparts were interested in a larger sample and 62 interviews were realized. Except for the percentage of doctors (33% of the total sample should have been doctors), the sampling cornerstones were met: two thirds of interviews from the public sector, one sixth each from the private and NGO sector; at least one third of respondents to be female or male. No requirement was defined for the age of respondents.

The study questions touched potentially delicate and personal issues relating to health workers' behaviour and attitude. Particular attention was therefore paid to triangulation. One means used was the knowledge of national and international GTZ staff involved in this study, who have detailed knowledge and long experience in the field that enables them to provide "external" assessments of certain problems and situations. Likewise, the focus group discussions reflected individual responses or drew out some delicate topics even more explicitly. Construct validity was enhanced by the consecutive use of similar questions and the reliance on several indicators to measure the same phenomena.

Ultimately, in order to find out what can be considered "true", it is also necessary to take into account what people can be expected to say on the basis of their interest and motives. Respondents may have stressed in particular the difficulties and challenges they are confronted with at their workplace. One may also expect individuals who feel very demotivated to be reluctant to admit so to the interviewer.

Certain questions by their type or content pose larger reliability and validity concerns than others, namely those asking respondents to rank themselves on a Likert scale. Such findings must be taken with some caution. They were included to provide a general impression.

Whether health workers really tell the "truth" cannot always be fully clarified. When this is the case, we clearly point it out in the text. On the whole, health workers appreciated the interest of "outsiders" in their personal concerns and opinions. There was no indication that they held back their views and judgements.

Given the sampling procedures as well as the small sample size, quantitative statements are not claimed to be representative for the entire health workforce of a country. Despite these limitations, the strength of this study lies in its exploratory and qualitative character. It sheds much light on what is considered important by health workers. By giving them a voice, we find out what really matters to them and which instruments have the potential to increase their motivation and job satisfaction and thus, ultimately, performance.

OUTLINE RESULTS AND DISCUSSION

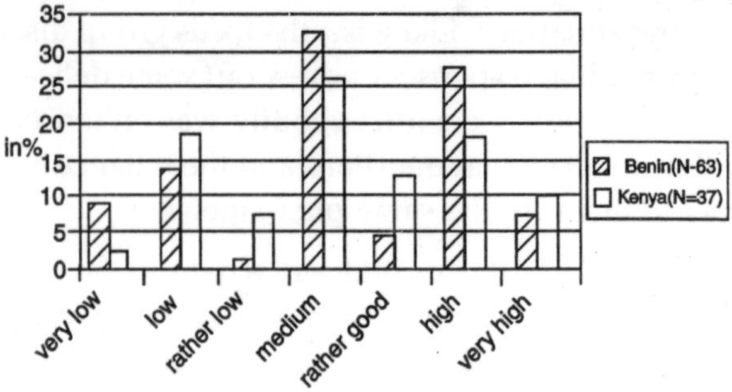

Fig; Self-assessment of motivation level

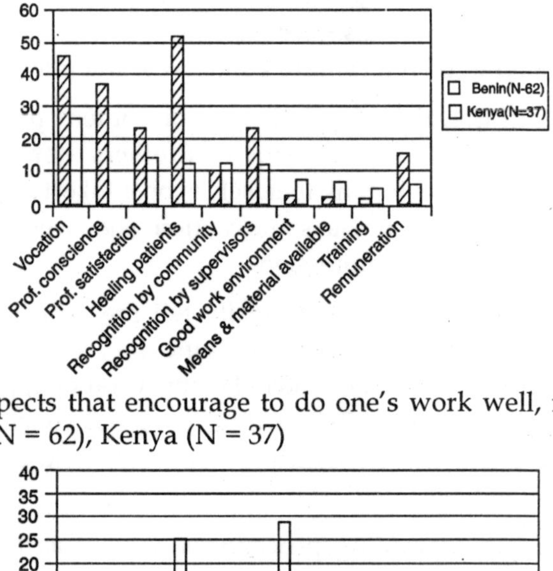

Aspects that encourage to do one's work well, in %, in Benin (N = 62), Kenya (N = 37)

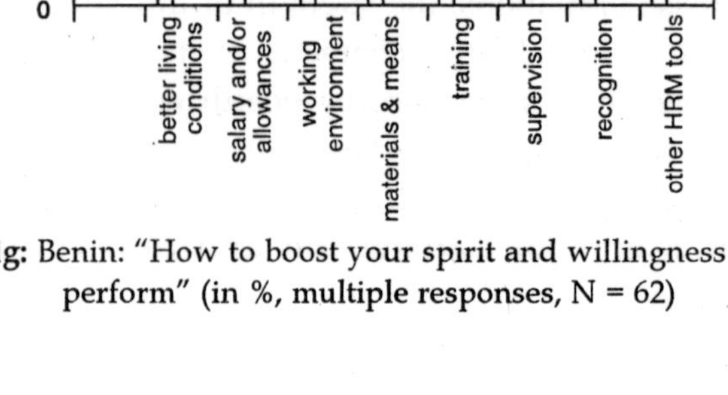

Fig: Benin: "How to boost your spirit and willingness to perform" (in %, multiple responses, N = 62)

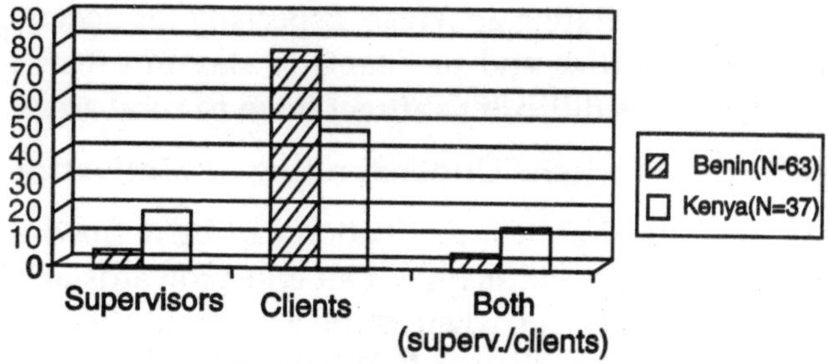

Fig: Preferred source of appreciation

COUNTRY INFORMATION

In both Benin and Kenya, the public sector is the greatest health service provider and employer of health workers. Both countries suffer from shortages in staff resources, inadequate skills and very low salaries, particularly for nurses and other lower cadres. For example, depending on the job group, Kenyan nurses earn today between KES 5757 (about USD 72) and KES 12 450 (about USD 155) per month.

In order to retain doctors in the public service and improve the situation in under-supplied areas, the Kenyan Government has introduced additional "extraneous" and "non-practising" allowances for medical doctors, dentists and pharmacists. For doctors who enter the public service with a basic wage of KES 11 690 (about USD 145) per month, the allowances in this job group amount to KES 25 000 (about USD 311) per month. This means that wages of doctors have de facto tripled. According to a key informant in the Ministry of Health of Kenya, this measure has so far attracted 500 doctors to seek employment in the Kenyan public service. While wages have therefore improved for this job category, the working conditions in government health facilities remain largely unchanged.

In Benin, a nurse earns around 40 000 XOF (USD 75). Although a variety of allowances are paid for various kinds of tasks or functions (responsibility allowance, risk allowance, remoteness allowances), it remains difficult to survive on just this income. Most health professionals therefore engage in other income-generating activities. Especially for doctors, it is much more attractive and profitable to stay in urban areas, which is why it is difficult to attract them to rural areas.

Hotel Health Workers' Understanding of Motivation

As mentioned above, motivation can be defined as the willingness to exert and maintain an effort towards attaining organizational goals. Yet, when health workers are asked about their definition of motivation ("What does being motivated mean to you?"), a different understanding emerges.

Out of these, one fourth explicitly mention financial encouragement. Another 40% consider "being motivated" as having the means and material to work, to get recognition, or other HRM tools, such as awards, supervision and good leadership. Hence, the majority understands motivation as a "motivator", i.e. an incentive, and not as a state of mind. Only 5% refer to motivation as the "willingness" or the "pleasure" to do one's work, similar to the above definition, from the literature, of motivation as an intrinsic process and state of mind. Not surprisingly, the latter groups are mainly doctors and health workers in the private sector.

In Kenya, one fifth understands motivation as encouragement. However, there is a larger share of health workers who refer to that intrinsic state of willingness and pleasure to do one's work. This difference in the connotation between Kenyan and Benin respondents may be due to the fact that so-called "motivation allowances" ("primes de motivation") have been introduced in Benin, that may have changed the meaning of motivation from a state of mind to that of an incentive.

This understanding of motivation matches health workers' perceptions of motivational consequences: For the majority of Benin respondents (70%), motivating someone serves to improve work performance, while only 30% perceive motivation as a means to increase job satisfaction and job attachment. Again, for Kenyans, there is a stronger focus on the satisfaction element (48%). Especially in Benin, this view of motivational consequences may represent a legacy from previous decades, when job satisfaction and pleasure were not part of the prevailing organizational cultures. As one key informant put it, individual health workers were merely seen as a part of the production chain.

The introduction of a quality management system, which is currently under way in Kenya and partly in Benin, may provide the opportunity to gradually change this mindset and to give the word motivation a new meaning. Alternatively, it may seem necessary to avoid the word motivation altogether and use a different terminology, such as for example "boosting one's work spirit or work morale".

In contrast to their own definition of motivation, health workers were asked to assess their level of motivation, by considering the following definition: "Willingness to do a good job, according to organizational objectives".

The health workers' replies suggest that they may not have responded in line with the given definition, but also referred to their own understanding of motivation. With the caveat that the validity of the answers may be somewhat limited, more so as the Likert scales for Benin and Kenya were not internally validated, the figure still provides an overall idea of how health workers see their own level of motivation: In both countries, more than 55% do not place themselves in the categories "rather good", "high" or "very high".

In Benin, health workers from the private sector/NGO facilities appear more motivated than those in public health facilities. Two thirds assess their level of motivation as "very high", "high" or "rather good" (14/21), compared to around a quarter from the public services (11/41). Nurses from the public sector appear to be the least motivated group and therefore a likely focus for efforts to increase motivation by means of human resources management and incentives. In Kenya, such clear tendencies cannot be derived, but then the sample size is also much smaller.

Motivational determinants: professional values and goals versus endangered self-efficacy.

To identify the motivational determinants that account for perceived level of health worker motivation, respondents were asked: "Which aspects currently encourage you to undertake efforts to do your work well?".

Health workers in Benin strongly referred to vocation and professional conscience, i.e. their personal professional values. Likewise, the wish to help patients and professional satisfaction were frequently mentioned. Pangu carried out a study in Benin on the reasons why health workers stay in function despite decreasing motivation and identifies exactly those four aspects. Among Kenyan respondents, vocation was equally very dominant. Also, healing patients, professional satisfaction and recognition were considered important. These aspects nurture health workers' goals. Both dimensions - values and goals - indicate a strong professional ethos and commitment and strongly appear to translate into the "will-do" component of the motivation process.

Other factors, such as work environment and HRM tools that relate more to the "can-do" component are also mentioned, but particularly in Benin they do not feature as prominently as values and goals. About 6% of respondents in Benin and Kenya mention regular salaries and allowances. Finally, half of the health workers in the private sector in Benin, that is 10% overall, consider that earning revenue is an important encouragement to do one's work well.

When health workers were asked, with respect to the future, what would have to happen so as to boost their spirit and increase their willingness to perform (this was asked only of Benin respondents), they emphasize to be able to perform one's work, namely having the materials and means available as well as further training and supervision. This corresponds with the findings of Alihonou et al. as well as with a staff survey from Zimbabwe cited in USAID, which revealed that the number one reason provided by health workers for resigning their government job was the lack of equipment and supplies.

Also, a more conducive working environment and atmosphere, recognition and feedback, and other HRM tools such as better leadership, management and participation, are reported to contribute to increasing health workers' self-efficacy, i.e. their self-perception of being able to do a good job and fulfill their duties ("can-do" component of motivation). It also emerged from the interviews that health workers appreciate small benefits as relevant to their motivation. For example, in public health facilities, unpaid holidays or small amenities such as free tea for staff on night duty were perceived as motivating. Their absence, temporary or permanent, was considered demotivating.

The two questions on current versus future motivational determinants accordingly revealed different answers: Several aspects that featured low under the question on current motivational factors - precisely due to their (perceived) non-existence or poor state, such as organizational factors - then emerged in the second question as potential motivating factors.

These aspects do not dominate, however. Instead, very prominent were health workers' request and need for available means and materials to carry out their work in a professional way. Subsequent questions, e.g. how health workers could improve their performance, persistently revealed the frustrations that health workers experience because of the lack of means and materials and the inadequate work environments as well as deficits in HRM.

It appears that these frustrations are so strong precisely because of the high professional commitment of health workers. In fact, there is a danger that perceived self-efficacy, constrained by inadequate HRM and work environment, becomes so weak that it may ultimately negatively affect health workers' commitment and professional ethos.

Health workers' commitment and professional ethos is, moreover, endangered by the existence of HIV/AIDS, which, as for example Aitken and Kemp have shown for Southern Africa, has a severe impact on health workers' behaviour and above all attitude to work. In fact, throughout the interviews, health workers refer to HIV/AIDS issues. Asked about their feelings and reactions with respect to HIV/AIDS at the workplace, few health workers feel sufficiently protected. Most health workers fear becoming infected and report reacting in general more reserved towards patients. Some respondents said that every patient is seen as a potential source.

The next section assesses some core HRM tools and derives their effect on the "will-do" and "can-do" component of motivation. Respondents were asked about their experience with and perceptions of certain non-financial incentives and HRM tools. The findings reveal present shortcomings, but also reveal further potentials in the application of such tools, which is supported by the vast evidence and examples collected by the WHR 2006.

Supervision as Control Versus Support Supervision and Recognition

Ideally, supervision is a formalized HRM instrument to correct shortcomings and to support good practice, on the basis of which recommendations are provided to help improve individual and facility performance. Supervision can contribute considerably to health workers' self-efficacy and relates therefore to the "can-do" component of Kanfer's model of motivation. To the extent that supervision is used to communicate a facility's goals and that it takes account of health workers' personal goals and needs, it also strengthens goal coherence and affects the "will-do" component of motivation.

The interviews revealed that 40% of respondents from Benin and more than 50% from Kenya perceive supervision as an exercise of control. As the following quotes reveal, existing schemes for supervision are sometimes perceived as unhelpful and distant, rather than personal and supportive:

"Supervision is not very useful. The supervisors remind nurses of the procedures they should apply. Right now, under given circumstances, you cannot implement them. They remind you of the rules and control you."

"While individual efforts go unnoticed, mistakes or shortcomings are noticed immediately."

"The supervision went without difficulties, but the supervisors did not give me any feedback afterwards."

Health workers criticize the low frequency and irregularity of supervision as well as the top-down approach used by supervisors. Supervision that involves discussions of health workers' conduct in the presence of patients is seen as particularly demotivating. Responses revealed that not knowing whether or when the next supervision takes place can also have a negative effect on health workers' commitment to improve their work.

In Kenya, almost half the respondents and one in ten of the respondents in Benin claimed that they do not receive any personal feedback from their superior. Judging from the answers provided, the feedback that health workers receive from their supervisors in rural facilities usually centres on specific shortcomings or technical aspects of service provision. It rarely appears to focus on the personal perspective of the health worker herself or himself. Feeling neglected by the superiors or the health administration has a strongly demotivating effect. There are indications that supportive supervision, recognition and personal feedback tend to be more common in religious and private health centres in Kenya than in public facilities.

Despite these shortcomings, health workers consider supervision useful and desirable to the extent that it helps improve personal performance, to avoid mistakes and to update knowledge. When personal needs and concerns are taken seriously, supervision provides the feeling of being cared for and of appreciation. This aspect appears particularly important for health workers posted to remote facilities with little contact with other professionals.

There is a large potential for improvement in the supervision process, according to the respondents' suggestions: Apart from a more frequent, regular and reliable supervision, many respondents ask for a different approach, in that supervision should be more supportive, instructive, needs-oriented, participatory and should provide a direct and timely feedback on their problems. There was also a call for more meetings to discuss problems and solutions. Direct observation of health worker activities is considered helpful to identify the bottlenecks in service delivery, provided that health workers are not criticized in front of the patients.

In conclusion, support supervision that exists appears to contribute significantly to health workers' self-efficacy. There are potentials to strengthen the "can-do" component of motivation through a more regular supervision routine and follow-up. Moreover, supportive supervision that takes account of the supervisee's personal and professional goals of recognition and learning and that communicates organizational goals clearly offers a potential for a positive motivational effect both in the "will-do" and "can-do" component that is so far not sufficiently used.

Lack of recognition versus institutionalized recognition and appreciation by superiors and communities.

Through an encouraging and supportive attitude, superiors can strengthen their subordinates' self-efficacy and thus foster personal efforts for the achievement of organizational goals: the "can-do" component of motivation. Community recognition and appreciation can have the same effect.

While most felt that their leaders are accessible, critique focused on lack of encouragement and insufficient consideration of staff views, as health workers did not feel adequately supported and recognized by their superiors. In other words, the leaders seemed to fail to contribute as much as possible to strengthening health workers' self-efficacy. In general, health workers criticized their leaders' inadequate communication and bad treatment of staff. When leaders fail to be role models by not adhering to organizational goals, health workers may wonder why they should adopt them, thereby reducing the drive for the "will-do" component. In fact, a good number of respondents wished for supervisors to receive training on management and leadership issues. Clearly, health workers highly value recognition and appreciation from superiors and colleagues as well as patients. The role of good working relationships with superiors and colleagues similarly emerged as one important motivational determinant in a study in Georgia by Bennett et al.

However, asked whose appreciation health workers find most relevant, 80% of Benin and 50% of Kenya respondents referred to the patients' appreciation. There is no correlation by type of institutions, hence client appreciation is not of greater importance to health workers from the NGO and private sector than from the public sector. This is not to say that in practice, health workers are indifferent to their supervisors' appreciation. After all it is important for career promotion and adequate postings, but as Buchan also notes, the "avowed first loyalty [of doctors and nurses] tends to be to their profession and their patients ..."

Appreciation from clients is seen as an indicator for successful professional conduct and the achievement of the health workers' goal to cure patients. The importance of patient appreciation stems primarily from health workers' search for professional satisfaction and their professional goals of helping patients, as revealed throughout the interviews, for example:

"Appreciation from the patients is most important, because it is sincere and heartfelt."

The above finding strongly supports ideas and efforts for strengthening community participation in health service provision. Client satisfaction surveys, community dialogue and interaction with health unit management committees should be managed in such a way as to not only ensure client orientation and accountability towards the community but also to convey appreciation and strengthen staff motivation. Such improved mechanisms may also help to reduce health workers' perceptions of too much interference by the community, lack of patient compliance or lack of cooperation by patients and their relatives. These issues formed frequent complaints by health workers and appeared to affect the "can-do" component of their motivation.

Inadequate training versus needs- and problem-adapted training.

Training and professional progress are important motivational determinants, as they nurture health workers' personal objectives and their value system. In fact, training as a tool of human resources management can serve several purposes. It can help health workers to cope better with the requirements of their job. It can also enable them to take on more demanding duties and positions and to achieve personal goals of professional advancement. Training can have strong motivating effects.

When asked about the effect of training courses they had taken over the past two years, nearly all health workers in Kenya and Benin mentioned that they felt more comfortable and confident with their work afterwards. Some 20% also mentioned increased interest and work commitment. These answers suggest a considerable effect of training courses on both the "can-do" and the "will-do" component of motivation. Overall, respondents were very interested to receive more continued medical education/continued professional development. This is similar to other study findings.

Contents of courses and seminars that were out of touch with the reality of the rural health facilities of developing countries were considered the most important problem by health workers. After a training course, those confronted with treatment guidelines based on standards of equipment and supplies that do not exist at their workplace experience their daily work environment as an insurmountable obstacle to the provision of "adequate" health care. Improvisation to make up for shortcomings in equipment and supplies was considered inferior practice.

Overall, training can have a strong effect not only on the "can-do" component, but also on the "will-do" component of motivation. Yet, to have this effect, i.e. to exploit this motivational potential, training courses must be adapted to the local context: the actual working conditions in rural facilities.

Non-transparent allocation versus equal opportunities for training and professional progress. Further education and professional progress rank highest among the professional objectives of the nurses and doctors interviewed in Kenya and Benin. These objectives were mentioned by about two thirds of respondents. The answers reveal that the interest in further education is motivated by the chance to rise within the hierarchy of the health system, to reach a higher status and to increase earnings.

In Kenya, the prospect of sponsorship for further qualifications in the public health system appears to make public sector jobs more attractive for health workers working in private and mission facilities, although working conditions were acknowledged to be better in some of the private facilities.

Health workers in the public sector, by contrast, often feel demotivated by the limited realistic prospects of professional progress and personal advancement and the rather slow and cumbersome promotion process. Where access to training and further qualifications is limited or granted in line with reasons that are not equitably available or merit-based, this can likewise have detrimental consequences for the motivation effect of training as a tool of human resources management.

Opportunities for training must be allocated in a transparent and fair way, since a sense of unequal treatment demotivates and leads to frustration. As such, it affects both the "will-do" and "can-do" component of motivation.

The use of training and further qualification as a human resources management tool is limited by financial resource constraints, of course. However, as individual examples show, there may be options for gradual improvement and needs-adapted training even in resource-poor rural settings. In Kenya, whereas the management of one facility ruled out Continued Medical Education for lack of funds to invite teachers, in another facility, the medical superintendent provided short information leaflets to update staff on basic guidelines and procedures. Given that 10% of health donor funds are spent on training activities, there is a great need - but also opportunity - in policies that address these deficits.

Passive Staff Involvement Versus Active Staff Participation

Staff participation and staff involvement is an important HRM tool. It permits making the best use of health workers' knowledge, hands-on experience and ideas for improvements. In addition, staff participation involves recognition and appreciation of health workers and their competences. It appeals to their need to be taken seriously. This has important implications for motivation, both for the "will-do" component (e.g., self-realization, professional satisfaction) and the "can-do" component (e.g., self-confidence, improvements around the workplace by taking account of health workers' knowledge and ideas).

Most respondents in Kenya and Benin felt they could contribute ideas and efforts, particularly with respect to daily activities. While Kenyan respondents seem to see this happen primarily through staff meetings, Benin respondents rather refer to their efforts on the job.

By contrast, 57% of Kenyan respondents felt they couldn't participate in decision-making at their facility, a perception shared by nearly 80% of Benin respondents. There was no difference between the different provider types. Still, nearly everybody considers participation as important and, with a few exceptions, the vast majority would like to be involved much more actively. The respondents indicate that the relevance of participation consists in sharing one's views and knowledge of a situation or of a problem-oriented solution, to be involved in decisions that concern oneself or to react where necessary in order to avoid frustrations.

Interestingly, under current conditions hardly any feeling of professional satisfaction or self-realisation among respondents appeared to result from participation. Staff involvement appeared to be a passive undertaking. It serves to collect ideas and proposals. It allows staff to get informed rather than to take part in actual decision-making.

Given that health workers are socialized in a rather top-down, hierarchical organizational culture within the public sector, which ultimately reflects cultural values and characteristics of the wider society, the idea of participation as a means of self-realization and particularly of recognition appears now to be hardly present.

The findings suggest that increased participation could have an effect on both the "can-do" component (ideas of staff are taken into account to improve the work process) and the "will-do" component (influence on decisions to the benefit of health workers - satisfaction with respect to personal goals, appreciation of health workers' skills and competences - satisfaction with respect to professional goals). Hence, there is a great need to institutionalize participation, e.g. by holding regular meetings, in which health workers not only share ideas and suggestions for improvements, but in which health workers ultimately participate in decision-making on issues that concern their work and immediate work environment.

Infrequent performance appraisals versus culturally adapted performance management. Performance management tools serve to improve performance of health workers. Performance management assists in setting, communicating and internalizing organizational goals, thereby nurturing the "will-do" component. At the same time, this provides feedback to health workers as regards their capabilities and skills to achieve these goals, hereby addressing the "can-do" component. One specific tool is performance assessment, which this section looks at specifically. Other tools include the communication of the organizational mission, vision and objectives, self-assessments, quality improvement teams, performance related payments, benchmarking and awards. Performance assessment constitutes a review of a health worker's skills and achievements.

In Kenya, government health workers must pass an annual performance review. The interviews revealed that not everybody appears to know what this is about and which indicators are applied. Attitudes regarding the relevance of the annual performance assessments seem to be mixed. Some health workers - especially those with a very good report - say it is motivating. Also, several think the performance assessment leads to a change in practice and behaviour. Yet, some few say that it has no effect on one's practice and behaviour. Moreover, less than 30% (27%) state that the performance assessment can potentially have an impact on one's promotion. A good assessment is required for a promotion, and even though bad assessments appear to be rare, promotions are not forthcoming, as they are contingent upon vacancies and the availability of financial resources. Also, as one respondent says,

"It is a slow and painful process; you have to follow up on the promotion you are meant to receive in Nairobi." (female nurse, government facility, Kenya, in focus group discussion)

Furthermore, individual award schemes at the district level ("best unit" of district health facilities), although carried out on the basis of a detailed performance assessment, were considered unfair and thus demotivating by the staff, probably because the method and criteria of the selection process had not been sufficiently communicated.

In contrast to Kenya, there are no such performance assessments in Benin. Instead, Benin respondents from the public sector referred to the biannual supervision process that serves to monitor key indicators. After the exercise, all facility managers in a district get together to receive feedback, advice and recommendations from the district health authorities, as well as congratulations in some cases. Health facilities are ranked, which allows health workers to find out about their relative facility performance. The majority of respondents report that that they know the procedures as well as the indicators by which facilities are monitored. However, according to some respondents, the responsible facility managers do not always share the results with the rest of the team, which is considered frustrating or annoying. In practice, the facility-based supervision process seems to be translated to the level of individual health workers and can hence be understood as a form of performance assessment.

Several health workers mentioned that good performance may be rewarded through participation in training or by means of a scholarship. However, on the whole, respondents appear to see no direct impact of good performance on career development. One positive effect are the so-called "primes de performance" (performance allowances), which are paid for good indicator results. The public ranking and public congratulations appear to have a strong effect on health workers.

By providing feedback on health workers' work, performance assessments have some effect on the "can-do" component overall, since they help improve knowledge and skills. Yet this effect is currently small, as is the effect on the "will-do" component. Although the responses suggest that health workers are performance-oriented, the potential of performance management as a motivating instrument has not been not fully realized yet. Given the fertile ground for performance orientation, there appears to be scope for the gradual introduction of a performance culture, the search for excellence. The responses also suggest that health workers are receptive to performance assessments. Any initiative to promote a performance culture must take into account cultural values, norms and characteristics, as shown by the following section.

Individual Success and Team-based Performance Promotion

The findings reveal certain cultural factors that may impinge upon motivation and performance. Respondents were asked whether there are barriers that impede personal efforts and act as barriers to better performance. They were prompted specifically on envy among colleagues.

In Kenya, nearly half the respondents stated that individual efforts are appreciated, while 30% confirm that envy indeed impedes individual efforts. In contrast, only a sixth of Benin respondents, among them all the private-sector doctors, feel it is possible and worthwhile to engage in individual efforts. Yet, nearly two thirds clearly expressed that individual efforts are futile and that team efforts are necessary to reach further. Half of the respondents mentioned envy as a barrier to individual efforts.

With respect to performance management, such feelings and views are problematic, because they may lead individuals to discount outstanding performance and the acceptance of responsibilities beyond theirs duties. The development of a performance culture, based on individual efforts, appears to be closely circumscribed by the social context. The findings indicate that it may be necessary to build performance management schemes upon group identities. This requires a focus on building teams and creating team spirit. Likewise, this suggests designing awards for groups rather than for individuals, more so as the latter creates conflicts within facility teams.

Supporting health workers and making them feel cared for: a call for quality management.

The previous section has shown that health workers are strongly guided by their professional conscience and similar aspects related to professional ethos overall, relating to the "will-do" component of motivation. Many health workers appear to be demotivated and frustrated precisely because they are unable to satisfy their professional conscience and impeded in pursuing their vocation due to lack of means and supplies and due to inadequate or inappropriately applied HRM tools. These appeared to negatively affect the "can-do" component of motivation. Due to the extent of the problems at hand, they also affect the "will-do" component of motivation.

In conclusion, efforts to strengthen health worker motivation must protect, promote and build upon the professional ethos of medical doctors and nurses. This entails appreciating their professionalism and addressing health workers' professional goals such as recognition, career development and further qualification. It must be the aim of HRM and quality management to develop the work environment so that health workers are enabled to meet personal and organizational goals. This requires strengthening health workers' self-efficacy by offering training and supervision, but also by ensuring the availability of essential means, materials and supplies as well as equipment and the provision of adequate working conditions that enable them to carry out their work appropriately and effectively.

The findings confirm our starting point that non-financial incentives and HRM tools do play an important role when it comes to increasing motivation of health staff. The findings suggest that HRM tools have the dual task to promote health workers' professional ethos and commitment, and to strengthen their perception of self-efficacy.

The discussion of HRM tools above showed that there are serious deficits in their application, resulting in and reinforcing health workers' low motivation, primarily within the "can-do" component, but also affecting the "will-do" component. On the other hand, the analysis of health workers' responses and suggestions indicates that the HRM tools analysed above clearly constitute motivational determinants. In fact, the "toolbox" of HRM appears to have a great potential for improving health worker motivation. Also, only a small range of the available HRM tools have so far been applied in the countries that have been assessed.

The key message obtained from the interview data is the need to make health workers feel they are cared-for. Health workers require support in a variety of ways, ranging from technical aspects to personal and psychological needs. It is necessary to move to a culture of support supervision, to institutionalize recognition of health workers, to allocate training opportunities in an equal and transparent way, to fulfil health workers' drive for learning and acquiring new knowledge, to increase participation opportunities and to strengthen leadership. Ultimately, this requires changes in the organizational culture and individual attitudes, which can improve only by means of a gradual process in an enabling environment.

Therefore, greater awareness among superiors is needed in relation to their role as leaders. Leadership must become clear part of a superior's function and skills. It is important to note that good leadership is more than one single tool of human resources management; it is a fundamental and cross-cutting element interrelated with the style of participation, supervision and feedback, performance management and quality improvement activities.

The analysis also showed the applicability and usefulness of Kanfer's and Franco et al's differentiation into the "will-do" and "can-do" component, thereby shedding some light into the black box of the motivational process. Policy implications and recommendations therefore can become more specific and targeted. There is a different angle to it when we take high professional commitment as the starting point for a strategy of improving motivation. Furthermore, when contextualizing these findings into a quality management approach, there is additional impetus and additional implications as well as clearer guidance for action.

There is substantial overlap between HRM and quality management in terms of contents. Staff is considered and valued as a key resource in all major QM frameworks. QM is about leadership and HRM. It aims at improved management capacity of health workers and strengthens the capacity for participatory problem-solving.

A QM perspective and approach offers numerous benefits when it comes to optimizing human resources management. The QM framework permits developing, applying and evaluating HRM tools comprehensively, coherently and systematically. It offers a comprehensive set of tools that can be adjusted to fit specific circumstances and requirements – whether of a district, a hospital or a health centre. Furthermore, QM introduces the perspective of a continuous improvement process that looks at both outcomes and process. The process orientation ideally provides for continuous efforts to improve HRM under given circumstances.

Moreover, QM aims not only at changing and improving HRM tools and working conditions, it may also affect (or address) organizational values and hence organizational culture. QM is concerned with both organizational as well as individual determinants of motivation, while recognizing the importance of cultural values. The most widely used QM methods include self-evaluation and quality improvement projects, in which a team sets realistic objectives for process (and outcome) improvement and monitors the realization of the plan. Equally important are staff and client satisfaction surveys, as well as training.

While we do not aim to promote a specific quality management model, the following process requirements are considered essential for a contribution of QM to HRM:

- Search for excellence: contribution of the whole staff body to quality improvement efforts;
- Orientation on quality as an outcome as much as on quality of the process;
- Strong emphasis on self-evaluation of individuals and organizations;
- More autonomy and responsibility for health workers;
- Focus on participation and self-realization, empowerment and to a certain extent emancipation of health workers.

The findings indicate that the values on which QM is based are equally shared and referred to by health workers in the two countries under investigation. While certain HRM tools have become increasingly popular, also in African countries, the potential of QM seems far from exhausted.

Recommendations and the Way Forward

Each country has a unique human resource situation, reflecting its stage in the health sector reform process. Accordingly, there is no overall blueprint on how to best improve health worker motivation. Each region, and even each facility, may require a specific mix of financial and non-financial incentives as part of a larger HRM or QM framework.

Findings from a survey on HRM experiences among health projects and programmes supported by GTZ in 29 countries (18 in Africa) suggest putting together a mix of incentives and HRM tools, aiming at both individuals' aspirations and organizational changes. These entry points can be realized incrementally even in resource-poor settings and make a difference when it comes to service delivery. This goes well hand-in-hand with the bundle of measures suggested by the World health report 2006 to enhance health worker performance.

Specifically with respect to performance management, there is a need to inform health workers about the process and indicators and to provide thorough feedback on the results. Also, consistently good performance should be the basis for promotional schemes by including elements of merit rather than length of service. This also necessitates streamlining the promotion process and making it more transparent. In Benin, the competition among facilities seems promising. However, within this ranking process, it is important to consider not only absolute scores, but also to take into account efforts and improvements over time. This is particularly relevant, as some facilities may suffer from much more serious drawbacks than others. Recognition and awards, which do not always have to be financial, appear to be highly appreciated. They should be applied in a systematic and transparent way.

Experience from the health projects supported by GTZ, which have relied on applying a mix of financial and non-financial incentives, shows that positive impacts can be achieved. For example, in Zambia, the introduction of refresher training for medical staff seems to have led to a higher retention rate. In Ethiopia a mix of continued medical education, the provision of housing, the establishment of a clear career structure and a defined number of services in hospitals has led to improved staff satisfaction and retention. An awards scheme, closer supervision and team-building efforts have improved both some service output indicators and the motivation to stay in rural districts of Ghana. As a result, higher antenatal care and EPI coverage as well as fewer applications for transfers have been reported.

These experiences call for a more systematic assessment. In fact, most countries, whether in the public or the private sector, in donor-supported programmes or NGO-run projects, apply a range of non-financial incentives. However, often this is not done systematically or specifically in relation to motivation and performance increases. As such, the impacts and effects of non-financial incentives are rarely monitored or evaluated. Hence there is great need to develop simple and practical methods to monitor the impact of incentives on staff motivation.

There are many challenges concerning the effective and sustainable implementation of incentive schemes and HRM tools, let alone comprehensive QM frameworks. With respect to allowances and financial incentives, the effect on staff motivation is often temporary in nature because such benefits become part of the general benefit package. Likewise, although training is seen as a good motivating instrument, high staff turnover may limit the sustainability of staff training.

Furthermore, there is a particular challenge with respect to introducing performance-related payment: It is difficult to define objective and commonly accepted performance criteria and even more difficult to implement and apply those performance criteria, given political interference and lack of good governance and transparency and the existence of corruption as well as nepotism.

In addition, it is very difficult to change old habits and long-term institutionalized norms and rules, such as promotion schemes that are based on age rather than merit. Another problem is caused by cultural norms that may negatively sanction an individual who is willing to show initiative beyond his or her duty, thus outperforming colleagues.

Hence, ultimately, HRM and QM measures must be imbedded in a good governance agenda in order to be effective and successful in the long run. Fostering transparency and accountability is necessary, since many of the factors that have a detrimental effect on health worker motivation are rooted in systemic or structural deficits. The role of donors and development partners is to strengthen institutional capacities at headquarters levels and at the district level to make a meaningful decentralization process, also in the field of human resources management, possible.

Likewise, we must be aware that the introduction and institutionalization of non-financial incentives and the various HRM tools or their improvement has its costs. It requires training, supervision from higher levels and follow-up. Change in organizational culture takes time. It is therefore important to develop realistic HRM plans and to provide for the financing to implement such measures.

Moreover, united action is needed from the donor community. The use and motivational effect of non-financial and financial incentive schemes in public health systems and private practice may remain limited as long as other development partners provide high top-up allowances as a financial incentive. Thus, donors should seek agreement on a code of conduct that establishes guidelines for orienting the development partners' activities – ranging from remuneration for health staff to sitting allowances, i.e. allowances paid for attending a training or a workshop.

Finally, we must be realistic: improved human resources management cannot compensate for many other factors, at both the macro and micro level, that seriously impinge upon work performance and staff retention, such as staff and supply shortages, heavy workload and difficult working conditions, migration pull factors originating from developed countries, as well as the threatening HIV/AIDS pandemic. Non-financial incentives and HRM/QM tools are not a magic bullet that solves the pressing HRH problem and compensates for the lack of investment and the structural deficits that characterize health systems in many low-income countries – there is no such magic bullet. However, as the discussion above indicates, these tools can make a difference and may be effective even in a resource-constrained context.

USE OF REWARD TO MOTIVATE EMPLOYEES

Since motivation influences productivity, supervisors need to understand what motivates employees to reach peak performance. It is not an easy task to increase employee motivation because employees respond in different ways to their jobs and their organization's practices. Motivation is the set of processes that moves a person toward a goal. Thus, motivated behaviours are voluntary choices controlled by the individual employee. The supervisor (motivator) wants to influence the factors that motivate employees to higher levels of productivity.

Factors that affect work motivation include individual differences, job characteristics, and organizational practices. Individual differences are the personal needs, values, and attitudes, interests and abilities that people bring to their jobs. Job characteristics are the aspects of the position that determine its limitations and challenges. Organizational practices are the rules, human resources policies, managerial practices, and rewards systems of an organization. Supervisors must consider how these factors interact to affect employee job performance.

Simple Model of Motivation

The purpose of behaviour is to satisfy needs. A need is anything that is required, desired, or useful. A want is a conscious recognition of a need. A need arises when there is a difference in self-concept (the way I see myself) and perception (the way I see the world around me). The presence of an active need is expressed as an inner state of tension from which the individual seeks relief.

OTHER THEORIES OF MOTIVATION

Many methods of employee motivation have been developed. The study of work motivation has focused on the motivator (supervisor) as well as the motivatee (employee). Motivation theories are important to supervisors attempting to be effective leaders. Two primary approaches to motivation are content and process.

The content approach to motivation focuses on the assumption that individuals are motivated by the desire to fulfill inner needs. Content theories focus on the needs that motivate people.

Maslow's Hierarchy of Needs identifies five levels of needs, which are best seen as a hierarchy with the most basic need emerging first and the most sophisticated need last. People move up the hierarchy one level at a time. Gratified needs lose their strength and the next level of needs is activated. As basic or lower-level needs are satisfied, higher-level needs become operative. A satisfied need is not a motivator. The most powerful employee need is the one that has not been satisfied. Abraham Maslow first presented the five-tier hierarchy in 1942 to a psychoanalytic society and published it in 1954 in Motivation and Personality.

Level I - Physiological needs are the most basic human needs. They include food, water, and comfort. The organization helps to satisfy employees' physiological needs by a paycheck.

Level II - Safety needs are the desires for security and stability, to feel safe from harm. The organization helps to satisfy employees' safety needs by benefits.

Level III - Social needs are the desires for affiliation. They include friendship and belonging. The organization helps to satisfy employees' social needs through sports teams, parties, and celebrations. The supervisor can help fulfill social needs by showing direct care and concern for employees.

Level IV - Esteem needs are the desires for self-respect and respect or recognition from others. The organization helps to satisfy employees' esteem needs by matching the skills and abilities of the employee to the job. The supervisor can help fulfill esteem needs by showing workers that their work is appreciated.

Level V - Self-actualization needs are the desires for self-fulfillment and the realization of the individual's full potential. The supervisor can help fulfill self-actualization needs by assigning tasks that challenge employees' minds while drawing on their aptitude and training.

Alderfer's ERG identified three categories of needs. The most important contribution of the ERG model is the addition of the frustration-regression hypothesis, which holds that when individuals are frustrated in meeting higher level needs, the next lower level needs reemerge.

Existence needs are the desires for material and physical well being. These needs are satisfied with food, water, air, shelter, working conditions, pay, and fringe benefits.

Relatedness needs are the desires to establish and maintain interpersonal relationships. These needs are satisfied with relationships with family, friends, supervisors, subordinates, and co-workers.

Growth needs are the desires to be creative, to make useful and productive contributions and to have opportunities for personal development.

McClelland's Learned Needs divides motivation into needs for power, affiliation, and achievement.

Achievement motivated people thrive on pursuing and attaining goals. They like to be able to control the situations in which they are involved. They take moderate risks. They like to get immediate feedback on how they have done. They tend to be preoccupied with a task-orientation towards the job to be done.

Power motivated individuals see almost every situation as an opportunity to seize control or dominate others. They love to influence others. They like to change situations whether or not it is needed. They are willing to assert themselves when a decision needs to be made.

Affiliation motivated people are usually friendly and like to socialize with others. This may distract them from their performance requirements. They will usually respond to an appeal for cooperation.

Herzberg's Two-Factor Theory describes needs in terms of satisfaction and dissatisfaction. Frederick Herzberg examined motivation in the light of job content and contest. Motivating employees is a two-step process. First provide hygienes and then motivators. One continuum ranges from no satisfaction to satisfaction. The other continuum ranges from dissatisfaction to no dissatisfaction.

Satisfaction comes from motivators that are intrinsic or job content, such as achievement, recognition, advancement, responsibility, the work itself, and growth possibilities. Herzberg uses the term motivators for job satisfiers since they involve job content and the satisfaction that results from them. Motivators are considered job turn-ons. They are necessary for substantial improvements in work performance and move the employee beyond satisfaction to superior performance. Motivators correspond to Maslow's higher-level needs of esteem and self-actualization.

Dissatisfaction occurs when the following hygiene factors, extrinsic or job context, are not present on the job: pay, status, job security, working conditions, company policy, peer relations, and supervision. Herzberg uses the term hygiene for these factors because they are preventive in nature. They will not produce motivation, but they can prevent motivation from occurring. Hygiene factors can be considered job stay-ons because they encourage an employee to stay on a job. Once these factors are provided, they do not necessarily promote motivation; but their absence can create employee dissatisfaction. Hygiene factors correspond to Maslow's physiological, safety, and social needs in that they are extrinsic, or peripheral, to the job. They are present in the work environment of job context.

Motivation comes from the employee's feelings of accomplishment or job content rather than from the environmental factors or job context. Motivators encourage an employee to strive to do his or her best. Job enrichment can be used to meet higher-level needs. To enrich a job, a supervisor can introduce new or more difficult tasks, assign individuals specialized tasks that enable them to become experts, or grant additional authority to employees.

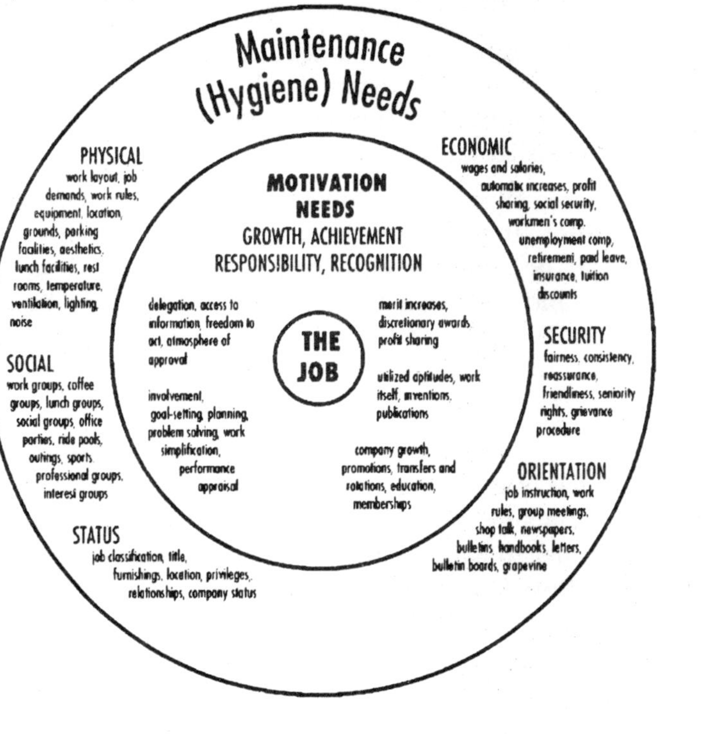

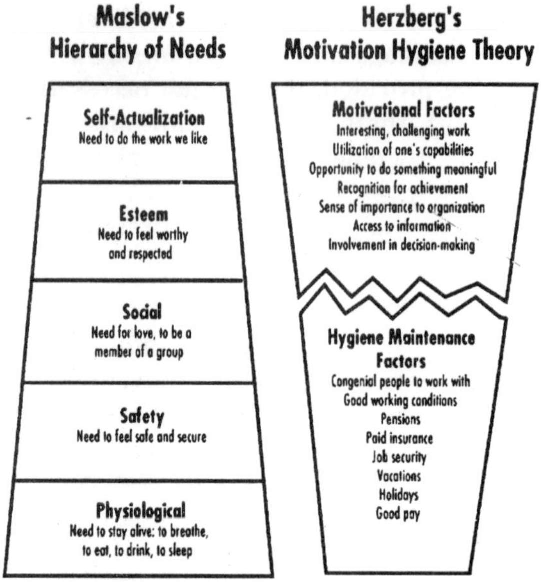

The process approach emphasizes how and why people choose certain behaviours in order to meet their personal goals. Process theories focus on external influences or behaviours that people choose to meet their needs. External influences are often readily accessible to supervisors.

Vroom's Expectancy Model suggests that people choose among alternative behaviours because they anticipate that particular behaviours will lead to one or more desired outcomes and that other behaviours will lead to undesirable outcomes. Expectancy is the belief that effort will lead to first-order outcomes, any work-related behaviour that is the direct result of the effort an employee expends on a job.

Equity is the perception of fairness involved in rewards given. A fair or equitable situation is one in which people with similar inputs experience similar outcomes. Employees will compare their rewards with the rewards received by others for their efforts. If employees perceive that an inequity exists, they are likely to withhold some of their contributions, either consciously or unconsciously, to bring a situation into better balance.

For example, if someone thinks he or she is not getting enough pay (output) for his or her work (input), he or she will try to get that pay increased or reduce the amount of work he or she is doing. On the other hand, when a worker thinks he or she is being paid too much for the work he or she is doing, he or she tends to increase the amount of work. Not only do workers compare their own inputs and outputs; they compare their input/output ratio with the input/output ratio of other workers. If one work team believes they are doing more work than a similar team for the same pay, their sense of fairness will be violated and they will tend to reduce the amount of work they are doing. It is a normal human inclination to want things to be fair.

Bowditch and Buono note that while equity theory was originally concerned with differences in pay, it may be applied to other forms of tangible and intangible rewards in the workplace. That is, if any input is not balanced with some fair output, the motivation process will be difficult. Supervisors must manage the perception of fairness in the mind of each employee. If subordinates think they are not being treated fairly, it is difficult to motivate them.

Equity Theory

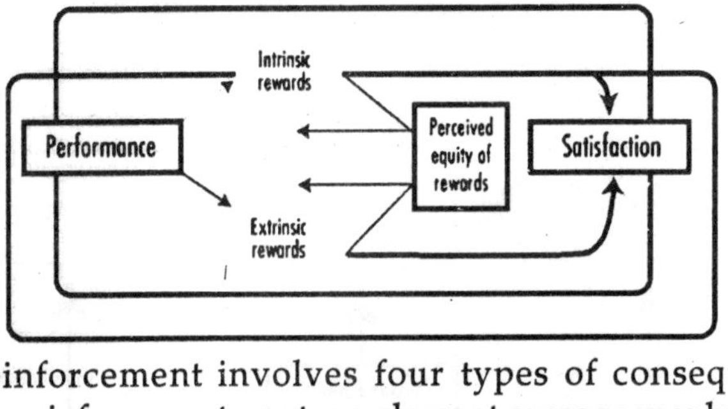

Reinforcement involves four types of consequence. Positive reinforcement creates a pleasant consequence by using rewards to increase the likelihood that a behaviour will be repeated. Negative reinforcement occurs when a person engages in behaviour to avoid unpleasant consequences or to escape from existing unpleasant consequences. Punishment is an attempt to discourage a target behaviour by the application of negative outcomes whenever it is possible. Extinction is the absence of any reinforcement, either positive or negative, following the occurrence of a target behaviour. Employees have questions about their jobs.

Reinforcement is based primarily on the work of B.F. Skinner, a psychologist, who experimented with the theories of operant conditioning. Skinner's work shows that many behaviours can be controlled through the use of rewards. In fact, a person might be influenced to change his or her behaviour by giving him or her rewards.

Employees who do an exceptionally good job on a particular project should be rewarded for that performance. It will motivate them to try to do an exceptional job on their next project. Employees must associate the reward with the behaviour. In other words, the employee must know for what specifically he or she is being rewarded! The reward should come as quickly as possible after the behaviour. The reward can be almost anything, but it must be something desired by the employee. Some of the most powerful rewards are symbolic; things that cost very little but mean a lot to the people who get them. Examples of symbolic rewards are things like plaques or certificates.

The Reinforcement Process

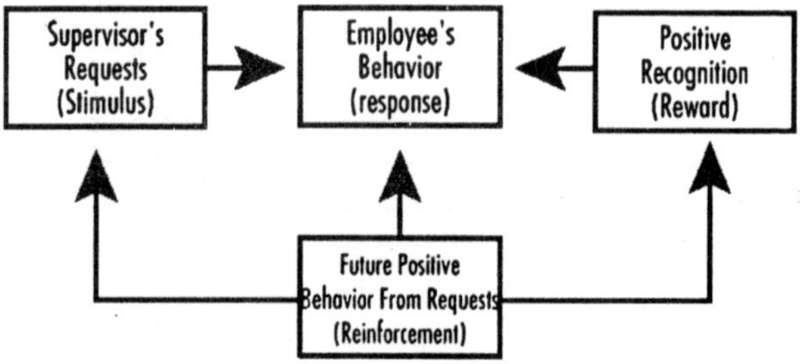

Chapter 6

Labour Relations

INDUSTRIAL RELATIONS

Good industrial relations, while a recognizable and legitimate objective for an organization, are difficult to define since a good system of industrial relations involves complex relationships between:

a. Workers (and their informal and formal groups, i. e. trade union, organizations and their representatives);

b. Employers (and their managers and formal organizations like trade and professional associations);

c. The government and legislation and government agencies l and 'independent' agencies like the Advisory Conciliation and Arbitration Service.

Oversimplified, work is a matter of managers giving instructions and workers following them - but (and even under slavery we recognize that different 'managing' produces very different results) the variety of 'forms' which have evolved to regulate the conduct of parties (i.e. laws, custom and practice, observances, agreements) makes the giving and receipt of instructions far from simple. Two types of 'rule' have evolved:

- 'Substantive', determining basic pay and conditions of service (what rewards workers should receive);
- 'Procedural,' determining how workers should be treated and methods and procedures.

Determining these rules are many common sense matters like:

- Financial, policy and market constraints on the parties (e.g. some unions do not have the finance to support industrial action, some have policies not to strike, some employers are more vulnerable than others to industrial action, some will not make changes unless worker agreement is made first, and rewards always ultimately reflect what the market will bear);
- The technology of production (the effect of a strike in newspaper production is immediate -it may be months before becoming effective in shipbuilding);
- The distribution of power within the community - that tends to vary over time and with economic conditions workers (or unions) dominating in times of full employment and employers in times of recession.

Broadly in the Western style economies the parties (workers and employers) are free to make their own agreements and rules. This is called 'voluntarism'. But it does not mean there is total noninterference by the government. That is necessary to:

- Protect the weak (hence minimum wage);
- Outlaw discrimination (race or sex);
- Determine minimum standards of safety, health, hygiene and even important conditions of service;
- To try to prevent the abuse of power by either party.

HR MANAGERS RESPONSIBILITIES

The personnel manager's involvement in the system of industrial relations varies from organization to organization, but normally he or she is required to provide seven identifiable functions, thus:

1. To keep abreast of industrial law (legislation and precedents) and to advise managers about their responsibilities e.g. to observe requirements in respect of employing disabled persons, not to discriminate, not to disclose 'spent' convictions of employees, to observe codes of practice etc. in relation to discipline

and redundancy, and similarly to determine organizational policies (in conjunction with other managers) relevant to legal and moral requirements (see also 4.).

2. To conduct (or assist in the conduct) of either local negotiations (within the plant) or similarly to act as the employer's representative in national negotiations. This could be as a critic or advisor in respect of trade etc. association policies or as a member of a trade association negotiating team. Agreements could be in respect of substantive or procedural matters. Even if not directly involved the personnel manager will advise other managers and administrators of the outcome of negotiations.
3. To ensure that agreements reached are interpreted so as to make sense to those who must operate them at the appropriate level within the organization (this can involve a lot of new learning at supervisory level and new pay procedures and new recording requirements in administration and even the teaching of new employment concepts - like stagger systems of work - at management level).
4. To monitor the observance of agreements and to produce policies that ensure that agreements are followed within the organization. An example would be the policy to be followed on the appointment of a new but experienced recruit in relation to the offered salary where there is a choice of increments to be given for experience, ability or qualification.
5. To correct the situations which go wrong. 'Face' is of some importance in most organizations and operating at a 'remote' staff level personnel managers can correct industrial relations errors made at local level without occasioning any loss of dignity (face) at the working level. 'Human resource management' and the obscurity of its reasoning can be blamed for matters which go wrong at plant level and for

unwelcome changes, variations of comfortable 'arrangements' and practices and unpopular interpretation of agreements.

6. To provide the impetus (and often devise the machinery) for the introduction of joint consultation and worker participation in decision-making in the organization. Formal agreement in respect of working conditions and behaviour could never cover every situation likely to arise. Moreover the more demanding the task (in terms of the mental contribution by the worker to its completion) the more highly-educated the workers need to be and the more they will want to be consulted about and involved in the details of work life. Matters like the rules for a flexitime system or for determining the correction of absenteeism and the contents of jobs are three examples of the sort of matters that may be solely decided by management in some organizations but a matter for joint consultation (not negotiation) in others with a more twenty-first-century outlook and philosophy. Human resource management is very involved in promoting and originating ideas in this field.

7. To provide statistics and information about workforce numbers, costs, skills etc. as relevant to negotiations (i.e. the cost of pay rises or compromise proposals, effect on differentials and possible recruitment/retention consequences of this or whether agreement needs to be known instantly); to maintain personnel records of training, experience, achievements, qualifications, awards and possibly pension and other records; to produce data of interest to management in respect of personnel matters like absentee figures and costs, statistics of sickness absence, costs of welfare and other employee services, statements about development in policies by other organizations, ideas for innovations; to advise upon or operate directly, grievance, redundancy, disciplinary and other procedures.

EMPLOYEE EVALUATION

An organization needs constantiy to take stock of its workforce and to assess its performance in existing jobs for three reasons:

- To improve organizational performance via improving the performance of individual contributors (should be an automatic process in the case of good managers, but (about annually) two key questions should be posed:
  - what has been done to improve the performance of a person last year?
  - and what can be done to improve his or her performance in the year to come?).
- To identify potential, i.e. to recognize existing talent and to use that to fill vacancies higher in the organization or to transfer individuals into jobs where better use can be made of their abilities or developing skills.
- To provide an equitable method of linking payment to performance where there are no numerical criteria (often this salary performance review takes place about three months later and is kept quite separate from 1. and 2. but is based on the same assessment).

On-the-spot managers and supervisors, not HR staffs, carry out evaluations. The personnel role is usually that of:

- Advising top management of the principles and objectives of an evaluation system and designing it for particular organizations and environments.
- Developing systems appropriately in consultation with managers, supervisors and staff representatives. Securing the involvement and cooperation of appraisers and those to be appraised.
- Assistance in the setting of objective standards of evaluation / assessment, for example:
  - Defining targets for achievement;

  - Explaining how to quantify and agree objectives;
  - Introducing self-assessment;
  - Eliminating complexity and duplication.
- Publicizing the purposes of the exercise and explaining to staff how the system will be used.
- Organizing and establishing the necessary training of managers and supervisors who will carry out the actual evaluations/ appraisals. Not only training in principles and procedures but also in the human relations skills necessary. (Lack of confidence in their own ability to handle situations of poor performance is the main weakness of assessors.)
- Monitoring the scheme - ensuring it does not fall into disuse, following up on training/job exchange etc. recommendations, reminding managers of their responsibilities.

Full-scale periodic reviews should be a standard feature of schemes since resistance to evaluation / appraisal schemes is common and the temptation to water down or render schemes ineffectual is ever present (managers resent the time taken if nothing else).

Basically an evaluation / appraisal scheme is a formalization of what is done in a more casual manner anyway (e.g. if there is a vacancy, discussion about internal moves and internal attempts to put square pegs into 'squarer holes' are both the results of casual evaluation). Most managers approve merit payment and that too calls for evaluation. Made a standard routine task, it aids the development of talent, warns the inefficient or uncaring and can be an effective form of motivation.

PROVISION OF EMPLOYEE SERVICES

Attention to the mental and physical well-being of employees is normal in many organizations as a means of keeping good staff and attracting others.

The forms this welfare can take are many and varied, from loans to the needy to counseling in respect of personal problems.

Among the activities regarded as normal are:

- Schemes for occupational sick pay, extended sick leave and access to the firm's medical adviser;
- Schemes for bereavement or other special leave;
- The rehabilitation of injured/unfit/ disabled employees and temporary or permanent move to lighter work;
- The maintenance of disablement statistics and registers (there are complicated legal requirements in respect of quotas of disabled workers and a need for 'certificates' where quota are not fulfilled and recruitment must take place);
- Provision of financial and other support for sports, social, hobbies, activities of many kinds which are work related;
- Provision of canteens and other catering facilities;
- Possibly assistance with financial and other aid to employees in difficulty (supervision, maybe, of an employee managed benevolent fund or scheme);
- Provision of information handbooks,
- Running of pre-retirement courses and similar fringe activities;
- Care for the welfare aspects of health and safety legislation and provision of first-aid training.

The location of the health and safety function within the organization varies. Commonly a split of responsibilities exists under which 'production' or 'engineering' management cares for the provision of safe systems of work and safe places and machines etc., but HRM is responsible for administration, training and education in awareness and understanding of the law, and for the alerting of all levels to new requirements.

Chapter 7

Orientation and Training

EMPLOYEE EDUCATION, TRAINING AND DEVELOPMENT

In general, education is 'mind preparation' and is carried out remote from the actual work area, training is the systematic development of the attitude, knowledge, skill pattern required by a person to perform a given task or job adequately and development is 'the growth of the individual in terms of ability, understanding and awareness'.

Within an organization all three are necessary in order to:

- Develop workers to undertake higher-grade tasks;
- Provide the conventional training of new and young workers (e.g. as apprentices, clerks, etc.);
- Raise efficiency and standards of performance;
- Meet legislative requirements (e.g. health and safety);
- Inform people (induction training, pre-retirement courses, etc.);

From time to time meet special needs arising from technical, legislative, and knowledge need changes. Meeting these needs is achieved via the 'training loop'. (Schematic available in PDF version.)

The diagnosis of other than conventional needs is complex and often depends upon the intuition or personal experience of managers and needs revealed by deficiencies. Sources of inspiration include:

- Common sense - it is often obvious that new machines, work systems, task requirements and changes in job content will require workers to be prepared;
- Shortcomings revealed by statistics of output per head, performance indices, unit costs, etc. and behavioural failures revealed by absentee figures, lateness, sickness etc. records;
- Recommendations of government and industry training organizations;
- Inspiration and innovations of individual managers and supervisors;
- Forecasts and predictions about staffing needs;
- Inspirations prompted by the technical press, training journals, reports of the experience of others;
- The suggestions made by specialist (e.g. education and training officers, safety engineers, work-study staff and management services personnel).

Designing training is far more than devising courses; it can include activities such as:

- Learning from observation of trained workers;
- Receiving coaching from seniors;
- Discovery as the result of working party, project team membership or attendance at meetings;
- Job swaps within and without the organization;
- Undertaking planned reading, or follow from the use of self-teaching texts and video tapes;
- Learning via involvement in research, report writing and visiting other works or organizations.

So far as group training is concerned in addition to formal courses there are:

- Lectures and talks by senior or specialist managers;
- Discussion group (conference and meeting) activities;

- Briefing by senior staffs;
- Role-playing exercises and simulation of actual conditions;
- Video and computer teaching activities;
- Case studies (and discussion) tests, quizzes, panel 'games', group forums, observation exercises and inspection and reporting techniques.

Evaluation of the effectiveness of training is done to ensure that it is cost effective, to identify needs to modify or extend what is being provided, to reveal new needs and redefine priorities and most of all to ensure that the objectives of the training are being met.

The latter may not be easy to ascertain where results cannot be measured mathematically. In the case of attitude and behavioural changes sought, leadership abilities, drive and ambition fostered, etc., achievement is a matter of the judgment of senior staffs. Exact validation might be impossible but unless on the whole the judgments are favourable the cooperation of managers in identifying needs, releasing personnel and assisting in training ventures will cease.

In making their judgments senior managers will question whether the efforts expended have produced:

- More effective, efficient, flexible employees;
- Faster results in making newcomers knowledgeable and effective than would follow from experience;
- More effective or efficient use of machinery, equipment and work procedures;
- Fewer requirements to implement redundancy (by retraining);
- Fewer accidents both personal and to property;
- Improvements in the qualifications of staff and their ability to take on tougher roles;
- Better employee loyalty to the organization with more willingness to innovate and accept change.

DIFFERENCE BETWEEN ORIENTATION AND TRAINING

Training constitutes a third set of practice modifications for effective team implementation. There is often a mistaken belief that people who are highly educated have the basic skills to work effectively in team settings. In fact, highly specialized individuals are often used to working alone and may lack some of the basic interpersonal skills necessary for collaboration. Training programmes designed for interpersonal skills in teams take one of two approaches: traditional classroom instruction in which a lecturer delivers material about techniques or strategies for working in teams and creative off-site team-building sessions in which teams participate in athletic, artistic, or competitive activities unrelated to their actual day-to-day responsibilities.

What is generally missing is the development of hands-on team capabilities, which is best accomplished by treating the team as a whole and applying the training as the team performs its actual tasks. In this way, the value of the training is established in the context of the work that the team does. In addition to teaching interpersonal skills, training must focus on establishing the skills necessary for self-management. First, considerable attention must be given to determining an optimal degree of autonomy. Self-managing teams are an appropriate response to situations where performance can be enhanced by taking decisions closer to the organization's environment. In contrast, self-management is not appropriate when the team is particularly large, when there is a high degree of functional diversity, or when the team is newly formed. In these situations, the team is faced with a high level of complexity, information-processing requirements are extensive, and managerial tasks are particularly challenging.

Having an external leader provide direction in these instances can improve team effectiveness. Perhaps the most substantial costs associated with increasing self-direction in teams are associated with the level of training and development needed to ensure that all or most of the members have the KSAs required to perform what were previously managerial responsibilities. In addition, on some teams employees are asked actually to carry out the training and development of their fellow members. Another training focus pertains to learning. In a team-based system, multidirectional learning is required across functions, levels, and organizations. This requires norms that are far different from those that prevailed in the traditional organization.

For example, learning requires the willingness to surface bad news and act on it. But that will not happen unless the traditional reaction— negatively evaluating the messengers of bad news—changes. Organizations that encourage experimentation and innovation and set up mechanisms for shared reflection can capitalize on this learning potential. Lateral learning must occur through dialogue and collaboration, and vertical learning must occur between teams at different levels in the organization. Local learning and innovation occurs through trial and error, but broader learning depends on whether organizations establish mechanisms for reflecting on and capturing learning from a variety of experiences.

If organizations wish to motivate teamwork, they must incorporate teamwork KSAs into their appraisal systems. It is important that the appraisal system not only reward good team players but also discourage behaviours that are not conducive to team effectiveness. An organization-specific job analysis should be conducted to determine the precise nature of the behavioural and performance measures to be included in the appraisal form for each individual team member.

Categories of teamwork KSAs such as conflict resolution, collaborative problem solving, communication, goal setting, performance management, planning, and task coordination could be translated into critical work behaviours or performance dimensions and incorporated into such an appraisal form. Equally important, however, is that team behaviours then be assessed. Imagine four teams, each performing the same task.

In the first team, each team member is given an individual goal. In the second, a goal is set for the team as a whole only. The third team is given both individual and team goals. The fourth is given no specific goal at all. Which team will do the poorest work? In an experiment that replicated this situation, the team with individual goals only was the poorest performer among all four teams. The team with both individual and team goals performed the best.

Most organizations might claim they have both individual and team goals if they have profit sharing or gain sharing. However, psychologically, these types of "team goals" are often overshadowed by individual goals, because the personal sense of control over performance lessens as one focuses on larger and larger groups, such as the entire organization. Each team should identify a set of critical measures representing a combination of results and process-oriented outcomes. Focusing only on results (for example, return on sales, revenue growth, and so on) does not help inform the team about which behaviours should be adjusted. Process measures (time spent per call, days before call returned, and so on) identify key behaviours that the team can change in order to improve results. Teams should avoid developing too many measures. If a measure is not critical in guiding the team's behaviour, then discard it. Most experts recommend that teams track six to ten performance areas.

Finally, in team-based organizations, people are responsible for collective performance at multiple levels. Individual, team, and business unit performance must be evaluated. Optimizing performance at any one level may hurt performance at other levels. The link between behaviour at one level and performance at another may be uncertain. People are often concerned that they will not get adequate feedback on how they are performing when the focus is on collective performance. Therefore, appraisal systems should assess behaviours that contribute to performance of other units or other levels within the organization. Team members should receive feedback from multiple sources, not just a manager. In small teams, each person can receive peer feedback, that is, feedback from all other team members and, where appropriate, feedback from customers.

Customers may be external to the organization (for example, a person who purchases a product or service) or internal (a person downstream in the process who receives the work of the team). It is also critical that feedback be given on multiple levels. It should be provided on individual performance, individual contributions to the team, team performance, and the team's contribution to the organization as a whole. Especially for the latter, feedback from customers and about competitors is critical. Whenever possible, it is best for teams themselves to document their own performance. This documentation should be developed and then discussed regularly at team meetings.

A final set of HR practices that should be examined when implementing teams pertains to compensation. Good practices for rewarding team performance require good processes for defining what the performance should be and for measuring and evaluating the performance. Some researchers have advocated that rewards should be the last component put in place in the transition to teams. This argument is made because team rewards are difficult to develop and have to be tailored to the organization.

Individual compensation should then be based on the accomplishment of these objectives. This is an intermediary step on the path toward team-based rewards; it allows recognition for teamwork and allows time for the organization to adjust other systems. Next, HR professionals can work to change the organizational compensation and reward practices. For example, team awards and team bonuses help team members focus on the performance of their own team. Profit sharing and gain sharing help team members focus on unit wide performance and orient employees to the larger performing unit by making it in everyone's interest to improve the performance of the enterprise as a whole.

This combination ensures that performance at each level is recognized and encouraged, in turn ensuring that individual behaviour is in the best interest of the team and that team behaviour is in the best interest of the organization. HR professionals may face several additional impediments. We see four challenges in particular: the inability of work teams to make a dramatic improvement in organizational performance quickly; the inevitable inter team conflict inherent in team-based organizations; resistance to work teams in foreign affiliates; and North American cultural barriers to working in teams. An unwillingness to communicate between teams destroys one of the reasons that organizations implement teams in the first place: to create a higher level of integration in a complex organizational environment.

Inwardly focused teams that fail to collaborate with others or communicate with external customers perform more poorly than externally focused teams. Several strategies are available to the HR professional for overcoming problematic inwardly focused teams. First, managers should keep teams focused on a higher level, or super ordinate, goal. Such a goal can be organization-, plant, or unitwide. A super ordinate goal keeps teams focused on the big picture, lowers competition between teams, and ties everything that all do more closely to overall organizational success.

A second strategy is to implement rewards (possibly based on goals) that are tied to the success of a set of teams as whole (a work unit, for example). Unit-level rewards are tricky in that all team members have to know how their contribution affects their rewards (also known as line of sight). A final strategy is to create linking or integrating teams composed of members from each of the competitive teams. Integrating teams tend to dilute original team member loyalties and ensure that each team's concerns are heard. Regardless of the strategy chosen, ignoring the problem of combative teams will inevitably erode any potential gains to be realized from the implementation of work teams.

HR professionals should take a proactive stand by designing strategies to reduce competition before the teams are allowed to become inwardly focused. A third impediment may arise when multinational organizations use work teams in their foreign affiliates. Organizations often wish to "export" their management practices because having similar HR practices in each country streamlines operations and reduces costs. For example, the Goodyear Tire and Rubber Company has begun using work teams in Europe, Latin America, and Asia; Sara Lee Corporation currently uses teams in Puerto Rico and Mexico; and Texas Instruments Malaysia has organized its entire workforce into teams.

Organizational scholars have pointed to national culture as a determinant of the success or failure of management initiatives that are developed in one culture and implemented in another. Some employees may resist management initiatives or react angrily when those initiatives clash with their deeply held cultural values.

HR professionals should learn about the cultures in which the company's work teams will operate. Through better understanding of cultural differences comes the knowledge of potential stumbling blocks to successful implementation before attempts are made to export work teams. Success stories about work teams in foreign affiliates exist, but that success depends on an understanding of the cultural forces that shape employee reaction to teams.

Just as some cultures are more individualistic or more collectivistic than others, individuals within cultures also vary on this dimension—even though there is, on average, more variation across cultures than within cultures. For example, when faced with the prospect of moving to a team-based work environment, some employees in a study conducted in the United States expressed concerns that reflected their individualistic values. Their comments included these: "Why should someone else's performance affect my pay?" "Will the team get credit for what I do?" "Individual achievement won't count anymore." "My achievement will be diluted by overall team success." These comments suggest that some employees may resist work teams because they are not compatible with their own work-related values.

Tests exist for measuring individualistic and collectivistic values at the individual level. Other measures such as preference for teams could be used as selection tools to evaluate prospective team members before they are placed on a team. If the teams are self-managing or autonomous, measures such as need for growth or need for achievement could be used to assess prospective member preferences for increased autonomy and responsibility. Whatever the measures used, HR professionals need to be aware of the role of individual differences in a team's success or failure in order to select more carefully individuals who are suited to working in a team. Barring the availability of such individuals, training must attempt to enhance employee receptivity to work teams.

Facilitators

First, in the years during which Total Quality Management enjoyed its heyday (the 1980s), many companies began a practice that had previously seemed contradictory to maintaining competitive advantage: benchmarking HR practices in other organizations. In years past companies viewed their internal operations as sources of extreme value.

But with the growth in international competition—especially in automobiles, electronics, and textiles—some businesses in the United States have realized the benefits of sharing information more openly to increase the global competitiveness of entire industries. This realization coupled with the work team success stories in the popular press have fueled an unprecedented exchange of both ideas and visits between companies and even competitors interested in adopting or improving work teams. For example, companies such as General Electric have looked to other seemingly unrelated businesses, such as Southwest Airlines, in order to adapt team-based practices. The benchmarking of HR practices also occurs within industries.

Several major semiconductor manufacturers (for example, Intel, DEC, Texas Instruments) have benchmarking agreements that allow for information exchange around HR best practices.

Second, in many industries, organizational environments are becoming exceedingly dynamic and complex. Scholars and practitioners alike have long realized the importance of aligning organizational structures with environmental characteristics. For example, the rapid changes witnessed in the computer industry forced companies such as IBM to restructure to achieve a better organizational structure-environment fit. There is general consensus that increasing environmental complexity will continue for the foreseeable future for organizations in many industries.

As these changes continue, the use of work teams will continue to serve as an integrated and flexible means of responding to organizational environments. Finally, regarding cultural change, researchers have suggested that there may be a substantial amount of cross-national convergence of management practices, values, and beliefs as a result of the interactions between organizations across cultures. As cultural convergence continues, a common set of values and assumptions may develop across national boundaries. This implies that eventually it may be possible to develop a universal set of best practices that will be appropriate no matter the cultural setting. In other words, less cultural adaptation may be necessary. Thus, HR practitioners in multinational corporations may gradually have an easier time dealing with cultural impediments.

We caution, however, that although some convergence is likely to take place, there are fundamental cultural values within nations that will remain stable. Researchers have referred to this phenomenon as the distinction between peripheral and core values. Therefore, it will always be necessary to adapt HR practices to some degree to fit the cultural context if the effectiveness of those practices across national boundaries is to be enhanced.

The Prospect of Teams Work

First, as the environment grows increasingly complex, temporary team structures will supplant more permanent work teams. As the forces outside organizations continue to change, the structures inside organizations will become more fluid. Rather than permanently assigning people to work teams, team composition will shift as projects, problems, or customers demand. Ad hoc teams or project teams will be more prevalent, placing extraordinary demands on employees to be flexible and demonstrate their value to organizations consistently through their team efforts. The challenge for HR managers will certainly involve compensation and evaluation for employees who may be constantly moving from one project team to another without a regular supervisor or team members with whom they have any long-term contact.

Second, the use of multicultural teams and globalized teams is likely to rise as trade barriers continue to fall. National culture plays a strong role in determining employee attitudes and behaviour. If a significant rise in these more culturally diverse teams occurs—and we feel strongly that it will—then HR managers must familiarize themselves with the cultures in which their organization operates. For example, if peer evaluations are part of the performance appraisal process on a multicultural team, HR managers must identify the key cultural characteristics that may serve as stumbling blocks to these evaluations.

If globalized teams are used, it is likely that entirely different compensation systems will be needed depending on the dominant cultural values of the areas in which an organization has business. Finally, with more telecommuting and flextime there will be less face-to-face time in work teams. We predict that traditional work teams will be replaced by virtual teams, whose members may seldom or never meet in person. Also referred to as "mobile, " these teams have no geographic centre. The members work out of their homes, automobiles, and clients' facilities and communicate via e-mail, fax, telephone, and videoconference. Team meetings may take place only once each quarter. The challenge for HR professionals is to assist managers in integrating team members, building cohesive teams, and facilitating communication and information exchange without having team members together in one place.

Teams are a powerful design option for organizations that hope to meet the challenges of increased global competition, improve output quality, and address the social needs of the ever-changing global workforce. However, the success or failure of work teams in multinational organizations will depend largely on the HR professional. Effective implementation of teams requires that HR practitioners adapt key assumptions about motivation, structure, and accountability. Adapted assumptions must support lateral thinking, collaboration, interdependence, a focus on process, permeable boundaries, and mutual responsibility. At the same time, HR practices must evolve to support teambased systems. Modifications in recruitment and selection, task design, training, evaluation, and compensation are all key to the effective use of teams in multinational organizations. Key to effective selection and recruitment for teams is the identification of teamwork KSAs.

Critical for task design is the development of teams around task processes and the integration of functional areas. Developing interpersonal, managerial, and learning skills are important training needs in team-based organizations. Finally, effective evaluation and compensation for teams requires a multilevel perspective and a balance between individual and team-based systems. Numerous impediments will challenge the effective implementation of teams across national contexts, including the inherent time lag between implementation and results, the often tenuous relationships between teams, cultural differences that require adaptations in practices to fit the context, and increasing domestic demographic diversity within nations.

To address these potential impediments, HR practitioners can encourage sharing practices within and between organizations, observe and adapt to organizational environmental trends, and maintain awareness of cultural convergence. HR professionals who can change their assumptions and are adept at modifying basic HR practices will be better poised to face future trends in the use of teams that are just on the horizon. As temporary team structures, multicultural teams, and virtual teams proliferate, these team-savvy practitioners will be able to lead their organizations through successful implementation and use of teams in multinational contexts.

DEVELOPING A HRM STRATEGY

Faced with rapid change organizations need to develop a more focused and coherent approach to managing people. In just the same way a business requires a marketing or information technology strategy it also requires a human resource or people strategy.

In developing such a strategy two critical questions must be addressed.

- What kinds of people do you need to manage and run your business to meet your strategic business objectives?
- What people programmes and initiatives must be designed and implemented to attract, develop and retain staff to compete effectively?

In order to answer these questions four key dimensions of an organization must be addressed. These are:

- Culture: the beliefs, values, norms and management style of the organization
- Organization: the structure, job roles and reporting lines of the organization
- People: the skill levels, staff potential and management capability
- Human resources systems: the people focused mechanisms which deliver the strategy - employee selection, communications, training, rewards, career development, etc.

Frequently in managing the people element of their business senior managers will only focus on one or two dimensions and neglect to deal with the others. Typically, companies reorganize their structures to free managers from bureaucracy and drive for more entrepreneurial flair but then fail to adjust their training or reward systems.

When the desired entrepreneurial behaviour does not emerge managers frequently look confused at the apparent failure of the changes to deliver results. The fact is that seldom can you focus on only one area. What is required is a strategic perspective aimed at identifying the relationship between all four dimensions.

If you require an organization which really values quality and service you not only have to retrain staff, you must also review the organization, reward, appraisal and communications systems.

The pay and reward system is a classic problem in this area. Frequently organizations have payment systems which are designed around the volume of output produced. If you then seek to develop a company which emphasizes the product's quality you must change the pay systems. Otherwise you have a contradiction between what the chief executive is saying about quality and what your payment system is encouraging staff to do.

There are seven steps to developing a human resource strategy and the active involvement of senior line managers should be sought throughout the approach.

STEPS IN DEVELOPING HRM STRATEGY

Get the 'Big Picture'

Understand your business strategy.

- Highlight the key driving forces of your business. What are they? e.g. technology, distribution, competition, the markets.
- What are the implications of the driving forces for the people side of your business?

- What is the fundamental people contribution to bottom line business performance?

Develop a Mission Statement or Statement of Intent

That relates to the people side of the business.

Do not be put off by negative reactions to the words or references to idealistic statements - it is the actual process of thinking through the issues in a formal and explicit manner that is important.

- What do your people contribute?

Conduct a SWOT Analysis of the Organization

Focus on the internal strengths and weaknesses of the people side of the business.

- Consider the current skill and capability issues.

Vigorously research the external business and market environment. High light the opportunities and threats relating to the people side of the business.

- What impact will/ might they have on business performance?
- Consider skill shortages?
- The impact of new technology on staffing levels?

From this analysis you then need to review the capability of your personnel department. Complete a SWOT analysis of the department - consider in detail the department's current areas of operation, the service levels and competences of your personnel staff.

Conduct a Detailed Human Resources Analysis

Concentrate on the organization's COPS (culture, organization, people, HR systems)

- Consider: Where you are now? Where do you want to be?
- What gaps exists between the reality of where you are now and where you want to be?

Exhaust your analysis of the four dimensions.

Determine Critical People Issues

Go back to the business strategy and examine it against your SWOT and COPS Analysis

- Identify the critical people issues namely those people issues that you must address. Those which have a key impact on the delivery of your business strategy.
- Prioritize the critical people issues. What will happen if you fail to address them?

Remember you are trying to identify where you should be focusing your efforts and resources.

Develop Consequences and Solutions

For each critical issue highlight the options for managerial action generate, elaborate and create - don't go for the obvious. This is an important step as frequently people jump for the known rather than challenge existing assumptions about the way things have been done in the past. Think about the consequences of taking various courses of action.

Consider the mix of HR systems needed to address the issues. Do you need to improve communications, training or pay?

What are the implications for the business and the personnel function?

Once you have worked through the process it should then be possible to translate the action plan into broad objectives. These will need to be broken down into the specialist HR Systems areas of:

- Employee training and development
- Management development
- Organization development
- Performance appraisal
- Employee reward
- Employee selection and recruitment
- Manpower planning
- Communication

Develop your action plan around the critical issues. Set targets and dates for the accomplishment of the key objectives.

Implementation and Evaluation of the Action Plans

The ultimate purpose of developing a human resource strategy is to ensure that the objectives set are mutually supportive so that the reward and payment systems are integrated with employee training and career development plans.

There is very little value or benefit in training people only to then frustrate them through a failure to provide ample career and development opportunities.

DEVELOPING AND DESIGNING A TRAINING PROGRAMME

Attracting the most qualified employees and matching them to the jobs for which they are best suited is significant for the success of any organization. However, many enterprises are too large to permit close contact between top management and employees. Human resources, training, and labour relations managers and specialists provide this connection. In the past, these workers have been associated with performing the administrative function of an organization, such as handling employee benefits questions or recruiting, interviewing, and hiring new staff in accordance with policies and requirements that have been established in conjunction with top management. Today's human resources workers manage these tasks and, increasingly, consult top executives regarding strategic planning. They have moved from behind-the-scenes staff work to leading the company in suggesting and changing policies. Senior management is recognizing the significance of the human resources department to their financial success.

In an effort to enhance morale and productivity, limit job turnover, and help organizations increase performance and improve business results, they also help their firms effectively use employee skills, provide training and development opportunities to improve those skills, and increase employees' satisfaction with their jobs and working conditions. Although some jobs in the human resources field require only limited contact with people outside the office, dealing with people is an important part of the job.

In a small organization, a human resources generalist may handle all aspects of human resources work, and thus require an extensive range of knowledge. The responsibilities of human resources generalists can vary widely, depending on their employer's needs. In a large corporation, the top human resources executive usually develops and manages human resources programmes and policies. (Executives are included in the Handbook statement on top executives.) These policies usually are implemented by a director or manager of human resources and, in some cases, a director of industrial relations.

The director of human resources may supervise several departments, each headed by an experienced manager who most likely specializes in one human resources activity, such as employment, compensation, benefits, training and development, or employee relations.

Employment and placement managers supervise the hiring and separation of employees and supervise various workers, including equal employment opportunity specialists and recruitment specialists. Employment, recruitment, and placement specialists recruit and place workers.

Recruiters maintain contacts within the community and may travel considerably, often to college campuses, to search for promising job applicants. Recruiters screen, interview, and occasionally test applicants. They also may check references and extend job offers. These workers must be thoroughly familiar with the organization and its human resources policies in order to discuss wages, working conditions, and promotional opportunities with prospective employees. They also must keep informed about equal employment opportunity (EEO) and affirmative action guidelines and laws, such as the Americans with Disabilities Act.

EEO officers, representatives, or affirmative action coordinators handle EEO matters in large organizations. They investigate and resolve EEO grievances, examine corporate practices for possible violations, and compile and submit EEO statistical reports.

Employer relations representatives, who usually work in government agencies, maintain working relationships with local employers and promote the use of public employment programmes and services. Similarly, employment interviewers—whose many job titles include human resources consultants, human resources development specialists, and human resources coordinators—help to match employers with qualified jobseekers.

Compensation, benefits, and job analysis specialists conduct programmes for employers and may specialize in specific areas such as position classifications or pensions. Job analysts, occasionally called position classifiers, collect and examine detailed information about job duties in order to prepare job descriptions. These descriptions explain the duties, training, and skills that each job requires. Whenever a large organization introduces a new job or reviews existing jobs, it calls upon the expert knowledge of the job analyst.

Occupational analysts conduct research, usually in large firms. They are concerned with occupational classification systems and study the effects of industry and occupational trends upon worker relationships. They may serve as technical liaison between the firm and other firms, government, and labour unions.

Establishing and maintaining a firm's pay system is the principal job of the compensation manager. Assisted by staff specialists, compensation managers devise ways to ensure fair and equitable pay rates. They may conduct surveys to see how their firm's rates compare with others and to see that the firm's pay scale complies with changing laws and regulations. In addition, compensation managers often manage their firm's performance evaluation system, and they may design reward systems such as pay-for-performance plans.

Employee benefits managers and specialists manage the company's employee benefits programme, notably its health insurance and pension plans. Expertise in designing and administering benefits programmes continues to take on importance as employer-provided benefits account for a growing proportion of overall compensation costs, and as benefit plans increase in number and complexity. For example, pension benefits might include savings and thrift, profit-sharing, and stock ownership plans; health benefits might include long-term catastrophic illness insurance and dental insurance. Familiarity with health benefits is a top priority for employee benefits managers and specialists, as more firms struggle to cope with the rising cost of health care for employees and retirees. In addition to health insurance and pension coverage, some firms offer employees life and accidental death and dismemberment insurance, disability insurance, and relatively new benefits designed to meet the needs of a changing workforce, such as parental leave, child and elder care, long-term nursing home care insurance, employee assistance and wellness programmes, and flexible benefits plans. Benefits managers must keep abreast of changing Federal and State regulations and legislation that may affect employee benefits.

Employee assistance plan managers, also called employee welfare managers, are responsible for a wide array of programmes covering occupational safety and health standards and practices; health promotion and physical fitness, medical examinations, and minor health treatment, such as first aid; plant security; publications; food service and recreation activities; carpooling and transportation programmes, such as transit subsidies; employee suggestion systems; child care and elder care; and counseling services. Child care and elder care are increasingly significant because of growth in the number of dual-income households and the elderly population. Counseling may help employees deal with emotional disorders, alcoholism, or marital, family, consumer, legal, and financial problems. Some employers offer career counseling as well. In large firms, certain programmes, such as those dealing with security and safety, may be in separate departments headed by other managers.

Training and development managers and specialists conduct and supervise training and development programmes for employees. Increasingly, management recognizes that training offers a way of developing skills, enhancing productivity and quality of work, and building worker loyalty to the firm, and most importantly, increasing individual and organizational performance to achieve business results. While training is widely accepted as an employee benefit and a method of improving employee morale, enhancing employee skills has become a business imperative. Increasingly, managers and leaders realize that the key to business growth and success is through developing the skills and knowledge of its workforce.

Other factors involved in determining whether training is needed include the complexity of the work environment, the rapid pace of organizational and technological change, and the growing number of jobs in fields that constantly generate new knowledge, and thus, require new skills. In addition, advances in learning theory have provided insights into how adults learn, and how training can be organized most effectively for them.

Training managers provide worker training either in the classroom or onsite. This includes setting up teaching materials prior to the class, involving the class, and issuing completion certificates at the end of the class. They have the responsibility for the entire learning process, and its environment, to ensure that the course meets its objectives and is measured and evaluated to understand how learning impacts business results.

Training specialists plan, organize, and direct a wide range of training activities. Trainers respond to corporate and worker service requests. They consult with onsite supervisors regarding available performance improvement services and conduct orientation sessions and arrange on-the-job training for new employees. They help all employees maintain and improve their job skills, and possibly prepare for jobs requiring greater skill. They help supervisors improve their interpersonal skills in order to deal effectively with employees. They may set up individualized training plans to strengthen an employee's existing skills or teach new ones.

Training specialists in some companies set up leadership or executive development programmes among employees in lower level positions. These programmes are designed to develop leaders to replace those leaving the organization and as part of a succession plan. Trainers also lead programmes to assist employees with job transitions as a result of mergers and acquisitions, as well as technological changes. In government-supported training programmes, training specialists function as case managers. They first assess the training needs of clients and then guide them through the most appropriate training method. After training, clients may either be referred to employer relations representatives or receive job placement assistance.

Planning and programme development is an essential part of the training specialist's job. In order to identify and assess training needs within the firm, trainers may confer with managers and supervisors or conduct surveys. They also evaluate training effectiveness to ensure that the training employees receive, helps the organization meet its strategic business goals and achieve results.

Depending on the size, goals, and nature of the organization, trainers may differ considerably in their responsibilities and in the methods they use. Training methods include on-the-job training; operating schools that duplicate shop conditions for trainees prior to putting them on the shop floor; apprenticeship training; classroom training; and electronic learning, which may involve interactive Internet-based training, multimedia programmes, distance learning, satellite training, other computer-aided instructional technologies, videos, simulators, conferences, and workshops.

An organization's director of industrial relations forms labour policy, oversees industrial labour relations, negotiates collective bargaining agreements, and coordinates grievance procedures to handle complaints resulting from management disputes with unionized employees. The director of industrial relations also advises and collaborates with the director of human resources, other managers, and members of their staff, because all aspects of human resources policy—such as wages, benefits, pensions, and work practices—may be involved in drawing up a new or revised union contract.

Labour relations managers and their staffs implement industrial labour relations programmes. Labour relations specialists prepare information for management to use during collective bargaining agreement negotiations, a process that requires the specialist to be familiar with economic and wage data and to have extensive knowledge of labour law and collective bargaining trends. The labour relations staff interprets and administers the contract with respect to grievances, wages and salaries, employee welfare, health care, pensions, union and management practices, and other contractual stipulations. As union membership continues to decline in most industries, industrial relations personnel are working more often with employees who are not members of a labour union.

Dispute resolution—attaining tacit or contractual agreements—has become increasingly significant as parties to a dispute attempt to avoid costly litigation, strikes, or other disruptions. Dispute resolution also has become more complex, involving employees, management, unions, other firms, and government agencies. Specialists involved in dispute resolution must be highly knowledgeable and experienced, and often report to the director of industrial relations. Conciliators, or mediators, advise and counsel labour and management to prevent and, when necessary, resolve disputes over labour agreements or other labour relations issues. Arbitrators, occasionally called umpires or referees, decide disputes that bind both labour and management to specific terms and conditions of labour contracts. Labour relations specialists who work for unions perform many of the same functions on behalf of the union and its members.

Other emerging specialties include international human resources managers, who handle human resources issues related to a company's foreign operations; and human resources information system specialists, who develop and apply computer programmes to process human resources information, match job seekers with job openings, and handle other human resources matters.

CREATING TRAINING SESSIONS

Human resources play a critical role in developing and implementing organizational strategies and structures. Successful HR professionals will be those who can align their organizational HR practices with the unique demands of team-based organizational structures.

First, we provide HR professionals with a brief history of the use of teams in the United States, reviewing definitions and types of teams, evidence regarding the impact of teams, and the factors that led to their proliferation. Second, we aim to provide the HR professional with tools to increase the effectiveness of teams, discussing the key assumptions underlying supportive conditions for teams. Third, we review modifications in HR practices that are necessary to implement teams effectively. Finally, we discuss potential challenges that HR practitioners may face in implementing teams in multinational organizations; looking to the future, we present guidelines for meeting these challenges. We conclude with some predictions about the use of teams that will likely develop as our team-based organizations continue to evolve.

What Teams Are

In general, a work team can be defined as a group of individuals working interdependently to solve problems or accomplish tasks. However, a single definition is not sufficient to capture the key differences that exist between the various types of teams being used in organizations. A number of key differences between these types of teams will determine the efficacy of HR practices designed to enhance their effectiveness. For example, compensation structures are normally altered for self-managing work teams to include team-based rewards to encourage cooperation between members and motivate them to reach team goals. Because self-managing members are working on permanent teams, the effort and expense involved in changing compensation structures is often justified. However, in more temporary teams, such as cross-functional or problem solving teams, other types of HR policy changes (for example, altering an evaluation system to include team behaviours) may be more appropriate to encourage positive behaviours.

Our point here is not to review all of the appropriate HR policies for each type of team but rather to acknowledge that our use of the term work team includes several different types of teams.

Contrary to popular belief, teams are not a new phenomenon. The origins of teams can be traced to the Tavistock studies of post–World War II and the Swedish socio technical movement generally associated with the Volvo Corporation. The first work teams in the United States were found in the Procter & Gamble Company in the early 1960s, the Topeka work system at a General Foods pet food plant in the late 1960s, and the Rushton Quality of Work Project in Pennsylvania in the mid–1970s. Given that teams were identified as a mechanism for improving employee performance as early as the 1960s, why has it taken over thirty years to implement work teams on a large scale in the United States?

We attribute the recent rise in the interest in and use of teams over the last ten years to three factors: a higher concern for the social component of work; the globalization of the U.S. economy and resulting downsizing; and the early adoption of work teams by highly visible companies such as General Motors, AT&T, General Electric, Xerox, and Motorola. Although many believe that organizations have adopted work teams to improve employee morale or productivity, the forces behind their adoption have been much larger in scale and much more connected to global patterns of international business. Organizations have adopted work teams because many had no choice. Dramatically reduced numbers of managers could not keep up with employee activities on a day-today basis.

Furthermore, the increased use of teams can be attributed, in part, to evidence of their success. Work teams have been associated with higher levels of productivity. It should be noted, however, that most of these studies have been conducted with self-managing work teams that have considerable control over their own structure and process. For traditional work teams, much of the evidence of impact has been collected on a case-by-case basis. Wellins, Byham, and Dixon (1994), for example, chronicle the pervasive positive impact teams have had in twenty companies. These companies claim that implementing teams resulted in improvements in bottom-line indicators such as cost savings, quality and service improvement, speed, absenteeism, and turnover.

This is not to say that teams are a panacea. Several studies on the impact of teams have failed to find effects for performance on more quantitative measures, such as productivity; others report only modest findings for productivity. Smaller effect sizes for productivity may be the result of using work teams in contexts where they are not appropriate. Clearly, work teams are not ideal for every task (even if you have a hammer, not every problem is a nail). Work teams are more effective under the right circumstances and situations.

For example, work teams are most effective when there is high task interdependence or a high degree of coordination and collaboration required between team members to accomplish tasks. Thus, a group of insurance sales agents who are geographically dispersed and have little interaction with one another to carry out their tasks would most likely be an inappropriate context in which to implement teams. The agents would probably see such an effort as an empty, poorly developed strategy designed to capitalize on a management fad.

Work teams are also more appropriate when the tasks that their members carry out are complex and well designed. If a group's work is routine and unchallenging, of dubious importance, and wholly preprogrammed with no opportunity for feedback, teams will probably not make much difference in productivity. As Johns (1996) has stated, "Taking a bunch of olive stuffers on a food processing assembly line, putting them in distinctive jumpsuits, calling them the Olive Squad, and telling them to self-manage will be unlikely to yield dividends in terms of effort expended or brainpower employed". Work teams, especially those that increase autonomy and responsibility, are most effective when members are given complex tasks that capitalize on their diverse knowledge and skills. Thus, teams should view their tasks as significant, the tasks should require the use of a variety of skills, and members should, where possible, assemble an entire product or deliver a complete service.

The effectiveness of work teams also depends on whether an organization has high integration needs as a result of operating in a complex environment. Complex environments usually force organizations to serve a wide variety of customers, deal with rapidly changing technology, and satisfy large numbers of different stakeholders. IBM, for example, faces a much more complex environment than McDonald's (compare the rate of change in PCs with that of Big Macs over the last fifteen years). Organizations must simultaneously deal with all of these issues—in other words, differentiate into smaller, more responsive units—and then integrate these widely dispersed efforts and units back into one cohesive organization. Teams will be most effective when a team structure is the best solution to obtaining the integration required to accomplish goals in a complex organizational environment. Without effective integration, the benefits attributed to work teams (increased productivity, higher quality, better job satisfaction) will not be realized.

Thus, companies implementing teams from a "bandwagon" perspective will not realize the benefits to be had from an appropriate fit between teams and context. In fact, many organizations are currently struggling with team effectiveness. We argue that this is the result, in part, of traditional assumptions about work that still prevail. In order to implement teams effectively, assumptions must change. We next discuss these adaptations.

Adapt Our Assumptions

We discuss the assumptions that shaped the decisions made by HR professionals in traditional hierarchical organizations in three areas: motivation; structure of work; and accountability. Traditional assumptions must be adapted in order to support effective implementation of teams.

Motivation

The first set of assumptions that must be examined pertain to motivation. National culture helps determine what motivates people. For example, some cultures can be classified as individualistic, where people tend to value their own self-interest and welfare over the interests of groups or societies; other cultures are known as collectivistic, where people tend to value the welfare of groups more than their own. Individualists are motivated by the opportunity to gain personal recognition. They resist working in teams more than people from collectivistic cultures. Such resistance lowers team effectiveness on outcomes such as productivity, job satisfaction, cooperativeness, and organizational commitment. It takes time and experience for people to adjust their notions of fairness and equity to include collective accountability. Taking a longer-term focus and understanding the eventual payoffs for early investments in team-based systems is essential for harnessing the motivational power of teams.

In understanding motivational assumptions, it is also important to consider expectations. Research attests to the importance of collective expectations in determining our level of motivation and subsequently our performance. When we believe we can accomplish objectives as a team, we are motivated to stick with our work tasks and prevail. But sometimes these high expectations get out of hand, to the point that teams hold unrealistic expectations. Cohesive teams often fall prey to this phenomenon, which is referred to as groupthink. Coinciding with extremely high expectations, teams suffering from groupthink also hold illusions of invulnerability.

They ignore important external information sources that might help them adjust their performance to fit the needs of customers better. Teams in individualistic cultures appear to be particularly susceptible to overconfidence. This may be because individualists view their team as an entity in and of itself rather than one that is connected to the external context and are therefore even less apt to use external sources of information to make corrections in their behaviour and improve their performance. Particularly in individualistic cultures, team-based organizations need to have systems that help teams set realistic expectations. This allows them to stay motivated while at the same time remaining open to learning from feedback and mistakes.

Work Structure

A second domain of assumptions concerns the structure of work. Traditional work groups were generally formed around common technical or functional skills and areas of expertise (for example, accounting, finance, or production). In recent years, it has become apparent that organizing work around a process (for example, new product development) rather than around a specific task or function is more effective. Doing so often requires extending team members' task skills. Multi skilled teamwork involves teams made up of individuals with multiple and overlapping skills that are deployed around the performance of a whole task, which represents a significant part of a larger work flow. Members are multi skilled so that work can be flexibly allocated among them.

In organizing work around processes, organizational boundaries must often be renegotiated. Increasingly, work teams include external customers and suppliers. For example, General Electric Medical Systems invites representatives from leading health maintenance organizations (HMOs) to serve on its sales and service teams. The American Red Cross has members of communities serving on key committees that set organizational objectives. Eastman Kodak allies itself with key competitors to form market segment task forces. These types of work structures require a whole new notion of collaboration—collaboration with external constituencies. Those who were previously viewed as "them" are now viewed as "us."

The reorganization of work around processes and across boundaries has numerous benefits. For example, multi skilling (the learning of new skills in addition to functional expertise) can result in reduced staffing as fewer workers can perform the same range of tasks. It can create efficiencies through more flexible task assignment. Multi skilling also often leads to lower inventories because there is more effective work flow coordination. It also makes the team more flexible in meeting fluctuating market demand through operational flexibility. Finally, it can lead to a more differentiated response to the needs of particular customer segments and so contribute to strategic flexibility. Multi skilling leads to greater awareness of the whole task and enables the team member to take part in problem solving, innovation, and strategic thinking. These same benefits do not accrue when tasks and organizations are structured under traditional assumptions of static, independent jobs.

Accountability

A third domain of assumptions that shape team effectiveness pertain to accountability. The focus of most HR departments has been on the individual. Individual accountability and responsibility have been the foundation on which all of the business practices in the United States have been built. Furthermore, accountability in traditional work organizations was vested in those with formal positions—the managers and supervisors. Individual employees showed deference to people in these positions. Reporting structures were vertical and a command-and-control philosophy reigned. Skills such as planning, coordination, personnel functions, quality management, health and safety, and boundary management were the domain of managers. But increasingly, these duties are becoming the domain of teams.

Managerial responsibility is shifting from individual accountability to collective, mutual accountability. As this has occurred, the notion of self-management has gained acceptance. Self-management grows as the team's operational tasks are delegated to the team itself. Many different terms have evolved to describe and distinguish varying degrees of autonomy, including self-directed work teams, empowered teams, and superior work teams. The common distinguishing characteristic of such teams is that they operate with some degree of autonomy.

As nonmanagers become collectively responsible for managerial duties, basic assumptions about the legitimacy of authority are challenged. Team members may begin to question what gives peers the right to set rules for others. They may have difficulty dealing with authority that does not stem from position. Rather than depending on a job description and direction from the manager, people work jointly with coworkers to determine what they do. Because personal success depends on collective success, an individual's fate is tied to coworkers. Feelings of mutual trust and partnership must develop. The organization must help people learn to deal with greater ambiguity, uncertainty, continual change, and collaborative relationships. Both managers and employees in the team-based organization need to adjust to this shift in accountability and responsibility. We discuss the HR systems that increase team effectiveness in the next section.

Modify HR Practices to Support Teams

In addition to recognizing and adapting the assumptions on which they base their practices, HR professionals must also modify those practices to support teams. The practices to be modified cluster in five areas: recruitment and selection; task design; training; evaluation; and compensation. In the following sections, we summarize the modifications and provide references for practitioners interested in exploring them in greater depth.

Recruitment and Selection

Working effectively in a team requires a particular set of knowledge, skills, and abilities (KSAs) that were not as critical in traditional organizations. Proficiency is needed in at least five areas: conflict resolution, collaborative problem solving, communication, goal setting and performance management, and planning and task coordination. During recruitment, organizations aspiring to create a workforce of effective team members should clearly communicate the importance of these proficiencies. Doing so provides a realistic job preview and can therefore help to reduce turnover. Recruiting individuals who prefer these activities also makes sense because team members' preferences for teamwork are related to team effectiveness.

It is also important to consider teamwork KSAs in the selection process. It might seem easy to include measures of KSAs in most selection systems, but most selection instruments focus on basic learning abilities (for example, math, language, perceptual skills) or specific technical abilities (for example, mechanical, electrical, and so on). In the last few years, employment tests designed to measure teamwork KSAs have been under development.

Early results suggest that the tests can predict subsequent performance beyond the level of prediction from a large battery of traditional employment aptitude tests. These initial findings offer encouraging support for such instruments. Interviews might also be a viable method of assessing social and interpersonal attributes that contribute to teamwork. There is evidence that a structured interview designed to measure social KSAs can predict future team effectiveness. Finally, selection techniques that involve collecting biographical information may be another way to assess teamwork KSAs.

Task Design

The second set of practices that must be modified relate to task design. Effective teams are designed around the tasks they perform. Two key considerations are that teams should be relatively self contained and handle many aspects of their own functioning. First, teams should be collectively responsible for an identifiable and substantial part of the work of the organization. To the extent possible, support services should be included in the team so that it has the resources necessary to accomplish its goals. Members should be multi skilled and dedicated to the team so that they do not have to split priorities. Finally, the team should report as a unit so that members do not have conflicting directions from different managers.

Second, the team should be responsible for many aspects of its own functioning. For example, it should be able to determine how to apply the team's resources, strategies for completion of work, and quality monitoring. It should also be responsible for working with internal and external customers. Finally, part of the team's task should be performance evaluation. Whenever appropriate skill levels and task conditions exist, team members should be involved in reviewing their own performance and determining their own rewards.

Beyond these two fundamental design principles, a third issue is whether teams should be functional or cross-functional. Functional organizations group people by common specialties and break work down into functional packets that translate into individual assignment. Project organizations combine different specialties required to perform the entire project but then break the work down for members of functional groups within the project. Team-based organizations require a shift away from a hierarchical breakdown to focus instead on the lateral distribution and integration of work.

Whether teams should be functional or cross-functional is a choice to be based on an analysis of the work to be accomplished. Process analysis can be used to determine the sets of activities that have to be carried out and integrated to deliver value to customers. If within an identifiable set of activities coordination must occur across different functional areas, then teams should be cross-functional. In the cross-functional teams members can integrate work across disciplines and make trade-offs that require a multidisciplinary perspective. But if the process analysis indicates that an identifiable set of activities occurs within a functional area, then teams should be functional.

EVALUATING THE TRAINING PROGRAMME

Long-term employment security is no longer promised or implied, and this has changed the degree of mutual commitment that employees and organizations feel toward one another. The consequences are paradoxical for many companies. On the one hand, they want to be freer to shed employees who are not needed; on the other hand, they want to encourage needed employees to stay as long as possible. But employees who know they have no long term security are often busy looking for better opportunities. Instead of a long-term relationship or even a "marriage, " both employees and companies can wind up in a "dating game" as they look for short-term selfish advantage.

As an HRM strategy in tight labour markets or when employees with rare skills are involved, some firms have committed themselves for specific contracted periods or offered stock options and incentive-based schemes to hang on to desired individuals. Nevertheless, at least one organizational survey consortium reports that employee attitudes on job security have become much less favourable in all companies over the last decade, even as other attitudes have remained relatively constant Corporation, private communication with the authors, January 1998). As several commentators have noted and as the chapters by Noer and others in this volume note, the psychological contract has changed. One noticeable effect of this change is in college recruiting, where companies no longer promise long-term careers and actually use "signing bonuses" to get the most talented graduates to join them. In other words, short-term payoffs are being used to make up for long-term inducements.

NONWORK OBLIGATIONS

Most companies now see family responsibilities as a more acceptable counterpoint to work obligations. Many employees desire flexible work schedules and supervisor support for emergencies and use these criteria to select employers when there is a choice. Some books have become best-sellers because they rate and describe "the best places to work". Underlying realities that have helped give voice to such concerns include changes in marriage patterns. Divorce rates have gone up substantially during recent decades, leaving many women dependent on their own efforts for economic well-being and creating many more single parents than in the past. For single parents, work is an economic necessity but it also competes with family for time and energy. In a related phenomenon, age at first marriage has increased by almost a year per decade for the last half century, so that it is now about twenty-four for women and twenty-six for men.

With this shift, many couples now live together without benefit of the clergy's blessing. Their concerns include many mutual career decisions, which may affect accepting a job or relocating. In recent years, this concern has sometimes emerged as a desire for company benefits to be extended to domestic partners. This has been especially noted when homosexual partners, who do not have the option of legal marriage, want such coverage. The open expression of such living arrangements and sexual orientations by workers represents another major shift in attitudes and values.

Assumptions

This review of the environmental forces affecting industry and HRM indicates that many of the assumptions made in the past about people in the work setting are no longer valid. If the assumptions are no longer valid, then the concepts and practices based on them may also be invalid. As we indicated in our opening discussion, many of these assumptions arose in the 1950s, and it is these beliefs that need to be reexamined and reevaluated.

Current Assumptions

The changes in the environment we have noted, which most companies operate in today, have required a new set of assumptions that are more appropriate for the times and that generate new HRM concepts and practices. These new assumptions may be subdivided according to their application to organizations and to individuals.

Organizations today contrast in several respects with those of the past. The shifts are evident in corporate forms and dynamics:

- More than ever, organizations are likely to be fluid, continually changing, and have many new relationships, from joint ventures, alliances, and partnerships to use of vendors and subcontractors.
- Embattled organizations are continually under pressure to increase outputs, improve cycle time, enhance competitiveness.
- A focus on short-term achievements is an imperative. Corporate acquisitions may often be seen as a better bet than undertaking long-term product development.
- Important skills and talent are to be hired as needed rather than developed internally over a long period. Conversely, unneeded employees should be quickly converted or disposed of.

HRM concepts and practices arise from a complex set of forces that form the operating environment for the organizations HRM serves. When the environment is stable, many of the changes are determined by the organization itself, often in a desire to give itself a competitive advantage in attracting, retaining, and motivating employees. Sometimes the concepts and practices arise out of the company founder's personal philosophy and preferences. But the environment has not been very stable during the last two decades.

Many of the operating assumptions on which HRM operates have been severely but gradually challenged in the last two decades in a series of inexorable changes. As a story popular in some management circles puts it, a frog dropped into a pot of boiling water will instantly jump out. But if the frog is placed in a pot of cool water that is gradually brought to a boil, the frog will simply grow warmer and doze off until it is too late. It is the suddenness of change that makes it vivid for people as well.

Many of the shifts noted have taken place gradually and in different spheres, and they may not have been given sufficient notice at the time of their occurrence. But when we look back over the last twenty-five years, it is obvious that many principles that were simply taken for granted are no longer true. This is as dangerous for us as the slowly warming pot is for the frog. To be effective, it is necessary for HRM concepts and practices to be lined up with assumptions that are based on the reality of our environments.

For organizations to assess their environments accurately it is useful periodically to go through a disciplined scan of their current and expected environments. In fact, many large firms and some consortia conduct environmental scans on a regular basis. This certainly seems like a healthy practice. We believe that a useful framework for doing environmental scans is one that looks at the DELTA forces around us, that is, the demographics, economics, legal and regulatory issues, technology, and attitudes and values. These are the forces that have greatly affected us in the past and seem the right places to look to for future change.

EMPLOYERS AND EMPLOYEES

Most knowledgeable observers in the field of human resource management (HRM) would agree that its major development as a profession came during the half century or so between the end of World War II and the early 1990s. As organizations employing as many as hundreds of thousands became dominant influences in the world of work and as questions about selection, training, work motivation, and compensation practices became more challenging in a growing, dynamic society, the need for professionally trained, skilled personnel became great. Also, despite occasional downturns in the economy, the professional growth of HRM took place against a general culture of prosperity, a belief that such good patterns would continue and even improve, and an assumption that work organizations should and would share in such growth.

Important too as HRM developed during this era was that the policies and practices developed and implemented were based in large part on the assumption that a desire for personal growth was the most important motivational characteristic of the workforce, along with the belief that more of everything (particularly economic outcomes) is better. Korman (forthcoming) has referred to this pattern as self-enhancing motivation and has cited as illustrative of this type of motivation such actions as making choices that match and fulfill one's personal needs, engaging in activities that foster self-growth, attempting to attain high levels of work performance, and working for goals that legitimately enhance oneself in one's own eyes and those of others. Given the cultural context and the assumption of the dominance of this type of motivational pattern, it was a relatively short step for HRM professionals during this era to develop a perspective that reflected them.

Characteristic programmes of this type included job enrichment, career management and career development, self-appraisals and peer performance appraisals, and income incentives of various kinds. Less significant as an influence on HRM during this era but still of some importance were programmes based on what Korman (forthcoming) has called self-protective motivation, defined as the desire to defend oneself from perceived threatening environmental and personal forces that might affect one's sense of identity. Korman suggests that it is this motivational force that underlies the need for personal and job security. Despite its importance, however, this need was generally viewed as less important than employee needs for growth, development, and achievement during the years of prosperity.

There were several reasons for this difference in emphasis. One factor, certainly, was the prosperity and the continued expectations of same. It was not a climate that generated a sense of anxiety, whether warranted or not. Second, the strength and membership of labour unions—organizations that have traditionally made job security a keystone of their efforts—were declining. With the assumption of continued prosperity and the weakness of labour unions, human resource (HR) managers and their allied professionals, such as industrial-organizational psychologists, worried less about providing job security than about providing the opportunity for growth, development, and achievement. Third, theorists on motivation in work organizations generally had a low level of interest in such concepts as anxiety, even though important research findings were beginning to be reported on the significance of such related variables as fear of failure in performance settings. Instead, theories were popular if they saw people as growth-oriented, desiring meaningful work achievement, and interested in attaining both intrinsic and extrinsic goals.

Nevertheless, despite these influences, there was some concern even during these years about providing a greater sense of security for employees. Prominent among those expressing such interest was Frederick Herzberg, an important management writer who saw in the reduction of anxiety that came with job security a significant approach to reducing job dissatisfaction. In addition, although their membership continued to decrease, labour unions and their emphasis on job security did not totally disappear from the work scene. Unions remained strong in some areas, particularly the federal, state, and local civil services, and their presence did much to ensure that job security remained on the table as an employee concern, at least in some instances.

There were, then, these two patterns of HR practice. One, the more influential, assumed that the more important motivational patterns were desires for growth, development, achievement, and self-enhancement. The second, less significant as an influence, assumed desires for job security and self-protection. Both were recognized, and both influenced HRM practices. Less recognized was that the disparity in influence of these patterns of practice encouraged another important underlying assumption. This assumption was that HRM policies and practices could be developed in a manner that would enable the attainment of two goals.

The first of these goals was to help organizations obtain their objectives. The second was that HRM could help employees meet their most important needs because the employees' desire to attain positive outcomes (both intrinsic and extrinsic), that is, self-enhancement, and their willingness to work for them were congruent with organizational needs for effective performance. Furthermore, this congruence could be maintained and encouraged because of the continuing expected affluence. In contrast, rarely if ever discussed was that these practices and policies and the assumed congruence between employer and employee depended on these assumptions of continued prosperity and that other approaches would become necessary if the situation changed.

The New World of Work

Now that time has come. A new and different world of work has begun to emerge, one that exists alongside the traditional work setting and that may eventually come to supplant it. It is a world characterized by at least three major trends that have implications for HRM.

- First, downsizing is now a frequent key component of managerial decision making, with all the potential short- and long-term anxiety-inducing effects on employee motivation that we would expect.

- Second, the work-family conflict is an endemic part of the lives of both employers and employees.
- Third, we live in a world marked by the extensive use of temporary workers, part-time employees, and outsourcing.

Workforce Reduction

Downsizing has become so much a part of the world of work during the past decade that it is a term familiar to almost all who work or who wish to. Table lists some of the more dramatic illustrations of downsizing that have occurred in American corporations during the past five years.

Downsizing is a phenomenon that continues to this day. Downsizing is a fact of the world of work that influences the lives, attitudes, and emotions of millions. That other jobs are continually being created—and they are—may not significantly affect those concerned about their long- and short-term job prospects.

Work-Family Conflict

Also part of this new world of work is conflict with the family, an inevitable fact of life as our society is increasingly characterized by women in the workforce, dual-career couples, and single-parent families. The increasing presence of women in the workforce contributes to this conflict, a conflict that is among the most serious facing American families and work organizations as we approach the new millennium. It is a problem, both actual and potential, that is becoming increasingly widespread. It is also one of the characteristics of the new world of work that has had and continues to have a major impact on the motivational and attitudinal characteristics of people in the workforce, both men and women.

Noncore Workers

We now also have a work setting marked increasingly by outsourcing agreements between companies, relocation of companies from high- to low-wage areas, globalization, a desire for individuals to develop multiskill capability rather than job specialization, and explosive growth in the use of temporary and contingent employees.

Feelings of ambiguity and conflict have resulted from these changes. On the one hand, there are now new ways for individuals to seek self-enhancement in the world of work, paths that have important implications for the practices and policies HRM may adopt. But on the other hand, the resulting anxiety from these changes has led to a high level of self-protective motivation. The outcome has been a world of work where the two different motivations are assuming equal significance. In other words, it is a world in which the desire and need for security has become as relevant as the need for achievement, growth, and development. It is therefore a world in which both motivational patterns will need to be addressed by HRM, but in different ways than they have been previously.

The New Assumptions

HRM needs new and different assumptions on which to base policy and practice. One necessary change, I believe, is to assume no longer that there is a congruence of interests between employees and employers. Sometimes there may be, but sometimes there may not be. Second, we need to assume that the key interpersonal and intergroup relationships in a particular work setting are as likely to be among individuals from different organizations with different investments as they are to be among individuals within the same organization. The following paragraphs elaborate on these recommendations in greater detail.

Because self-enhancement was assumed to be the dominant work motivation during the years of the growth of the field, it is not surprising that HR professionals operated on the belief that it was both possible and desirable to design and implement policies and practices that could and would integrate the goals of both employees and organizations. In fact, one of the major books of this era, and one which served as a sort of conceptual guideline for many, was titled Integrating the Individual with the Organization. In a similar vein and serving as further illustration of this assumption of congruence between employer and employee was the growth of job enrichment as a management tool, fueled by the belief that individuals would respond to the challenge of enriched jobs. According to this perspective, the enriched job provided a mechanism for self-enhancement and, in satisfying such desires, the individual would be more highly performance motivated and contribute more to the attainment of organizational goals.

Now, however, we need to change this assumption. More specifically, we need to view the individual and the organization as separate entities who will be able to integrate their efforts and cooperate with one another under certain conditions but not under others. Furthermore, determining what those conditions might be will be an important objective for HRM professionals in the coming years.

A second assumption about people and organizations during the years of growth and prosperity was that the interpersonal and inter group relationships HRM needed most to be concerned with were those that took place within the organization, that is, intra organizational relationships. In other words, the focus was on the relationships between people in different jobs, in different functions, and at different hierarchical levels, but all within the same organization. Although it was recognized that individuals often met with salespeople, suppliers, and others, such meetings with "outsiders" were generally limited to specifically designated occupational groups. Now, however, more attention will have to be paid to relationships between those with primary allegiance to a particular organization and those who may work in that organization but not have primary allegiance to it.

Today, individuals work full-time in an organization to which they have primary loyalty while next to them or with them are individuals on temporary assignments, part-time workers, and people working in joint venture settings and in outsourcing situations. The result may therefore be individuals working together whose allegiances and concerns may involve differences that are highly important to us. Relationships, views, and expectations among those who are all part of one group—or who view themselves as part of the same company or as "insiders"—are different from the types of relationships and communication patterns that develop among those who view themselves as belonging to different groups. For example, Korman (1988) has proposed that in situations in which we find insiders and outsiders, the former are more likely to discriminate and act in a prejudicial manner toward the latter.

The result may be unnecessary conflict and sometimes even "tribalistic" patterns, where each group cares only about itself and not about the other or joint goals. Although cases of severe conflict may be extreme—because there are usually some reasons for these different groups and individuals to at least try to work together— the potential for conflict between groups and individuals exists in this new work setting and there will be a need to take account of such possibilities in developing future HRM programmes. These new assumptions, which I believe to be more appropriate for the emerging work setting, suggest the need for new HRM approaches, techniques, policies, and practices that will allow satisfaction of both the self-enhancing and the self-protective motivational processes.

Some Programme Suggestions

Programmes consistent with the new assumptions need to be developed for HRM as it confronts this new world of work. The remainder outlines four such programmes, with each discussed in greater detail in the following sections.

- Effective self-career management programmes based on the desire for self-enhancement.
- Labour pool associations designed to meet needs for both self enhancement and self-protection.
- Performance incentive programmes that are not based on organizational commitment, including financial

rewards providing direct income as well as health, welfare, and pension benefits.

- Insider-outsider training programmes.

Self-Career Management

Self-career management programmes are designed primarily for those individuals who view themselves as relatively independent professionals or "businesses, " rather than as organizationally dependent job holders. These are individuals who can and do make their own decisions about their careers, know their capabilities, and understand where they can find the types of work opportunities where they can "sell" themselves as a business or service. Self-career management is a different way of looking at oneself and one's work capabilities.

It is a mechanism for declaring oneself independent of an organizational control system but at the same time being willing to negotiate mutual terms of acceptability concerning work contributions to that system. Self-career management—thus defined as the giving up of relatively permanent organizational relationships in favour of more self-controlled career decision making—has become increasingly recommended to and by HRM professionals as a possible approach to dealing with challenges presented by the emerging world of work, a world still dominated in great degree by the use of downsizing as a management strategy despite continuing questions about its outcomes.

Clearly, there are reasons for such positive evaluation. Self career management recognizes the tentative nature of a specific employment relationship while also emphasizing the need for employee skills and meaningful contributions and the opportunity to fulfill the desire for self-enhancement that is so important in the work setting. In addition, for the appropriate individual and the appropriate situation, self-career management also provides an approach to meeting the need for self-protection, because this can be negotiated by the individual involved. The key, however, is in the word appropriate. Self-career management is appropriate when the individual has or can develop both meaningful self-knowledge and the types of skills and abilities that are in demand. In addition, self-career management is appropriate when the individual has knowledge of the job market and the freedom to respond to the opportunities available.

A variety of techniques reflect self-career management when it is defined in this manner. Perhaps the most important and first question that needs an answer (for which the HRM professional must provide input) is whether a specific organization should provide financial and other resources for developing and implementing self-career programmes for its employees, particularly programmes emphasizing personal growth. This is not an easy question to answer. At first glance, there are clearly reasons for companies to undertake such programmes.

They provide recognition of the frequently temporary nature of contemporary work settings while at the same time encouraging positive relationships between individuals and organizations over the long run. Both of these outcomes may serve the individual and the organization in good stead at once or at some time in the future. In addition, these programmes may serve to illuminate and develop skills in the participants not previously realized and thus eventually prove beneficial to the individual and the organization. Finally, such programmes help the organization in situations where downsizing may become inevitable. Clearly, preparing individuals to deal with the loss of employment before it happens is to be preferred over sudden notices of termination.

Still, some negative aspects also need to be recognized before a corporate decision is made to undertake a personal growth programme encouraging self-career management. One obvious problem is the cost involved. The cost may be considerable, depending on the number of individuals involved and the type of programmes chosen. Second, there is the continuing reality that all the benefits the programmes may provide to employees may never be of value to the organization that pays for them (and, indeed, may turn out to be of value to competitors).

Third, it needs to be realized right from the beginning that such programmes are not for everyone. They should not be oversold as "the answer" to the problems of the new world of work. Rather, companies need to keep in mind that other programmes will be necessary regardless of what they decide about self-career management programmes (for more on this, see the following section). To be blunt, self-career management is not and cannot be appropriate for those who have neither the personality nor the technical skills, educational levels, or likelihood of developing the skills to the degree needed to make the approach fruitful. For these individuals, other alternatives will be necessary.

Assuming these pros and cons have been considered and the company decides to proceed with such programmes, how might they do so? One possible procedure is to make self-career management programmes a voluntary aspect of the HRM process. Such an approach would increase the probability of successful outcomes by making it likely that the individuals participating in the programmes possess the skills, abilities, interests, or personality that would enable them to benefit from the programmes.

In addition, once the decision to proceed is made, HRM can increase the effectiveness of self-career management programmes by generating and making available as much information as possible about the nature of potential and actual career possibilities in a particular job market for those participating in the programmes. Self career management programmes are much concerned with personal growth but are not aimed at personal growth alone. They also have career and work-oriented goals.

The more work opportunities available that the participant knows about and the more the participant has the time, knowledge, and personal characteristics to carry out a job or career search, the more self-management career programmes will be useful. A further advantage of providing job knowledge to those undergoing self-career management is that doing so will help identify those for whom such programmes might not be useful, that is, those who will not have job opportunities for the skills they have or are likely to develop. For this latter group, other types of programmes will be necessary, perhaps programmes of the type we now turn to.

Labour Pool Associations

HRM also needs to begin to develop mechanisms that are appropriate in assisting the adaptation of current and potential employees for whom the concept of self-career management is inapplicable. Among these are the unskilled and semiskilled, immigrant workers, single parents whose job freedom is limited, and people with little growth potential. Two factors concerning these individuals are crucial. First, there are great numbers of such employees and they may, in fact, be increasing relative to the population at large. Second, despite their numbers, economically they are falling farther and farther behind people with higher skill levels, as evidenced by the findings of an increasing disparity in income between those at the higher and lower levels of our population.

Yet despite their numbers and this disparity, it is fair to say that little attention has been paid to how the new world of work can meet the needs of these people. For these individuals, basic educational training may have been insufficient, job training opportunities may not be available, and financial resources to keep up skill development may not be there. Also, the habit and encouragement of self-reliance in the occupational sphere may be more foreign to these individuals than those who are higher on the occupational hierarchy. Rather, these individuals may have, perhaps, more of a tendency to rely on traditional employment relationships and organizational reward systems as sources of meeting self enhancement and self-protection needs. Because the characteristics of the emerging world of work makes this pattern increasingly unlikely, it is even more important to pay attention to helping these groups adapt to the new and different setting.

Such associations can be conceived of as organizations based on cooperative relations among different companies (and perhaps government agencies) that focus on maximizing the human resources available to all of them. As cooperatively managed HR personnel from different organizations, labour pool associations would have several objectives. First, they would keep a continuing registry of individuals and their skills, thus ensuring a labour supply as needed by member organizations, large or small.

Second, they would serve as training-retraining-counseling centres for occupational entry and upgrading as desired and available. Third, and perhaps most uniquely, they would serve as "permanent employers" who, besides supplying and making available job and training opportunities, would also provide such "security type" benefits as health insurance and pension plans. These benefits would be paid into accounts maintained for each individual by the organizations. They would thus replace the security systems traditionally used by organizations, which are increasingly difficult to maintain in this era of downsizing and rapid corporate change.

One step toward this type of organization is the Talent Alliance (TA), an association of companies that has been operating since spring 1997 and includes such members as AT&T, Du Pont, GTE, Johnson & Johnson, Lucent Technologies, NCR, TRW, Unisys, and UPS. The TA, has several goals. One is to keep individuals employed in companies and settings where they are most needed when they are needed. It is therefore an employee allocation system (or labour pool association) of the type we envision here. A second objective is to increase employee marketability; this is done in a number of ways, including through career growth counselors, training and retraining programmes for employees, and strategic planning seminars for corporate management aimed at adapting HR practices to the new world of work.

The TA is, therefore, a step toward the type of organization suggest here because it has some of the aspects recommend. However, it lacks at this time a focus on the necessity of meeting the needs underlying self-protective motivation, that is, the desire for the security of health and welfare benefits and pensions. A second possible limitation is that it is designed for the occupational spectrum of relatively big organizations employing large numbers of individuals, a considerable percentage of whom may be at a high technical level. Such organizations are, of course, crucial as major employers and these occupational groups are of legitimate concern. However, believe that labour pool associations need also be concerned with those individuals who, though working for small, sometimes marginal organizations, nevertheless have traditionally looked to organizations as the mechanisms through which they will meet their needs for both enhancement and protection.

One Further Note

Labour pool associations may be of value to those for whom self-career management programmes are appropriate as well as for those for whom it is not. This is because systems need to be developed to bring individuals and organizations at all levels together for their mutual benefit in this emerging world of short-range assignments as well as long-range jobs and rapidly changing skill and competency demands. Labour pool associations, as we have envisioned them, would satisfy this need.

In sum, we need organizations like the TA and others like it, such as Job Link in Louisville, Kentucky, to meet self-enhancement needs but also to meet the need for self-protection. It is basically a referral and counseling centre that makes training available as a final resort.) We need organizations such as the TA and Job Link because the two major motivations in work settings—self-enhancement and self-protection—increasingly may not be met by individual companies. For some organizations, self-career management will be an appropriate alternative mechanism.

However, for others, cooperative efforts like labour pool associations will be needed to help them find qualified workers and to help workers find jobs that meet both self-enhancing and self-protective needs. Key here is the need for cooperative activity among different organizations, including accepting the principle of having these associations serving as an "employer" designed to meet self-protective concerns. This is perhaps a somewhat different perspective from that we are used to, but it is an idea that reflects the new world of work and the needs it has generated.

Nonorganizationally Linked Incentive Systems

Financial incentive systems for performance have long been one of the staples of HRM and there is little reason to think they would or should lose their relevance in the new world of work. On the contrary, they may become even more relevant as other types of incentives—those that assume organizational links and commitment, such as promotion and transfer opportunities—will become less relevant to those who see their future as falling into the self-career management pattern or who are attaining employment through "labour pool associations."

Purely financial incentives, on the other hand, are not limited to any specific type of setting. Bonuses tied to individual or unit performance are innately transferable (or fungible) and do not have to be linked to any particular organization. That is, the value of financial incentives as mechanisms to self-enhancement are not limited to any particular context and will usually hold their meaning regardless of where they are offered. Financial incentives will, then, retain significance in the new world of work and may become even more significant as the ties of organizational loyalty become less common and less relevant. First, direct monetary income in this changing world of fewer commitments will gain increased significance.

Second, incentive programmes that enable individuals to meet their needs for self-protection will have increased value.

Such needs might be met by developing and applying incentive payments directly into health, welfare, and pension programmes even though the employees involved may be temporary workers who frequently change employers. Consistent with the logic underlying the labour pool associations described earlier, HR professionals might well consider developing financial incentive programmes using individual "benefit" accounts into which employers (and employees) would contribute based on employment, no matter how temporary or varying that employment might be.

These would be financial incentives for performance designed to satisfy self-protection needs by paying into health, welfare, and pension accounts maintained by the labour pool association. In addition to being of value to the individuals involved, such contributions are likely to increase commitment and loyalty to an organization's needs. (One might note that the type of account we are referring to here is somewhat analogous to Social Security accounts. However, there are two major differences. First, these accounts are linked to individual work patterns and individual work behaviour in a more immediate manner. Second, these plans focus on health and welfare benefits as much as if not more than pay and pension concerns.)

Insider-Outsider Training Programmes

Training programmes designed to integrate individuals of diverse backgrounds and views into cohesive work teams are not new. They have been a standard part of HRM programmes in recent years as cultural and ethnic diversity has become a major challenge for organizations. Some of these training programmes have proved fruitful and some have not. However, the challenge to HRM here is somewhat different in that the programmes we refer to have generally made one major assumption that we cannot make in the new context: that the individuals and groups in these programmes, diverse though they may be, all wish to maximize the effectiveness of the same organization, that is, the organization to which they are all committed by reason of employment. In the new world of work, group members may include permanent employees committed to the same organization and work unit as well as temporarily assigned employees who rotate from assignment to assignment within the same organization and are sent to different units with not always consistent goals.

Even more difficult, however, will be dealing with people who are individual contractors or temporary workers who go to different organizations once a specific job is finished. It is not just that there will be changing memberships and changing interaction patterns in these organizational settings. Rather, there are and will also be individuals working together who have different, perhaps even conflicting loyalties. How does one get these groups to work together for some superordinate goal when some are truly insiders and some outsiders?

It is not clear how one proceeds here. Appeals to superordinate goals may not be appropriate over the long run (although they may be for the short run). In addition, the need for emotional cohesion may not be great because the groups may not be conceived of as even quasi-permanent. It is also uncertain which type of development programme might be most appropriate and which type of incentive programme might be best. One possibility may be the extensive use of financial incentives to integrate such groups into a common effort because financial benefits are not tied to any particular organization or setting. These incentives may be performance based, perhaps even providing stock options keyed to the length, level, and quality of performance in a particular setting.

We really do not have any answers to these questions at this time, but the potential for conflict between insider-outsider groups within organizations is great, as is the potential for conflict among those with different perspectives who also need to work together, such as suppliers and vendors. Hence, it is in the development of appropriate training and performance incentive programmes to meet this need that HRM may make another significant contribution in the new world of work. A work setting is beginning to emerge that is radically different from the one that has traditionally provided the context for

HRM policies and practices. In this world downsizing is a tool of managerial decision making, work-family conflict is a fact of life for millions and, increasingly, contingent workers, part-time workers, and outsourcing are used. It is a work setting where opportunities to meet self-enhancement and growth needs exist for some individuals but not for all, and where opportunities for self-protection such as job and benefit security are increasingly difficult to come by.

These changes have made it necessary for HRM as a profession to reevaluate its traditional practices and begin to develop and implement programmes that meet these needs for self-enhancement and self-protection in the new work setting. This offered illustrations of such programmes, including effective self-career management programmes based on personal growth principles; labour pool associations for those for whom self-career management is inappropriate; performance incentive programmes not based on organizational commitment, including financial rewards of both direct income and health, welfare, and pension benefits; and insider outsider training programmes.

Underlying these recommendations is my view that HRM professionals, regardless of specific training, need to take an active role in meeting the demands of the new world of work. Key to this process is recognizing that the opportunities for meeting and satisfying the primary motivational patterns of self-enhancement and self-protection are no longer what they used to be, whatever level of the occupational spectrum we are focusing on. For the benefit of both organizations and individuals, developing new mechanisms for responding to these changes is a major challenge facing HRM today.

Index